The Public Administration Workbook

Fourth Edition

Mark W. Huddleston

Department of Political Science and International Relations,
University of Delaware

 LONGMAN

An imprint of Addison Wesley Longman, Inc.

New York • Reading, Massachusetts • Menlo Park, California • Harlow, England
Don Mills, Ontario • Sydney • Mexico City • Madrid • Amsterdam

To my family
Emma, Andy, Katherine, and Giles

Editor in Chief: Priscilla McGeehon
Acquisitions Editor: Eric Stano
Director of Development: Lisa Pinto
Marketing Manager: Megan Galvin-Fak
Supplements Editor: Mark Toews
Project Manager: Ellen MacElree
Design Manager: Wendy Ann Fredericks
Cover Designer: Wendy Ann Fredericks
Cover Photo: © EyeWire
Art Studio: ElectraGraphics, Inc.
Technical Desktop Manager: Heather A. Peres
Electronic Page Makeup: Alice Fernandes-Brown
Printer and Binder: Courier Kendallville
Cover Printer: Phoenix

Please visit our website at http://www.awlonline.com
ISBN 0-80133268-0
12345678910—CRK—0302010099

Contents

Preface

I wrote this book because I wanted to use it. After listening to my public administration students complain, year in and year out, about the mind-numbing dullness of their textbooks, I decided that there must be a better way to approach this material. Public administration is not, after all, an inherently dull subject. It just seems dull sometimes.

Public administration seems this way, I am convinced, because much of what is interesting about the field cannot be captured in prose alone. Simple written or spoken descriptions are inadequate. This is not true of all public administration topics, to be sure. As a discipline, we have done a good job writing provocatively, even in textbooks, about questions such as democracy and bureaucracy, and politics and administration. But position classification? TQM? Performance budgeting? it is hard for students to appreciate that these are (or can be) exciting topics, just by reading about them. But give students a chance to try these things out, and the world changes: The mist rises, eyes focus, and minds engage. The text suddenly becomes meaningful—even interesting—and worth thinking about.

This point needs careful elaboration, lest my intent be misconstrued. I view the exercises in this book as instruments and little more. Paradoxical as it may sound coming from one who has written a book of hands-on exercises, I am chary of teaching techniques. Or, to put the point less perversely, I try to avoid teaching techniques for their own sake. Frankly, I do not believe that it is ultimately very important for undergraduates to learn how to evaluate a job or construct a program budget. What is important is that their interest be piqued and that they be stimulated to think about fundamental problems in public administration. These exercises do that.

To provide maximum flexibility for instructors, most of the exercises in this book have been designed so that they can be done by students individually, as out-of-class assignments; only the leadership (Exercise 4), administrative law (Exercise 5), and collective bargaining (Exercise 11) exercises require an in-class group effort. My own experience very strongly suggests, however, that students get more from the exercises when they work on them in small groups during class. This approach also provides an added dash of realism, as students learn the delicate arts of compromise and cooperation, so essential to good public administrative practice. Whatever one's preferences, the accompanying *Instructor's Manual* provides detailed suggestions for using (and modifying) the exercises to fit a variety of course needs.

For those instructors who have used previous editions of *The Public Administration Workbook*, I should note that this fourth edition contains two entirely new exercises, one on organizational design (Exercise 2) and another on Total Quality Management (Exercise 3). To help make room for these new additions, one of the previous exercises—the rather complex and time-consuming politics of budgeting simulation—has been excised.

I am immensely grateful to the many people who have helped make this fourth edition of *The Public Administration Workbook* possible. These include not only the able staff of Longman and the various editors and reviewers they have engaged, but my colleagues in colleges and universities around the country who have adopted the book over the years, and who have taken the time to write to me with comments and suggestions. I am particularly thankful for the reviewers who provided feedback on the manuscript for this edition: Carol Botsch of University of South Carolina—Aiken; Craig Donovan of Kean University; Lynn H. Leverty of University of Florida; David C. Powell of Eastern Illinois University; Daniel M. Russell of Springfield College; and Daniel W. Williams of Baruch College.

I am very glad indeed that you continue to find this book a useful tool to introduce your students to the endlessly fascinating world of public administration.

Mark W. Huddleston

About the Author

Mark W. Huddleston is Chairman of the Department of Political Science and International Relations at the University of Delaware, where he has taught since 1980. He has written extensively in the field of public administration, especially in the area of executive personnel management. He was rapporteur for the Twentieth Century Fund's study of the Senior Executive Service and author of its subsequent book *The Government's Managers* (1987); he is also the co-author of *The Higher Civil Service in the United States: Quest for Reform* (1996).

In addition to teaching courses at the University of Delaware, in recent years Professor Huddleston has conducted public administration training and served as a consultant in several interesting overseas settings, including Bosnia, Slovenia, Kazakstan, Mexico, Botswana, Zimbabwe, and South Africa. He described his work in Bosnia in detail in a recent article entitled "Innocents Abroad" published in *Public Administration Review* (59, 2 March/April 1999).

Professor Huddleston is a graduate of the State University of New York at Buffalo (B.A., 1972) and the University of Wisconsin Madison (M.A., 1973; Ph.D., 1978).

Introduction

OVERVIEW OF THE PUBLIC ADMINISTRATION WORKBOOK

One thing that makes public administration fun to learn is that you can roll up your sleeves and actually *do* some of it in the classroom. What would otherwise be simply a collection of arcane concepts and impenetrable jargon can become accessible and—lo and behold!—even interesting when you slide behind an administrator's desk and become familiar with some of the principal techniques of public management.

The exercises in this book introduce you to 18 of the most important skills in the professional administrator's kit bag. Part One includes six exercises in public management broadly defined. In the first exercise, you hone one of the most critical skills of all—clear writing. Exercises 2 and 3 deal with organizations—how to design them and how to manage them for quality. The fourth exercise, on administrative leadership, is based on the design and manufacture of paper airplanes (it really is!) and is probably one of the most fun exercises in the book. Exercise 5 deals with administrative law and introduces you, through a role-playing game, to the intricacies of the Americans with Disabilities Act, an especially topical concern. The final exercise deals with an equally pertinent and current issue—administrative ethics—and asks you to make some tough decisions about how you would respond to some potentially serious breaches of professional ethics.

Part Two includes five exercises in public personnel administration. You begin by learning how to conduct a job analysis and by writing a job description, the foundations of virtually everything else in personnel management. You then design a performance appraisal system, devise a valid selection system, and decide how much a job is worth. Finally, you are thrown into the thick of a labor-management dispute and have to negotiate a new contract with a union of firefighters.

Part Three introduces you to the field of public budgeting. Four successive exercises based on the same organization—a county library system—provide you with a tour of the four major budget formats used in the United States: line-item budgeting, performance budgeting, program budgeting, and zero-base budgeting. You begin by compiling a basic line-item budget for the system and proceed by transforming the budget, step by step, into the remaining three formats.

Part Four presents three exercises in decision making and policy analysis. As with Parts Two and Three, the exercises here build on one another. After applying a simple cost-effectiveness model to a problem in transportation decision making in Exercise 16 (and making, it is to be hoped, a rational decision), you learn a technique in Exercise 17 that allows you to plan the smooth implementation of your policy choice. In the final exercise, you are exposed to some of the rewards and difficulties of policy evaluation: Did your policy work? How can you know?

By the way, several of the exercises include what I call "information technology (IT) options." These encourage you to complete the exercise by downloading data from the World Wide Web or constructing an Excel spreadsheet or preparing a presentation for your class using PowerPoint or a similar software package. Not only will following these IT options make the exercises easier and more fun, but they will also help you acquire the skills that professional public administrators must use on the job every day.

THEORY AND TECHNIQUE IN PUBLIC ADMINISTRATION

Techniques alone do not a discipline make, of course. It is essential that you understand the theory behind each technique so that you know when, why, and how to use it. In fact, the real reason for doing these exercises and learning these techniques is to learn the theory. After all, techniques come and go with fair frequency—even faster, believe it or not, than theories. And you will seldom find exactly the same technique, used in exactly the same way, in any two governmental jurisdictions. But if you know the theory that generates the technique, you are way ahead of the game. You can walk into almost any administrative office, shuffle a few of your categories, and figure out in no time what your administrative colleagues are doing.

So why learn these techniques at all, you ask? Simple. They provide a useful and pleasant entrée to the theories themselves. It's much more fun to learn about zero-base budgeting by writing a zero-base budget than it is just to read about one. Moreover, you'll remember much more about zero-base budgeting that way. And that's the important thing.

To help you make the connection between *theories* of public administration and *techniques* of public administration, each exercise is preceded by a brief theoretical introduction. You should read these carefully. They contain valuable hints about how to complete the exercise and also explain why the technique is important and how it is anchored in the field of public administration.

Assuming that your interest in one or more of these subjects will be sufficiently aroused that you'll want to know more about it, each exercise is followed by a short bibliographic essay directing you to further reading that you will find useful. In general, the books and articles cited in the essays are quite accessible—you don't need a master's in public administration to make sense of them.

One last point before you begin: It is possible to do almost all of the exercises on your own, outside of class. In fact, only three of them—the leadership exercise, the administrative law exercise, and the collective bargaining session—actually require a group effort. Nevertheless, you should, whenever your instructor allows, work on these exercises in small groups. Not only will you learn more and have more fun, but it is more realistic—administrators often cooperate with one another!

PART ONE

Public Management

WHAT IS PUBLIC MANAGEMENT?

The millions of men and women who comprise the public sector in the United States represent an extraordinary variety of skills and occupations, from architecture to zoology. Indeed, it is difficult to imagine an occupation that does not have a few of its practitioners laboring away in one corridor or another of American government. One consequence of this diversity is that the terms we commonly apply to their collective activities—public administration or public management—are not as descriptive as we might like. Even if we reserve our usage of "public manager" (as we probably should) for those who exercise some supervisory or discretionary authority, we can still encounter difficulties. Although they are all public administrators by this definition, a virologist at the National Institutes of Health, for instance, will likely not feel a close kinship with either an air transportation safety specialist at the Federal Aviation Administration or a regional administrator for the U.S. Department of Housing and Urban Development. As we shall see in Part Two, our rank-in-job personnel system, which nicely accommodates technical specialists while frustrating administrative generalists, is largely responsible for this phenomenon.

But while the day-to-day work of public managers does vary tremendously in substance, there are important similarities in how they do what they do, similarities that mark them both as managers (as opposed to nonmanagers) and as public managers (as opposed to private managers). In what is perhaps the best-known formulation of the tasks of an executive, Luther Gulick and Tyndall Urwick offered the mnemonic acronym POSDCORB: planning, organizing, staffing, directing, coordinating, reporting, and budgeting. Other theorists—and most textbook authors—have compiled similar lists.

Exactly what elements should begin and end such a list of managerial requisites is an argument we shall avoid here. For our purposes in *The Public Administration Workbook,* we shall simply focus on six skills or sensitivities that are core managerial elements on anyone's list. These are the abilities to communicate clearly in writing, to design appropriate organizational structures, to manage for continuous improvements in organizational performance, to lead other people effectively, to be aware of the constraints of law, and to maintain a high degree of sensitivity to questions of administrative ethics.

FURTHER READING

Two classic attempts to define public administration and public management are Woodrow Wilson, "The Study of Administration," *Political Science Quarterly* 2 (June 1887); and Dwight Waldo, "What Is Public Administration?" in Waldo, *The Study of Administration* (New York: Random House, 1955), both of which have been reprinted in Jay M. Shafritz and Albert C. Hyde, eds., *Classics of Public Administration,* 4th ed. (Fort Worth: Harcourt Brace, 1997). For a discussion of the differences between public and private management, see Graham T. Allison, "Public and Private Management: Are They Fundamentally Alike in All Unimportant Respects?" *Proceedings for the Public Management Research Conference,* November 19–20, 1979 (Washington: Office of Personnel Management, OPM Document 127-53-1, February 1980), also reprinted in Shafritz and Hyde.

Exercise 1

The Administrative Memo

AN IMPORTANT TELEPHONE CONVERSATION

Professor Jones is sitting at his desk grading term papers and rubbing his forehead when the telephone rings:

PROFESSOR JONES: Hello?

PERSONNEL OFFICER: Professor Jones? This is Molly MacIntyre from the Department of the Interior in Washington. I hope I'm not interrupting you.

PROFESSOR JONES: No, no, not at all. What can I do for you?

PERSONNEL OFFICER: Well, I'm calling to follow up on a letter of recommendation you wrote last fall for a young man named Jeff Stone. Do you remember Jeff?

PROFESSOR JONES: Yes, of course. He took . . . let me think . . . two courses with me. That's right—he took my introductory undergraduate public administration course and later my course in organization theory.

PERSONNEL OFFICER: Good. Well, Jeff has applied for a position as an entry-level analyst in our budget office. He is one of the finalists for the job, and now I'm trying to get a little more information to help us make the decision.

PROFESSOR JONES: I'll be happy to help. Jeff is a very bright fellow.

PERSONNEL OFFICER: Yes, he seems to have quite a strong record. And in the initial interview we had with him, he came across very well. Very articulate and personable.

PROFESSOR JONES: I recall using similar adjectives in my letter.

PERSONNEL OFFICER: Yes, you did. But there is one thing that troubles us.

PROFESSOR JONES: What's that?

PERSONNEL OFFICER: His writing.

PROFESSOR JONES: Ah.

PERSONNEL OFFICER: Yes, you know, on the recommendation form you filled out for Jeff, you checked "excellent" for all the characteristics except writing.

PROFESSOR JONES: Jeff is a really bright guy. He has great problem-solving abilities. He works well with other people. And he's motivated.

PERSONNEL OFFICER: But his writing?

PROFESSOR JONES: I also remember that he made a terrific oral presentation to the class.

PERSONNEL OFFICER: But he can write?

We will cease our eavesdropping here, as Professor Jones tries to frame a response that is both honest and fair to Jeff. How the conversation ends in this particular case doesn't really concern us anyhow. What is important is that similar exchanges occur all the time. When you graduate and begin applying for your first professional job, you will need to provide references from professors or other people who know your work. They will be asked to evaluate, among other things, your analytical skills, your motivation, your maturity, and, very importantly, your ability to write. Public agencies—and private sector employers—want to hire people who can write well. You may be a natural leader and as sharp as a tack, but if you can't write, you will be at a tremendous disadvantage.

In some respects, the idea of good administrative writing may seem to be a contradiction in

5

terms. Certainly we are all painfully familiar with examples of "bureaucratese," that bloated form of prose that seems designed to obfuscate rather than communicate, where *kill* becomes "terminate with extreme prejudice" and *to be fired* is rendered as "subjected to involuntary outplacement." Breathes there a person who has not been confounded from time to time by the "EZ" instructions for Form 1040 or by the baleful opacity of insurance policies? Probably not, for as Max Weber noted long ago, bureaucracies—public and private—hide behind language, and bureaucracies are ubiquitous.

These tendencies notwithstanding, the ability to write well is an important administrative skill. What sort of things will you have to write? Memoranda, annual reports, budget narratives, personnel evaluations, policy proposals, legislative testimony, and press releases are all examples.

Writing is a skill like any other. It is honed through practice. No single course, much less any single exercise in a book of this sort, can magically turn you into a good writer. It can, however, help you learn some of the fundamentals. And you *can* learn them. Great writers may be born, but good writers are made.

THE ABCs OF GOOD ADMINISTRATIVE WRITING: ACCURACY, BREVITY, AND CLARITY

Accuracy   Good writing is accurate writing. This is true in two senses. First, the statements that you make in your writing—the facts on which you rely—should be true. If you are writing a report for the county office of social services and you note that last year its social workers had an average case load of 75 clients each, make sure that is a correct figure. Everyone makes mistakes occasionally; good writers minimize them. Nothing causes the credibility of an administrator to plummet as quickly as a reputation for error.

Accuracy is important in a second sense as well: Your spelling, punctuation, and grammar all should be correct. There is an old saying: "You can't expect anyone to take your writing more seriously than you appear to take it yourself." If you draft a memo or prepare a report that is sloppy, filled with run-on sentences or misspelled words, you clearly have not taken your writing seriously. Others will treat it accordingly.

This rule is not hard to follow. One clearly does not need to have "natural writing talent" to be careful in the use of facts or to use a dictionary.

The U.S. General Accounting Office: A Paragon of Accuracy

The United States General Accounting Office, often called the investigative arm of Congress, is an independent federal agency responsible for evaluating the performance of federal programs and agencies. You may have seen some of its blue-covered reports on such topics as "Medical Waste Regulations: Health and Environmental Risks Need to Be Fully Assessed" and "Navy Ships: Status of SSN–21 Ship Construction Program." Because it almost always serves as a critic of bureaucratic performance, it has to get its facts right to maintain its credibility—and it does. Over the years, GAO staffers have developed an intricate system of fact checking and report verification that is unrivaled in thoroughness. As a report reaches its final stages of drafting, a GAO employee marks it up with a red pencil, cross-referencing every assertion, phrase, and number in the manuscript to a set of supporting documents in GAO files, creating, in effect, hundreds, even thousands, of invisible footnotes!

Brevity   The best administrative writing is short and to the point. Administrators are busy people. So are the legislators, contractors, clients, and others with whom they interact. Almost no one has the time or patience to wade through a memo that runs on like a Norse saga. In many offices, the rule is that if a document is longer than three or four pages, it must have an "executive summary" attached to the front for interested parties to scan quickly. You need to exercise judgment in following this rule of brevity, of course. If your assignment is to write an evaluation of a major agency program, you likely will need to say more than "This program has failed to meet its objectives."

A Brief Poem on Brevity

In general those who have nothing to say
   Contrive to spend the longest time in doing it,
They turn and vary it in every way,
   Hashing it, stewing it, mincing it, *ragouting* it.
         —James Russell Lowell,
         An Oriental Apologue, Stanza 15

Clarity Good writing is clear writing. It is writing that takes the work—and the guesswork—out of reading. When you write clearly, your audience knows exactly what you mean, and that should be your primary goal.

To keep it clear, keep it simple. Too many people knit their words together as if they were weaving an oriental carpet, producing awesomely intricate and ornamented patterns of prose. Even if you think your readers enjoyed diagraming sentences in tenth-grade English (a doubtful proposition, by the way), don't construct your sentences as if they were puzzles to be solved. For those who aspire to clear writing, there is no better friend than the simple declarative sentence, arranged in subject-verb-object form (e.g., "The Department of Transportation [subject] awarded [verb] 300 contracts [object]").

Avoid unnecessary jargon and fancy words. Though you may be justly proud that you have mastered the foreign language of your profession (Pentagon-speak, legalese, accountingish, or whatever), don't assume that all your readers are equally adept. As the great essayist E. B. White wrote more than 40 years ago, "Do not be tempted by a twenty-dollar word when there is a ten-center handy, ready and able."[1]

Clarity does not come cheap. In fact, there is an inverse relationship between the ease of reading and the ease of writing. As Hemingway put it, "Easy writing makes hard reading."[2] Thus it is a good guess that the crisper and clearer the sentence, the longer it took to write. The key is to rewrite, and then rewrite some more.

A Writing Checklist

1. Know your main point, state it at the outset, and build the rest of your writing around it.
2. Verify your facts.
3. Check your spelling and grammar.
4. Eliminate unnecessary words and phrases.
5. Use the active voice.
6. Keep it short, simple, and to the point.

FURTHER READING

William Strunk Jr. and E. B. White, *The Elements of Style,* 3rd ed. (New York: Macmillan, 1979), is one of the pithiest and most useful volumes on good writing. A companion volume by Margaret D. Shertzer, *The Elements of Grammar* (New York: Collier, 1986), provides a solid grounding in the rules of our language. Probably the best advice for someone who wants to write well is this: Read a lot of good writing. No one ever learned to write a snappy sentence by watching television.

Overview of Exercise

This exercise has two parts. First, you will read a short memorandum drafted for the signature of your boss by one of your coworkers and make any corrections you deem necessary. Next, you will write a brief memorandum on a subject as specifically assigned by your instructor or as outlined in Step Two of the instructions.

INSTRUCTIONS

Step One

You are J. Wilson, a staff assistant to A. Babcock, Secretary of the Department of Environmental Protection. Secretary Babcock has sent you a brief note asking you to review—and revise as necessary—a memo drafted for his signature by someone else in the department. Read Babcock's note to you (Form 1) and the draft of the memo (Form 2). Bearing in mind the ABCs of good writing (summarized in a memo on Form 5) and the points in Babcock's note, rewrite the memo on Form 3.

Step Two

You are the student representative on the college or university committee charged with making recommendations for improving parking, registration, or food service (pick one) on your campus. Use Form 4 to write a brief memorandum (no more than one page) setting forth your views to the other members of the committee, all of whom are either faculty members or administrators. Use the situation on your own campus as the basis of your memo.

---

[1]William Strunk Jr. & E. B. White, *The Elements of Style,* 3rd ed. (New York: Macmillan, 1979), p. 63.
[2]Quoted in Samuel Putnam, *Paris Was Our Mistress: Memoirs of a Lost and Found Generation* (New York: Viking, 1947).

Office of the Secretary
Department of Environmental Protection

April 1, 2000

J———

Please read and fix the attached. It's supposed to be a brief cover memo to our field staff officially informing them of our new responsibilities under the Wetlands Protection Act. Because we'll be attaching copies of Titles II and III, you can keep it short. Just summarize the main points, which I hope you can ferret out of this mess. And please send a note to the folks down in personnel and ask them to tighten up our screening for writing ability.

Thanks,
A.B.

April 1, 2000

TO: Feild Personel

FROM: A. Babcock, Commissioner
         Department of Enviromental Protection

SUBJECT: Wetlands Conservation Act of 1999

Being that the Wetlands Protection Act of 1999, which was passed finally into law last year in 1999 and signed by the Governor has many ramifications and implications for personnel who work in this Department. I am writing to all field personel to bring them to their attention. First I will exactly explain the purposes and previsions of the law. The first part of the law, which is called Title I, sets forth the purposes of the Act, which was to protect the wetlands and to generally improve the quality of life. The second part of the law, which is called Title 2 and also called "Wetland Protection" assigns to this Department the authority to issue rules and also the State Transportation and Agriculture Departments. A copy of which is attached.

Briefly it says that it is the responsibility of this Department to survey and catalog wetlands in the State and propose rules about proper uses, where to for fines would be levied, which we would propose, when violated. Finally, the last part concludes with Title III which is also called the "Wetland Support Program" which provides grants and loans to private citizens which own lands which have been designated wetlands which need to be protected. A copy of this title, too, is attached, the information which it contains within may be dissembled by you to interested partys.

Funding for all parts of program have been recomended by the Administration. The amount of funding which has been recomended by the Administration is $14 million dollars for the next fiscal year which is expected to increase. But not more than ten percent. Which would mean that expenditures would be about $20 million the year after that. Some of this money, which would be dedicated, or about half, would be in a special loan fund, at low interest rates, which be available and paid back by farmers and private citizens who own lands which have been designated wetlands over twenty years to prevent unnecessary destruction.

As further information becomes available which is revelant to your role in the program it will be made available to you.

FORM 5

April 7, 2000

TO: Student Readers

FROM: Mark W. Huddleston, Author, *The Public Administration Workbook*

SUBJECT: Hints on Writing a Good Memo

I am writing to give you some hints about how to write a good memo—and how to complete this exercise. To begin a memo, tell the persons to whom you are writing why you are writing to them. If you don't know what I mean, go back and read the first sentence.

A good memo redeems the promise made in the first sentence or two by making a lucid, concise, and logically ordered set of points. Bear in mind the ABCs of good writing:

1. *Accuracy.* Make sure that your writing is correct in both form and substance. Check your facts as well as your spelling, punctuation, and grammar.
2. *Brevity.* Keep your memo short and to the point.
3. *Clarity.* Make your meaning clear by using appropriate language arranged in intelligible sentences and logical paragraphs.

© 2000 Addison Wesley Longman, Inc.

17

Exercise 2

Designing Organizations

APPROACHING ORGANIZATION DESIGN

Not long ago, designing the structure of a new government organization—or a business organization, for that matter—was a fairly simple matter. Although people might disagree about things such as who should report to whom, how many layers there ought to be between the boss and the lowest-level worker, and whether it was better to organize around process or place or function, the basic template was seldom in dispute. The finished organization would resemble a pyramid, wide at the base and narrow at the top. And inside the pyramid, the sinews of the organization would reflect the military principles of command and control. Authority would emanate clearly and invariably from the top of the structure. Orders would cascade down the chain of command like water down a mountainside, from agency head to bureau chief to mid-level manager to frontline worker. At least that was the theory.

Today, designers of organizations have a much broader array of models from which to choose. Depending on their purpose and the inclinations of the individuals who devise and manage them, organizations can be tall or flat or round—really any shape at all. Similarly, the authority systems that structure organizations can be as tight and centralized as the military or as loose and fragmented as a beach party.

THREE MODELS OF ORGANIZATION

Although there are many types of organization in contemporary public administration, most of them derive from one of three basic organizational designs. These are the *bureaucratic, matrix,* and *team* models of organization. Although the bureaucratic model is still by far the most common, matrix and team-based organizations are becoming increasingly popular. Let us look at the structure of each in turn and consider their advantages and disadvantages.

Bureaucratic Model

The *bureaucratic model* has a traditional pyramidal form (see Figure 2.1). According to the great political sociologist Max Weber, bureaucracy is the organizational face of rational thought, the essence of modernity. Bureaucratic organization is hierarchical, highly specialized, governed by clear rules and procedures, and impersonal.[1]

Although examples of bureaucratic or at least quasi-bureaucratic organizations have been known for centuries—the Roman Catholic church is one especially influential example—bureaucracy really came into its own in the late eighteenth and early nineteenth centuries with the blossoming of the industrial revolution. Organizing bureaucratically, with each worker responsible for one small task, proved to be far more efficient for large-scale manufacturing than traditional craft-style production. Adam Smith tells us, for instance, that one man responsible for all the operations that go into making a pin—drawing the wire, straightening the wire, cutting the wire, pointing the tip, grinding the head, and so forth—could, "with utmost industry, make one pin in a day, and certainly not more than twenty." But when that man works as part of a bureaucratic organization, with clear division of

[1] See Max Weber, "Bureaucracy," in *From Max Weber: Essays in Sociology,* ed. and trans. H. H. Gerth and C. Wright Mills (London: Oxford University Press, 1946), reprinted in Jay M. Shafritz and Albert C. Hyde, eds., *Classics of Public Administration,* 4th ed. (Fort Worth: Harcourt Brace, 1997), pp. 37–43.

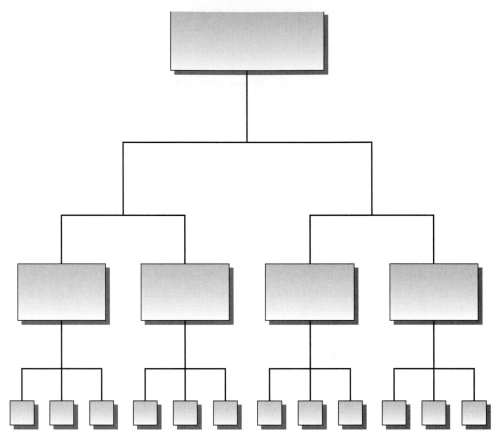

Figure 2.1
Bureaucratic Model of Organization

labor and specialization of function, productivity soars: Ten people working in such an arrangement "make among them upwards of forty-eight thousand pins in a day."[2]

Governments, too, have found bureaucratic organization useful. Just as in the private sector, bureaucracy in government affords relatively high levels of production—allowing more chickens to be inspected, more checks to be issued, more forms to be processed—than earlier, more casual methods of organization permitted. Bureaucracy has also proved to be a powerful tool in the fight against discrimination, patronage, and other types of organizational misbehavior. At least in principle, the color of your skin, whom you know, or which political party you support is irrelevant in a bureaucratic organization structured by formal regulations and committed to impersonality. Moreover, the bureaucratic model has facilitated control over organizational outputs.

In a well-run bureaucracy, there are no surprises about what the organization does because employees follow prescribed rules. Control over outputs in turn simplifies democratic accountability. Citizens dissatisfied with public services can hold the elected officials who supervise the bureaucracy directly responsible for what the bureaucracy does.

It hardly needs to be said, however, that whatever its merits in theory, bureaucracy has disadvantages in practice. Indeed, the word *bureaucratic* has become a common pejorative, synonymous with "red tape." One prominent sociologist, Michel Crozier, even defines bureaucracy as organizational dysfunction.[3] Bureaucracies are said to be by nature unresponsive, overly cautious, maladaptive, and even unproductive. Bureaucrats—now there is a real epithet!—are charged with caring only about procedures, not about goals. Lower-level workers in bureaucracies, in particular, are thought to be

[2] Adam Smith, *The Wealth of Nations* (1776), quoted in Jay M. Shafritz and J. Steven Ott, eds., *Classics of Organization Theory*, 2nd ed. (Chicago: The Dorsey Press, 1987), pp. 30–31.

[3] Michel Crozier, *The Bureaucratic Phenomenon* (Chicago: University of Chicago Press, 1964).

"dehumanized." Clients are treated like numbers, not like people.

Some critics argue that the problems of bureaucracy can be fixed either by modest changes in *structure* or by modifying organizational *processes*. Structural remedies generally entail making the bureaucracy flatter, reducing what are perceived as unnecessary layers of supervision. Process-related strategies typically focus on "human relations" and seek through training or other forms of organizational development to change the way people think and interact with one another in the workplace. Both such approaches hold considerable appeal for public managers because they are seen to address some of the major faults of bureaucracy without discarding its essential benefits.

Matrix Model

The *matrix model* of organization represents a sharp structural departure from traditional bureaucracy. In a matrix organization, specialists are arrayed in a functional structure (much like a traditional bureaucracy) for housekeeping purposes. The work that the organization accomplishes, however, is organized along project lines, which cut horizontally across the functional structure. The term *matrix* derives from the crosshatching created by these intersecting lines.

Figure 2.2 helps explain this idea. The lines running up and down connect each employee to a functional home—environmental engineering, biological sciences, licensing and inspection, and so forth. The lines running side to side connect each employee to a specific project—wetlands preservation, agricultural runoff mitigation, reforestation, and so on. Each employee is thus answerable in theory to two management structures. The functional structure represents, in effect, his or her permanent address, the place that issues the paycheck and provides administrative continuity. The project structure is where he or she lives at the moment—and in a matrix organization, one is almost always on the

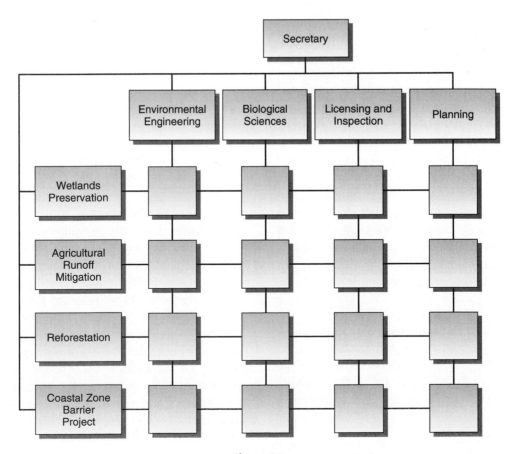

Figure 2.2
Matrix Model of Organization

road. On a day-to-day basis, it is the project management structure that provides leadership and coordination.

Matrix organizations are still not widespread in government, but they are growing in popularity. They constitute a prime example of what organization theorist Henry Mintzberg terms *adhocracy*.[4] Indeed, the key advantage of the matrix organization is flexibility and fluidity. As problems come and go in an organization's environment, project structures can be created and dissolved to match them. Matrix organizations are especially suitable for bringing together groups of specialists to work intensively on well-defined, time-limited projects. In the private sector, high-technology research and development companies have been the keenest advocates of matrix organization. In the U.S. federal government, NASA has been the chief exponent of matrix organization, not surprisingly given its mission of melding diverse specialists and innovative technologies to undertake unique projects.

But although the matrix form seems to work very well for NASA and many Silicon Valley firms, it does have some downsides. The chief disadvantage of a matrix organization is a mirror image of its chief advantage: dual lines of authority. Every matrix employee reports to two supervisors, one functional and one on the project to which he or she is attached. This clearly violates the old administrative maxim that no person can serve two masters. Certainly, life in the matrix organization demands an unusual degree of diplomacy, compromise, and delicate bargaining over shared resources. When these attributes are not in evidence, matrix organizations can be paralyzed by conflict. In fact, even proponents of matrix organizations suggest that this form is probably not appropriate when operations are routine, a service or product is highly standardized, and the environment is very stable.

Team Model

The third model is the *team approach* to organization, sometimes known as the *horizontal model* in recognition of its emphasis on decentralization. The team approach is integral to Total Quality Management (TQM), which we will examine in

[4] Henry Mintzberg, *The Structuring of Organization: A Synthesis of Research* (Englewood Cliffs, N.J.: Prentice Hall, 1979).

detail in Exercise 3. More generally, though, this model of organization is built on the premise that small, integrated groups of people drawn from diverse disciplines but with a focus on a common *process* can most effectively deliver administrative services.

Figure 2.3 presents a chart of a team model of organization. In this particular example, the teams are drawn from several different departments; thus each of the five teams, designated by the five circles, has members from Departments A, B, and C. It is also possible to assemble teams from within single departments or even from within single subunits of single departments.

To illustrate the advantages of the team model, look again at Figure 2.3. This time, cover up the bottom half of the diagram with your hand or a piece of paper, and mentally relabel the departments as the Department of Labor, the Department of Education, the Department of Social Services, and the Department of Transportation. Now imagine that you are an unemployed single mother in the state that has this departmental structure and that you are trying mightily to remove yourself from the ranks of the unemployed and find a decent job. Here is the administrative trek that you will have to make: First, you will have to visit the Department of Labor to get information about openings; next, you will have to go to the Department of Education to learn about job training opportunities; finally, you will have to call various agencies within the Department of Social Services to try to get help with child care and other logistical support.

Now uncover the rest of the diagram. The team model of organization that your state has implemented has suddenly simplified your life enormously. Instead of having to thread your way through a labyrinthine bureaucracy, you can now walk into a single State Job Center, a facility staffed by representatives of all relevant state departments, where in one visit the team of complementary specialists can assess your needs, identify appropriate job openings, design a training program, and arrange for the various social service supports necessary to get your on you feet as an employee.

The team and matrix models are obviously similar in certain respects, especially in their essentially antibureaucratic ethos. However, several key differences should be noted. First, the team model orga-

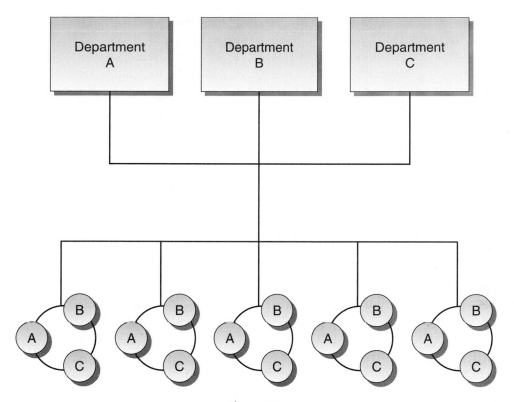

Figure 2.3
Team Model of Organization

nizes around process, the matrix model around pro-ject. Teams are usually assembled to deliver routine, ongoing services, while matrix projects generally have a specific time-limited mission to accomplish. In the employment example we used earlier, for instance, the expectation is that this service is one that will continue indefinitely. A matrix organiza-tion would be more appropriate to a task that had a clear beginning and end, one in which the project group would dissolve and move on to other things once the mission was accomplished. A second dif-ference between the team and matrix models is that official lines of authority remain functional in the team form of organization. The team member from the Department of Labor in the employment exam-ple continues officially to report to his or her super-visor in the Department of Labor. Although teams may designate leaders, there is no equivalent of a project manager to confuse reporting relationships under this mode of organization. Finally, as noted earlier, matrix organizations are by definition cross-functional. Teams may cross departmental lines or they may not. The key to a team model of organiza-tion is to identify the needs of a government's "cus-tomers" and to design administrative processes in ways that facilitate meeting those needs.

These observations may seem to suggest that the team model really isn't much different from the bureaucratic model. After all, it allows for routine services, doesn't disrupt traditional vertical lines of authority, and need not even cross departmental lines. This would be an incorrect interpretation, however. Central to the team concept is a degree of decentralization inimical to the bureaucratic model. Top managers retain formal authority over a team's work—that is, the vertical lines remain in place—but as a practical matter they cede day-to-day con-trol to frontline workers. The main operating assumption in the team model is that those who are actually delivering the services know best what needs to be done. This doesn't mean that these frontline workers don't need training and support and continued direction from above. Clearly they do. It does mean, though, that properly designed and managed teams can provide very high levels of service and can often be depended on to assume responsibility for continuous improvement in qual-ity and productivity.

No model of organization is without disadvantages, of course. Some of the drawbacks of the team concept are implicit in the remarks made in this text. First, team-based organizations require more than just rearranging boxes on an organizational chart. They require heavy investments in training to ensure that employees understand and are capable of accepting their new responsibilities. Second, team-based organizations also need to allow for a fair amount of "downtime," periods when team members are meeting and discussing team issues rather than processing clients, reviewing forms, or otherwise engaging in the actual work of the organization. Third, decentralizing authority sometimes means diffusing authority. Whenever a group rather than an individual is made responsible for an issue, it becomes more difficult to hold particular people to account when things go wrong.

WHICH MODEL IS BEST?

It is probably tempting to conclude that the matrix model or team-based model of organization is always better than the traditional bureaucratic form of organization. And if you were to browse the shelves of popular management books at your local bookstore, you'd find that there are a lot of titles in print that would support that conclusion—management theory tends to be rather faddish. But let us not be hasty. Battered though it is, bureaucracy should not be counted out just yet. In fact, many reputable organization theorists would suggest that there are plenty of circumstances when "bureaucracy" is still the right answer to the question, "Which model is best?"

The idea that different organizational designs are appropriate for different circumstances is called *contingency theory*. Contingency theory suggests that in some circumstances, traditional hierarchical organizations—or "mechanistic" organizations, to use the jargon of the field—work very well. At other times, in other circumstances, flatter and more "loosely coupled" organizations—or "organic" organizations—work better.

What are the times and circumstances when one is better than another? Actually, several contingency theories of organization are available, each emphasizing different factors—technology, size,

environment, and so forth. This makes it difficult to generalize with full confidence. But here are some things one should take into consideration when thinking about organizational design:

- *Environmental stability.* Traditional bureaucracies are well suited to stable environments (for example, a revenue department in a small city with an established population). Matrix organizations are well suited to unstable environments (for instance, a planning agency in a town experiencing explosive population growth). Teams can be used in either environment.

- *Control.* Traditional bureaucracies are the best choice when centralized control is paramount (for example, the Department of Defense and decisions about the use of strategic nuclear weapons). Team-based organizations are the best choice when on-the-spot decisions are needed (such as physician–nurse–rehabilitation therapist–social worker teams and long-term care programs for elderly outpatients). Matrix organizations are often the best choice when overall control of highly specialized but nonetheless intersecting projects is needed (for instance, NASA and the construction of the space station).

- *Nature of work.* Organic structures—matrix or team-based—are generally more suited to highly trained specialists (for example, researchers in the National Institutes of Health). Traditional bureaucratic structures *may* be more congenial for employees who engage in routine work (such as data entry clerks in an accounting department).

- *Expectations.* The workforce in general has developed expectations about participation and responsibility that favor organic structures. The continuing transformation of the American economy away from its traditional manufacturing base toward services and high technology is likely to nurture these expectations. Thus, other things being equal, matrix and team-based organizations may represent the wave of the future.

- *Nonexclusivity.* It is possible—though not always easy—to mix styles within the boundaries of a single organization. For instance, an organization that generally corresponds to the contours of a traditional bureaucracy can embrace teams for some of its activities. Other combinations are also possible.

FURTHER READING

Books that promote a particular perspective on organizational theory—especially simplified, applied, management-in-five-easy-steps sorts of books—are legion and not particularly helpful. For collections of readings that provide general, balanced overviews of organizational theory and behavior, see Jay M. Shafritz and J. Steven Ott, eds.,

Classics of Organization Theory, 4th ed. (Fort Worth: Harcourt Brace, 1997), and Jerald Greenberg, ed., *Organizational Behavior: The State of the Science* (Hillsdale, N.J.: Erlbaum, 1994). See also Andrew Du Brin, *Fundamentals of Organizational Behavior* (Cincinnati: South-Western, 1997), which draws together much of this material in a highly readable form. For more focused treatments of organizational design, see David K. Banner and T. Gagne, *Designing Effective Organizations: Traditional and Transformational Views* (Thousand Oaks, Calif.: Sage, 1995), and Robert Keidel, *Seeing Organizational Patterns: A New Theory and Language of Organizational Design* (San Francisco: Berrett-Koehler, 1995).

Overview of Exercise

This is an exercise in organizational design—or rather organizational *redesign.* Based on the models discussed in the text, you will be asked to review the structure of a state agency—the Department of Economic Development—and make some recommendations as to how it might be reconfigured.

INSTRUCTIONS

Step One
Read the background information presented on Form 6.

Step Two
Review the organization chart presented on Form 7.

Step Three
Redesign the structure of the Department of Economic Development so as better to serve the

needs of the state's citizens. Use Form 8 to sketch your reconfigured organization chart. Everything is up for grabs in terms of structure. The only given is that the current missions, outlined briefly on the existing organization chart, must still somehow be performed.

IT Option
- Download the file **orgchart.opx** from *www.awlonline.com/huddleston* and edit as a Microsoft Word document.
- Make a presentation on your organizational design to the class using Microsoft PowerPoint.

Step Four
Answer the questions on Form 9.

Background on the Department of Economic Development

For the past 20 years, the Department of Economic Development (DED) has been the state government's lead organization for stimulating exports, promoting the state to tourists, attracting new businesses to the state, and helping existing businesses grow. It has a total of 57 employees deployed across three main divisions: Business Development, Workforce Development, and Tourism. The DED's top staff, including the director, three associate directors, and two special assistants, are all exempt, non–civil service employees, meaning that they are essentially political appointees of the governor. Four of these five managers—the exception being the special assistant for communications, a young woman who had worked on the governor's last campaign—are former business executives. All other department employees are career members of the state merit system.

Despite the private sector experience of its top leadership, the DED has been criticized in recent years for its unresponsiveness to the state's business community. Young entrepreneurs seeking assistance with loans, business development opportunities, employment problems, and other issues are, it has been said, "given the runaround": They are asked to fill out unnecessary paperwork, put on hold on the telephone for long periods of time, told to contact someone else (who turns out to be equally unhelpful), and so on.

Although he is proud of the state's economic growth during his first term, the governor is worried about his likely opponent labeling him "antibusiness" as he heads into his reelection campaign. Consequently, the governor has ordered the DED's director to shake the organization up and make it more responsive to its clientele by fundamentally redesigning its structure.

Organization Chart for the Department of Economic Development

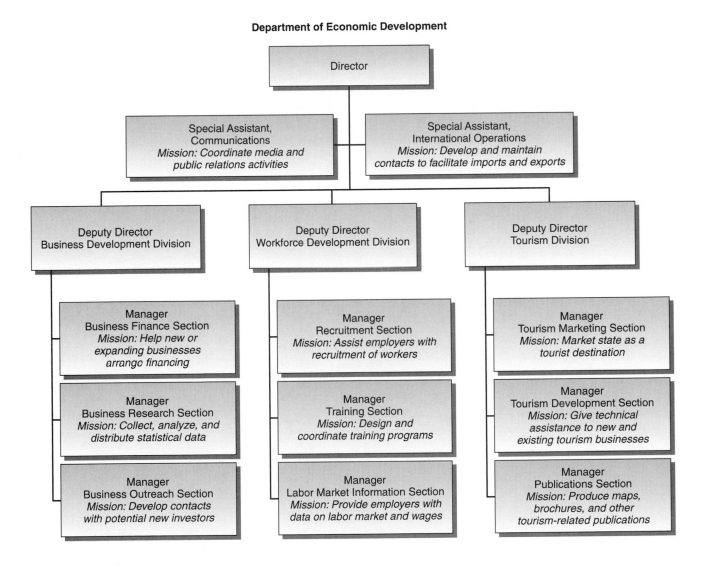

Reconfigured Organization Chart

Questions

1. How would you describe the organizational structure you created on Form 8? Is it a bureaucratic, matrix, or team model—or is it some new hybrid?

2. Why exactly did you design this structure? What impact do you expect it to have on the DED's effectiveness? Will the governor be pleased?

3. Would you like to work in this sort of structure? Why or why not? In general, which type of organization do you think you would find most congenial?

4. What sort of organizational structure do you in fact expect to work in when you graduate and take a professional job?

Exercise 3

Managing Organizations: Techniques for Total Quality Management

TOWARD QUALITY IN PUBLIC ADMINISTRATION

"Hey, Al," said Pete, pointing with his paintbrush. "You missed a spot in that corner."

"Aw," responded Al, "it's close enough for government work."

Close enough for government work. Now there's a telling phrase that everyone has heard and most of us have used at one time or another. What we mean when we say this is: "It's not that important. There's no penalty for doing a less than perfect job—just like in government."

Although tales of government inefficiency have always been exaggerated, it was probably true that not so long ago, quality of work received less than systematic attention in many government agencies. Government, after all, is a monopoly. It has no competitors nipping at its heels, keeping it on its toes. Managers may become complacent. Good performance may go unrecognized, poor performance unpunished. Without the discipline of the marketplace, innovation may be discouraged, with results subordinated to rules.

However much this used to be true, times have changed. A fundamental transformation in the character of public management has been under way in the United States for the past 15 or 20 years. Beginning in quiet corners of state and local government in the 1980s and spreading outward and upward in the 1990s, public agencies have increasingly been "reinvented." Out have gone traditional, knee-jerk bureaucratic, rule-bound remedies to every problem. In have come ideas that are innovative, entrepreneurial, and "outside the box." David Osborne and Ted Gaebler, the chief chroniclers and

advocates of this movement, outline the core principles of reinvented government as follows:[1]

- Promote *competition* between service providers.
- Focus on *outcomes,* not inputs.
- Be driven by *missions,* not by rules and regulations.
- Treat clients like *customers,* giving them meaningful choices.
- *Prevent* problems before they emerge, rather than waiting to solve them.
- *Decentralize* authority and embrace participatory management.
- Prefer *market* mechanisms to bureaucratic mechanisms.
- *Catalyze* all sectors—public, private, voluntary—to address community problems.

What sparked this revolution? No one single event was responsible. Declining public confidence in government in the aftermath of Vietnam and Watergate set the stage. The fiscal crisis that hit the public sector—epitomized by California's Proposition 13 in 1978—gave added impetus. The success that some large corporations seemed to have reinventing themselves in the face of mounting global competition in the late 1970s and early 1980s provided a tantalizing model for government leaders.

Whatever the cause of the reinvention revolution, the thread that ties all of its elements together is *quality.* Reinventing government is not about

---

[1] Adapted from David Osborne and Ted Gaebler, *Reinventing Government: How the Entrepreneurial Spirit Is Transforming the Public Sector* (Reading, Mass.: Addison-Wesley, 1992), pp. 19–20.

making government cheaper or smaller (or bigger and more expensive). Reinvention is about making government work better. It is about relegating the line "close enough for government work" to the dustbin of history.

As you might guess by looking at Osborne and Gaebler's list of principles, governments use many different methods to try to improve the quality of their services. Not all of them are new. Some of them—Management by Objectives (MBO), Planning Programming Budgeting System (PPBS), and zero-base budgeting (ZBB)—we will consider in other exercises. In this exercise, we will focus on what has become one of the most widespread and accepted of the quality-in-government initiatives: Total Quality Management (TQM).

TOTAL QUALITY MANAGEMENT (TQM)

Like many of the other techniques that may be considered under the broad heading of "reinventing government," TQM has been borrowed from the private sector, where it has been used to great effect in corporations such as Xerox, Federal Express, IBM, Delta Airlines, and Citicorp. In essence, TQM involves reorienting the culture of an organization toward quality and customer service. To that end, TQM requires a high degree of employee participation, careful measurement of performance, and the relentless pursuit of "continuous improvement" in organizational processes.

Although the roots of TQM stretch all the way back to Frederick Taylor, Scientific Management, and subsequent efforts to develop statistically based quality control systems in industry, the real credit for TQM is generally accorded to W. Edwards Deming (1900–1993), an American engineer and physicist who played a key role in helping rebuild Japanese industry after the Second World War under the auspices of General MacArthur's occupation command. The work of Deming and his colleagues—some American and some Japanese—helped shape the economic miracle of postwar Japan. Deming is probably best known for his "14 points for management," which distilled his philosophy into a relatively simple list of directives (point 7, for example, is "Adopt and institute leadership"), and for his Plan-Do-Check-Act (PDCA) Cycle. As

shown in Figure 3.1, the PDCA Cycle is a reminder that quality is a continuous commitment to planning, doing, checking (reviewing), and acting, not a linear path with a beginning and an end. Successful quality management requires unceasing planning, doing, checking, and acting.

What exactly does TQM require beyond these philosophical abstractions? The short answer is, a lot of hard—though often fun—work. TQM implementation is complex and time-consuming; it is anything but a "quick fix" to an organization's problems. Because it entails nothing less than a wholesale change in organizational culture, TQM generally necessitates both an initial intervention by trained consultants and a commitment by top management to ongoing training of employees (and of themselves). This means that the sort of short summary of TQM practices that can be offered here does not begin to describe the full range of organizational changes that the method requires.

With that caveat, it may be said that TQM implementation consists of six basic steps:

1. *Create teams* of employees whose work intersects to deliver a product or service.
2. *Establish incentive systems* so that team members can realize the benefits of increased pro-

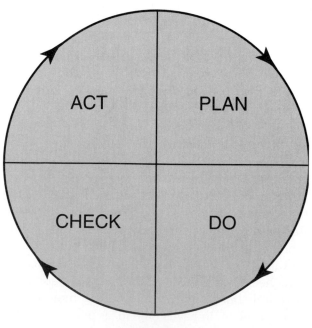

Figure 3.1
PDCA Cycle

ductivity and offer suggestions for improvements in quality without anxiety or fear.

3. *Identify the needs of the customers or clients*— both those outside the organization (the final or "external" customers) and those inside the organization (the intermediate or "internal" customers) served by each team.

4. *Map existing work processes* of each team and each employee. All teams should ask how they might improve processes better to help meet customer needs.

5. *Measure performance.* Develop baseline and benchmark measures for all aspects of work. The aim should be continuous improvement toward zero defects.

6. Identify suppliers and subcontractors whose work bears on the final product or service. *Forge partnerships* to ensure that quality orientation infuses suppliers and subcontractors.

Although some observers suggest that TQM is not as well suited to the public sector as it is to the private sector,[2] It is clear that governments all across America are forging ahead with one variant or another of TQM. The Department of Defense has a Quality Management Office located in the Office of the Secretary. Most other cabinet-level agencies, including the Departments of Agriculture, Energy, Interior, Labor, Commerce, and Treasury, have implemented TQM initiatives of one sort or another. The National Performance Review (NPR), headed by Vice President Al Gore, has supported TQM projects as part of its broader mission. States governments from California to the Carolinas and from Texas to Oregon have adopted TQM. So, too, have cities large and small.

---

[2] They argue, for instance, that although some government agencies may have unambiguous customers that they can aim to please, many do not. The National Park Service will never be able to make all of its "customers"—tourists, vendors, nearby businesses and industries, and so on—happy at the same time. And can we really expect the "customers" of the IRS to be "delighted"—the frequent measure of success cited by TQM advocates? Would we *want* the "customers" of various regulatory agencies—the Security and Exchange Commission, the Federal Communications Commission, and so forth—to be really pleased with the fruits of their labor? Perhaps not. For an elaboration of these arguments, see James E. Swiss, "Adapting Total Quality Management (TQM) to Government," *Public Administration Review* 52, 4 (July-August 1992), pp. 356–362.

TQM TECHNIQUES

Implementation of a full-scale TQM program necessitates the use of a wide array of specific administrative technologies and managerial techniques. These range from simple questionnaires that can be administered to vendors and clients to sophisticated strategies of leadership and team building. Somewhere in between are the tools that allow managers and workers to measure and track their performance. Such tools are essential if defects are to be minimized and quality is to be maximized— the real goal of TQM.

Six especially useful TQM tools, which can easily be mastered and applied even by beginning students of public administration, are cause-and-effect diagrams, flowcharts, Pareto charts, run charts, histograms, and scatter diagrams. Each of these tools is designed to display information visually in a way that is simple but powerful. Managers (and workers) who use these charts and diagrams are often able to gain insight into the sources of production or service delivery problems that would otherwise elude them—and thus to strive for continuous improvement. In the next few pages, you will learn about each of these techniques as we build a set of charts aimed at solving the following illustrative problem: Why am I not getting better grades? After reading through this section, you will be asked in the exercise that follows to apply what you have learned and chart some data from a case study.

CAUSE-AND-EFFECT DIAGRAMS

The cause-and-effect diagram is sometimes called a "fishbone diagram" because of its distinctive shape and sometimes an "Ishikawa diagram" in honor of its creator, Kaoru Ishikawa, a prominent Japanese quality control engineer. Whatever its name, the purpose of this chart is the same: to stimulate thinking about the factors that enhance or impeded quality.

As is shown in Figure 3.2, each of the lines angling into the main axis of this diagram represents a major category of quality-affecting factors. "Machines," "Materials," "Methods," and "Manpower" are the four categories used most commonly in TQM exercises, though one should feel free to use whatever categories best reflect the

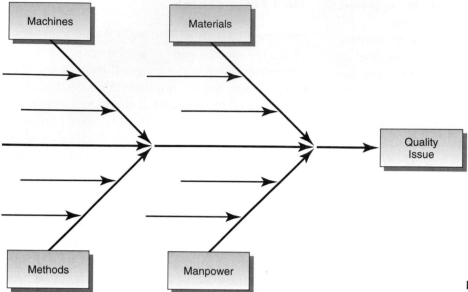

Figure 3.2
Cause-and-Effect Diagram

needs or practices of an organization. Each of the shorter lines shooting off from the major category lines marks a related, subordinate potential factor.

It is important to stress that one doesn't need to know for certain what the cause of a problem is before one produces this sort of chart. In fact, cause-and-effect diagrams are usually created at an early stage of problem solving, to assist brainstorm-ing and to get people actively involved in thinking an issue through. It is also important to note that cause-and-effect diagrams can be constructed for any sort of problem, from the simplest to the most complex.

To illustrate, let us take the problem of your grades in your college classes. And by the way, before you object that you have no problems with

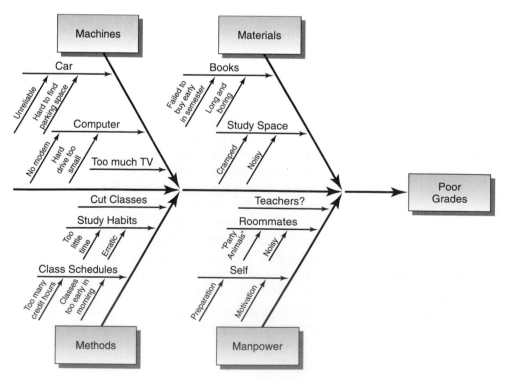

Figure 3.3
Cause-and-Effect Diagram
for Poor-Grades Problem

your grades because you are a good (or even excellent) student, remember that this is a chapter on Total Quality Management, with an emphasis on continuous improvement: Every student, no matter how good, can get better. Ideally, we would begin by sitting down in a brainstorming session with you and a group of people who know you well—friends, family, roommates, teachers. Looking at the bare skeleton of a cause-and-effect diagram, we would try to list all of the possible things—a hectic schedule, inadequate study time, cutting classes, noisy roommates, an outmoded computer, and so forth—that interfere with you doing your best, labeling the bones as we went along. Ultimately we might produce the sort of creature shown in Figure 3.3.

Note that no one solution necessarily jumps out of this (or any such) diagram. In and of itself, the chart in Figure 3.3 does not tell us if your primary problem is, in fact, inadequate time with your books or too much time with noisy roommates. Instead, the chart serves to focus discussion and to initiate a process whereby possible causes can be weighed and remedies identified.

FLOWCHARTS

In general, a flowchart is a visual description of a *process*. Where cause-and-effect diagrams provide a schematic overview of possible sources of problems, flowcharts seek to depict the sequence of events in some operation that is of interest. For instance, the flowchart in Figure 3.4 indicates that a "no" at gateway 1 requires a detour through activity A, whereas a "yes" leads directly to gateway 2. Although symbols vary from flowchart to flowchart, in general it is useful to distinguish between gateways or yes-no decision points on the one hand and activities that result from particular yes-no decisions on the other. A gateway in a flowchart serves as a sort of sentry, checking ID before allowing us to pass the guardhouse: Has step *x* in the process been completed? If yes, do *a*; if no, do *b*.

Professionals in many different fields—computer science and engineering prominent among them—use flowcharts to try to put into systematic form on paper what may be a complex series of interdependent activities. TQM uses flowcharts to depict the process of work in an organization. The idea is that by representing work processes graphically, one can begin to identify areas susceptible to

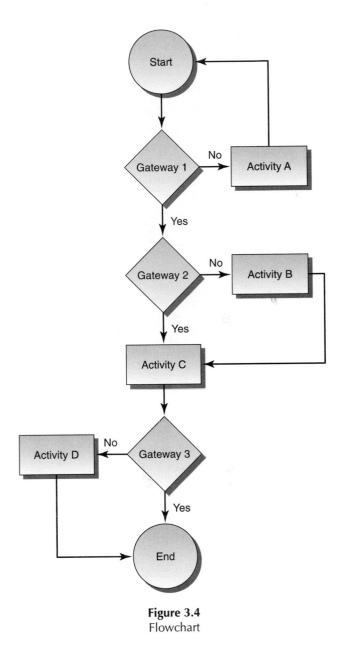

Figure 3.4
Flowchart

improvement. Effective flowcharts do not have to be sophisticated. They can even be sketched in pencil on the back of an envelope. The point is to try to capture all of the elements that go into a finished product or service.

Let's say we decide, based on our "fishbone diagram," that one of the root causes of your less than perfect GPA is your propensity to procrastinate when it comes to tackling term papers and other writing projects. We could then sit down and sketch a flowchart that links all the events and activities that optimally ought to take place between the

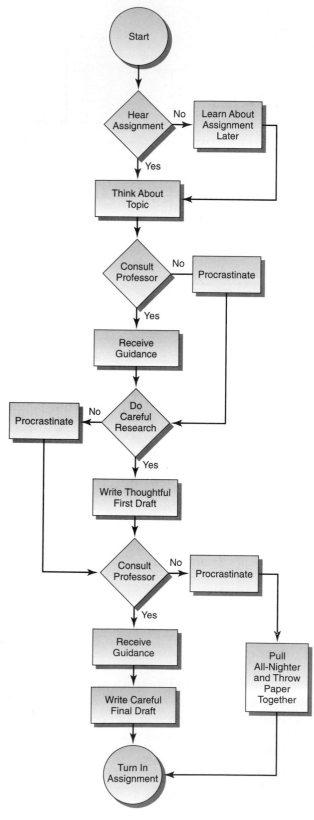

Figure 3.5
Term Paper Flowchart

announcement of the assignment and your turning in the final draft of the paper, as in Figure 3.5.

Note that we have also included in the chart alternative flows of events that take place when the optimal path isn't followed. These alternative flows are sometimes called "no loops" by TQM cognoscenti. In effect, the "yes" path constitutes the normative ideal; the "no loops" are drawn from an honest appraisal of real-life behavior. A good flowchart identifies "no loops" as a first step in the battle to improve performance; indeed, honesty in flowcharting is essential to addressing shortcomings in quality. In this case, we know we need to eliminate the "no loops" of not hearing about the assignment in a timely fashion, failing to consult the instructor, not undertaking careful background research, and so on.

PARETO CHARTS

A Pareto chart displays data on the types and frequency of problems in the delivery of a product or service (see Figure 3.6). A good Pareto chart gives a TQM team a clear idea of what factors are most responsible for product or service defects and thus what to work on first. Pareto charts stimulated the so-called "80–20 rule" in TQM: 80 percent of an organization's problems stem from only 20 percent of the causes. With a clear idea of which items are most responsible for compromising quality, a manager can, at least in the near term, focus like a laser beam, ignoring factors that are relatively trivial.

A good use of Pareto charting in our effort to improve your grades would be to compile written comments from all of your instructors on all of your papers. This would allow us to count and compare the frequencies of each type of criticism. As we can see in our hypothetical illustration in Figure 3.7, grammatical errors were cited far more often than any other problem in your writing. This suggests that spending a few hours each week with a tutor in the university's writing center would be the best investment of your time and energy—even more useful than investing in a new spellchecker, poring through the library for an extra fact or two, or learning a new system of footnoting (although the logic of continuous improvement would suggest that sooner or later you'll have to address these matters too).

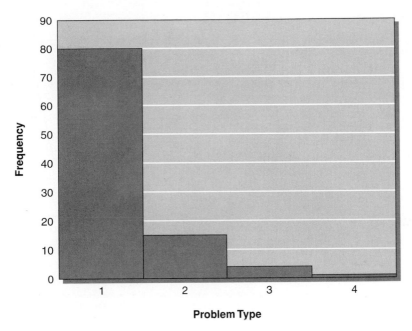

Figure 3.6
Pareto Chart

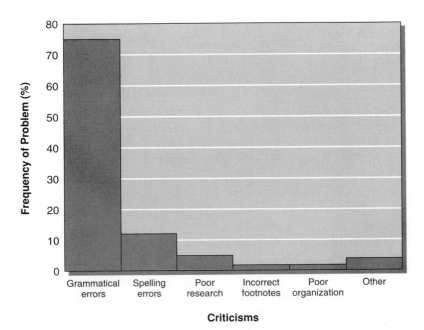

Figure 3.7
Pareto Chart of Criticisms of Writing Assignments

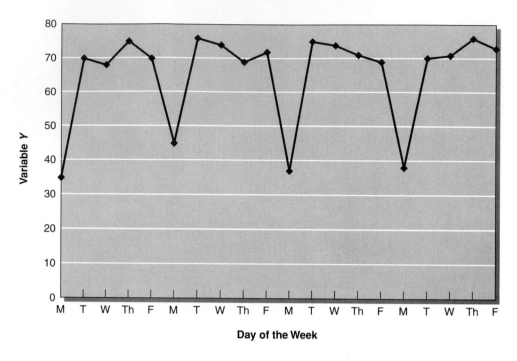

Figure 3.8
Run Chart

RUN CHARTS

A run chart is simply a graphic display of some variable over time. For that reason, run charts are also often called "trend charts." Figure 3.8 shows a simple run chart that plots some variable (production defects? the Dow Jones average? hospital admissions?) over four weeks of time. Run charts allow managers to glance at this display of data and get a sense of pattern—if there is any. If these data were charting defects on an automobile assembly line, for instance, the production supervisor might want to investigate what kind of condition the workers are in on Monday mornings and to try to do something about it.

As you will have guessed, we could use a set of run charts to deal with some of our grade performance problems. For instance, let's assume that after going through the cause-and-effect exercise, you have decided, sensibly enough, to set aside a certain amount of time each day to study. Because

of other obligations—part-time job, sports, social life—the amount of time you budget varies from day to day. It might be two hours on Monday, three hours on Tuesday, Wednesday, and Thursday, only an hour on Friday, and so on. In any event, you decide (like a good TQM manager) to keep careful track of how close you are to the budgeted mark each day over a four-week period. You are then able to produce a run chart that displays, day by day, the discrepancy between the amount of time you planned to study (in your search for continuous improvement) and the amount of time you actually studied (see Figure 3.9).

Of what use is such a chart? If in fact you were to see the sort of pattern that this set of charts displays, you would know that you have some serious problems focusing on schoolwork during weekends (assuming you budgeted your time properly in the first place). It may be time to adjust your social schedule, watch one or two fewer football games, or get up before noon on Saturday and Sunday.

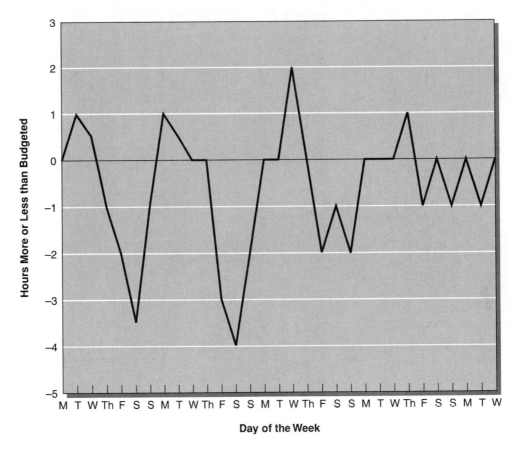

Figure 3.9
Run Chart of Study Times

HISTOGRAMS

Although a histogram may sound like something unpleasant that your doctor prescribes, actually it is nothing more than a chart that displays the frequency with which something occurs. Typically, a histogram takes the form of a bar chart, with frequency measured along the *y*-axis and the levels of occurrence (expressed in "bins") measured along the *x*-axis, as in Figure 3.10.

Although histograms may resemble Pareto charts on the surface, in fact they measure different sorts of things. Where a Pareto chart uses vertical bars to compare the relative frequency of different types of phenomena (apples vs. oranges vs. bananas), histograms use vertical bars to show the frequency with which a single phenomenon occurs

at different levels or intensities (small apples vs. medium apples vs. big apples).

Histograms are useful in many different circumstances. For instance, a college admissions office might create a histogram to chart how often students with various SAT scores apply to that college. A police chief might use a histogram to display emergency response times. A hospital administrator could use a histogram to show how many multiple-bypass patients spend ten days in the hospital, as opposed to 12, 14, or 16 days.

And you can use histograms to improve your academic performance. How? Let's assume that one of your problems is that you seldom get all of your reading done on time. Let's further assume that at least part of the reason for this is that you simply don't do a very good job estimating how long it will

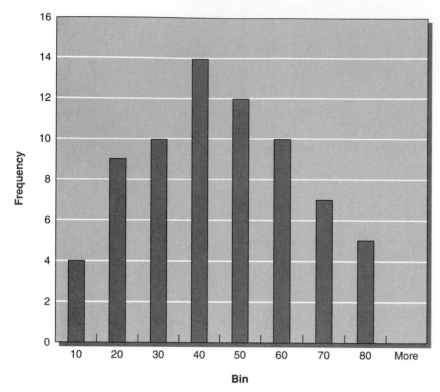

Figure 3.10
Histogram

take to plow through your various assignments. You sort of eyeball that novel from Brit Lit 101 or that textbook chapter from Physics 200, guess that you'll have to spend an hour with each—which you are sure you can do the night before the classes—and proceed to head out to a party with your friends.

Let's say that for a few weeks you kept track of how many minutes it took you to read each of the

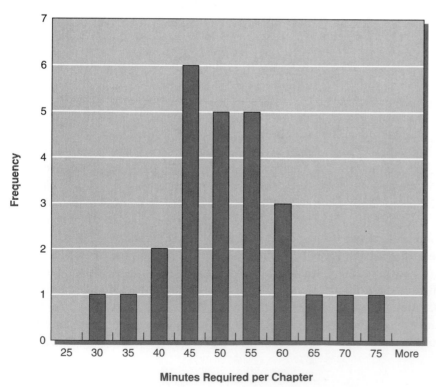

Figure 3.11
Histogram of Reading Times

various chapters of text you were assigned (51, 23, 46, 65, and so on). This would allow you to produce the sort of histogram displayed in Figure 3.11, which in turn would tell you that it generally takes you 45 to 65 minutes to read each chapter of text. Only very infrequently does it take you less than 40 minutes or as much as 70 minutes or more. Knowing this about yourself, you could add up the number of chapters you had to get through each week and budget a realistic amount of time to get your work done.

SCATTER DIAGRAMS

Except for cause-and-effect diagrams and flowcharts, which are by design only tentative approximations of reality, the graphic displays that we have discussed so far have dealt only with the relative frequency of discrete variables. At most they have told us that x happened this often and y happened that often. They have not really told us anything about the relationship between x and y. Probing such relationships is the point of a scatter diagram. In a scatter diagram, two variables are plotted against one another on the same chart, as is illustrated in Figure 3.12.

In the scatter diagram shown in Figure 3.12, it appears to be the case—just by eyeballing things—that an increase in variable x tends to be associated with an increase in variable y. We do not know from these data if the relationship is causal—Does x

cause y? Does y cause x?—nor do we know how strong the relationship is; these and related questions require more sophisticated statistical tools than we now have at hand.

But knowing that there appears to be some relationship is useful. If this scatter diagram were displaying data on the number of broken windows (x) versus the number of serious crimes committed (y) in a particular area, for instance, then a police department might want to explore deploying more resources in deterring quality-of-life or nuisance crimes. Similarly, if this scatter diagram were plotting the length of time it took welfare recipients to find employment (x) against distance in minutes from a major public transit line (y), then a social service manager might want to consider stimulating alternative transportation programs for welfare-to-work candidates. Again, in neither case (or in others that we might imagine) can we be sure that there is in fact a causal relationship between these variables. Such a diagram does serve as a starting point for further analysis, however. It may even provide a reasonable basis for action, if the two variables are closely related logically as well as empirically. For instance, if this scatter diagram were representing number of hours worked (x) and the number of errors made by keyboard operators (y), it would probably not be unreasonable for a manager to hire additional keyboard operators rather than to encourage existing employees to work a lot of overtime.

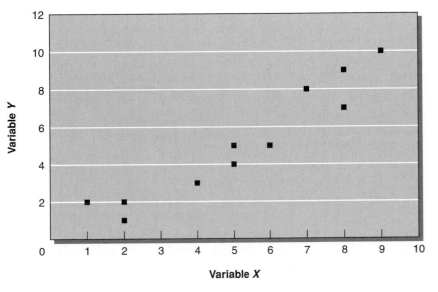

Figure 3.12
Scatter Diagram

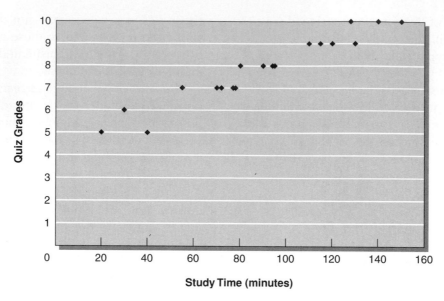

Figure 3.13
Scatter Diagram of Quiz Scores and Study Time

One obvious candidate for a scatter diagram in our academic improvement program may be found in Figure 3.13. Here we have carefully plotted grades received on a series of quizzes against the amount of time you invested in studying for each quiz. Not surprisingly, this scatter diagram suggests a pretty strong relationship between the two variables. Although we can't know for sure which way the causal arrow runs—or even if there is a causal arrow—it seems pretty likely that the more time you spend studying for a quiz, the better the grade you will receive.

FURTHER READING

There are many guidebooks to TQM written for managers. One of the most useful and most accessible is Mary Walton, *The Deming Management Method* (New York: Perigee Books, 1986). For a description of how TQM can be successfully applied to the public sector, see Steven Cohen and Ronald Brand, *Total Quality Management in Government* (San Francisco: Jossey-Bass, 1993).

Overview of Exercise

This exercise allows you to practice the six common TQM techniques—cause-and-effect diagrams, flowcharts, Pareto charts, run charts, histograms, and scatter diagrams—described in the narrative portion of this exercise. You will read a brief case study about the state Department of Motor Vehicles (DMV) and, working in TQM teams, use the information provided to produce the required charts and diagrams.

INSTRUCTIONS

Step One
Read the case study provided on Form 10.

Step Two
Form in TQM groups as directed by your instructor.

Step Three
Brainstorm within your group and use Form 11 to sketch a cause-and-effect diagram of the DMV's slow processing problem.

Step Four
Use Form 12 to flowchart the reregistration process at DMV. Be prepared to discuss the "no loops" that you have identified and how to eliminate them.

Step Five
Use Form 13 to translate the raw complaints data contained in the case study (see Box 1 on Form 10)

into a Pareto chart. Be prepared to discuss which problems seem to be serious and which relatively trivial. Do these data conform to the 80–20 rule?

IT Option
- Use the Bar Charting feature of Excel to do this problem.

Step Six
Construct a run chart on Form 14 using the average processing time and days of the month data from the case study (see Box 2 on Form 10). Is there a discernible pattern here? Assume that the first Monday was the first of the month. Does this suggest a pattern? Based on your run chart, how might the DMV management address this problem?

IT Option
- Use the Line Charting feature of Excel to do this problem.

Step Seven
Create a histogram on Form 15 using the processing time data from Box 3 on Form 10. For the purposes of this step, ignore the third column, the times-of-day data. Your y-axis will display frequency; your x-axis will designate discrete sets of time, measured in minutes. In constructing the x-axis, pick an interval (a "bin," to use the technical term) that is neither too wide (0–50, 51–100, etc.) nor too narrow (0–2, 2–4, 4–8, etc.). What do we learn from this chart?

IT Option
- Use the Histogram feature of Excel to do this problem.

Step Eight
Use Form 16 to produce a scatter diagram that plots processing time against time of day. All the data necessary may be found in Box 3 on Form 10. Plot the time of day along the x-axis and the minutes in processing time along the y-axis. What does this scatter diagram suggest? What remedial actions might management take?

IT Option
- Use the XY Charting feature of Excel to do this problem.

Step Nine
Answer the questions on Form 17.

Case Study

The Department of Motor Vehicles (DMV) is an independent state agency responsible for titling, licensing, and inspecting cars, trucks, and motorcycles and for testing and licensing drivers. In most respects, the DMV's operations are the epitome of bureaucratic routine. In each of the state's 17 counties, there is a DMV inspection and licensing center staffed with lower-level civil servants who check headlights and windshield wipers, scrutinize proof of liability insurance, administer driving tests, collect fees, stamp forms, and otherwise push paper for the 4 million owners and operators of motor vehicles in the state.

Despite some administrative improvements in recent years, the DMV remains almost every citizen's worst governmental nightmare. Once every five years, each licensed driver must report to the local DMV center for license renewal, a process that involves standing in seemingly interminable lines for pictures to be taken, vision to be checked, forms to be completed, and fees to be paid. Even worse, once a year the owner of every motor vehicle—car, truck, bus, van, RV, motorcycle, and so on—must report to the center for vehicle relicensing, a process that is even more complex and time-consuming. Discontent with DMV procedures has become so widespread that it has become an issue in state politics. The chairman of the state assembly's transportation committee has even introduced legislation that would privatize the DMV, a move vigorously opposed by the civil service employees' union and viewed skeptically by other legislators. Other proposals have included opening more centers, moving to biennial or even triennial inspections and relicensing, and privatized inspections coupled with mail-in renewals.

The DMV's single biggest problem is the time it takes for vehicles to be inspected and relicensed. On average, it takes 75 minutes from the time a driver pulls into one of the vehicle inspection lanes to the time he or she walks out the door of the processing center with a new license plate sticker. The crawl through the inspection lane is almost always painfully slow but is at its worst during the lunch hour (when the DMV is at half-staff) and on the fifteenth and thirtieth of each month (when tags expire). Once a driver has made the start-and-stop journey from the end of the line to the inspection bay, a state employee checks headlights (high and low beams), taillights, turn signals, horn, windshield wipers, emergency flashers, emissions, and brakes. The inspection itself takes only five minutes or so. Vehicles that fail the inspection are given 48 hours to remedy the problem and return for a reinspection.

Once a vehicle has passed inspection, the driver parks it in a lot and walks into the processing center with all of the necessary relicensing paperwork. This includes (1) the form from the vehicle inspector stating that the vehicle passed all safety and emissions tests, (2) a current "insurance card" from a state-approved insurance company attesting to the fact that the driver carries appropriate liability insurance, and (3) the current vehicle registration. Vehicles being registered for the first time also have to present (4) proof of title and (5) a notarized bill of sale specifying the price paid for the vehicle. Most of these forms must be checked against a computer database and then stamped by a DMV employee, a set of operations that requires the driver to stand in three or four separate lines—one for each form other than the bill of sale.

The final stop for the reregistering driver and the penultimate stop for the newly registering driver is a cashier, who collects the stamped documents and receives payment for the registration. The cashier also collects a 4 percent motor vehicle excise tax on all vehicles, new or used, being registered for the first time. Separate checks are required for registration (payable to the DMV) and for the excise tax (payable to the Division of Revenue); credit cards are not accepted. After payment has been received, the cashier gives the driver two small stickers bearing a four-digit month-year code that are to be applied to the bottom right-hand corner of the front and rear license plates. The driver who is registering for the first time has to go to yet one more station and stand in yet one more line—to receive the set of vehicular license plates.

As noted, even when this process works smoothly, it is aggravatingly time-consuming for the DMV's customer-clients. And unfortunately, the process doesn't always work smoothly. Massive traffic jams occasionally plague the inspection lanes when one of the four bays has to be closed—when a machine breaks or a staff shortage arises suddenly—and the scores of drivers who had been in that lane try to squeeze into one of the other crowded lanes, already filled with exasperated drivers. Drivers may or may not remember to bring their registration with them as they go through the lanes, and without this document (which contains the previous odometer reading), inspectors are unable to test a vehicle—necessitating a return trip. The inspection itself offers myriad opportunities for failure—a headlight slightly misaligned, brakes that pull slightly to one side or another, an obscure bulb burnt out, and so forth.

Once inside the building, having the proper documents becomes even more important. A missing or out-of-date insurance card, a forgotten checkbook, or an improperly written or unnotarized bill of sale are just a few of the problems that can derail the process. Given the possibilities for fraud and other forms of corruption, employees are not permitted to deviate from published procedures. Consequently, pleas to accept photocopies of documents or to "call my insurance company—they'll tell you I'm properly covered" fall on deaf ears.

In an effort to address some of these problems, the governor announced six months ago the appointment of a new DMV director. The director, in turn, immediately announced that she had contracted with a major outside consulting firm to diagnose DMV problems and to make recommendations for reform. Preliminary data from the consulting firm's studies have already started to come in. Box 1 presents partial findings from a "customer satisfaction" survey of the state's drivers. As you will see, there is little satisfaction among the customers.

Box 1 presents a breakdown of the complaints about DMV's registration process. Box 2 provides raw data on the processing times experienced by 100 different drivers randomly selected over a monthlong period. Box 3 tracks processing times for 50 drivers at various times of the day.

Box 1
Survey Results: Driver Complaints About DMV Registration Process

Complaint	Number
Number of inspection lanes is insufficient	17
Employees are rude or discourteous	6
Process is too slow	187
Inspection procedures are unfair	8
Rules are inflexible	22
Business hours are inadequate	18

Box 2
Mean Processing Time (to the Nearest Ten Minutes) for a Four-Week Period

Day	Mean Processing Time
Monday	90
Tuesday	80
Wednesday	70
Thursday	70
Friday	50
Monday	50
Tuesday	60
Wednesday	50
Thursday	60
Friday	90
Monday	100
Tuesday	90
Wednesday	70
Thursday	70
Friday	70
Monday	60
Tuesday	80
Wednesday	70
Thursday	70
Friday	80

Box 3
Processing Times for 50 Customers at Various Times of the Day

Customer	Time in Minutes	Time of Day (Start)	Customer	Time in Minutes	Time of Day (Start)
1	95	12:38	26	50	14:25
2	72	12:35	27	70	14:45
3	41	9:15	28	60	15:33
4	85	11:55	29	36	9:37
5	60	14:20	30	41	10:05
6	71	11:20	31	52	10:02
7	87	12:18	32	38	10:20
8	33	9:05	33	49	11:02
9	48	10:50	34	83	12:47
10	61	10:42	35	84	13:05
11	92	12:45	36	81	13:10
12	77	11:49	37	91	13:25
13	70	13:35	38	102	13:00
14	52	10:55	39	81	13:55
15	88	12:40	40	90	13:39
16	56	11:10	41	43	14:55
17	75	12:05	42	50	15:15
18	86	12:10	43	75	15:47
19	65	11:31	44	62	15:44
20	70	14:10	45	77	16:02
21	68	12:00	46	82	16:15
22	90	13:14	47	91	16:22
23	100	12:30	48	97	16:27
24	31	9:10	49	96	16:44
25	46	9:45	50	102	16:38

Cause-and-Effect Diagram of Slow Processing Times

Flowchart of Reregistration Process

Pareto Chart of Complaint Types

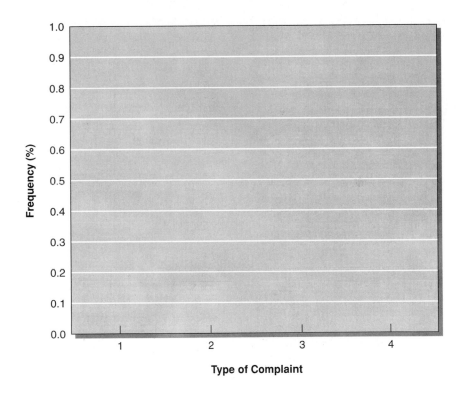

Run Chart of Weekly Processing Times

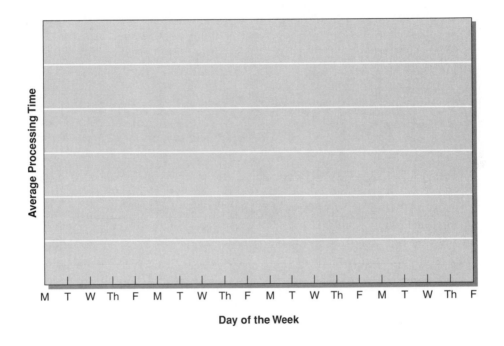

Day of the Week

Histogram of Processing Times

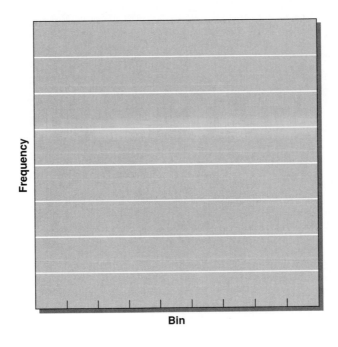

Scatter Diagram of Processing Times and Times of Day

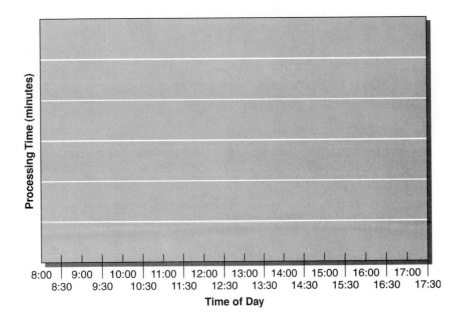

Questions

1. How useful are the various TQM techniques? Do you find one technique particularly useful or not useful? Why?

2. What would it take to get various members of an organization to use these techniques and otherwise to engage in a process of "continuous improvement"? Do you believe that the DMV can turn things around using these methods? Why or why not?

3. Is government in general more or less suited to TQM techniques than the private sector? Explain your answer.

4. What can citizens do to encourage political leaders to pursue quality in public management? Do citizens really care enough about quality to pursue the issue?

Exercise 4

Leadership and Administration

THE IMPORTANCE OF LEADERSHIP

Leadership is one of the most fundamental and enduring features of human society. No group, from the largest nation-state to the smallest gathering of children, seems to function without a leader. Some leaders are formal and official; others are informal and unofficial. Some are permanent; some are temporary. Some are benign; some are malign. Some are elected, some are selected, and others just seem to emerge. The only real constant is the idea of leadership itself. When a group suffers a leadership crisis—when a leader dies or resigns or proves incompetent or when, like the Italian parliament, a group seems unable to agree on a leader for more than a few days at a time—it often becomes immobilized, adrift in a sea of purposelessness and indecision. Groups that have healthy and stable leadership prosper; those that do not stagnate and eventually disintegrate.

Why are leaders so important? The answer is that we cannot accomplish collective purposes without them. Coordination among diverse individuals seldom arises spontaneously. Without a conductor, players in a symphony orchestra can merely bow, toot, pluck, and generate a lot of noise. Under a well-wielded baton, they make music. Similarly, absent a head coach or at least a captain, a football team of all-stars turned loose on a Sunday afternoon is likely to produce little more than fodder for an edition of "NFL Bloopers."

Of course, not just any conductor or football coach will do. Effective groups need effective leaders, men and women of vision and judgment, who can guide, motivate, and inspire followers to reach peak levels of performance. This is obviously also true for public administration. Translating public policy into efficient and effective organizational action requires strong and enlightened administrative leadership. The difference between an agency that is robust and successful and one that just plods along is very often to be found in the quality of leadership.

But this requirement is more easily stated than it is fulfilled—or even fully comprehended. There isn't much agreement about what makes for an effective leader, administrative or otherwise. Is an effective leader bold and authoritative? Consultative and democratic? Goal-oriented? People-oriented? Should a leader flourish a carrot or brandish a stick? Establish clear goals or encourage subordinates to set their own? "Well, yes . . . and no . . . and maybe," say the experts.

This uncertainty reigns despite the fact—or perhaps because of the fact—that the study of leadership is nearly as old as history itself. It is not unlikely that our earliest ancestors spent their evenings sitting around fires in the mouths of their caves trying to sort out who could best lead the hunt. And ever since that time, a search for leadership has been woven into the fabric of our most treasured myths and legends. Lessons on leadership fill the Old and New Testaments, cover the walls of Mayan temples, course through the Upanishads, and have a prominent place in the writings of Confucius. Leadership was a major concern of the ancient Greeks and Romans, preoccupied Machiavelli, and has been a key theme in modern political theory. Military commanders from Julius Caesar to Norman Schwartzkopf have thought and written about their own leadership. And of course, hundreds of professors have written thousands of books and articles on leadership. As Warren Bennis and Burt Nanus, two well-known leadership theorists, have put it, "Leadership is the most studied and least understood topic of any in the social sciences."[1]

THEORIES OF LEADERS

But even though we may not be able to specify one theory of leadership on which everyone agrees, we can at least sketch the contours of the discussion. Most early theories of leadership tended to emphasize one of two factors—*traits* or *situations*. Trait theories suggest that there is something about a person, some unique combination of strength, ambition, character, vision, charisma, and so forth, that marks that person as an effective leader. Leaders, according to this view, are born, not made. The Napoleon who swept the field at Austerlitz was foreshadowed by the boy who dominated his playmates on the hillsides of Corsica, fearless in the face of superior numbers.[2] Even when leadership qualities are not held to be exactly genetic—neither of Napoleon's parents was particularly remarkable, after all—trait theorists insist that they are formed so early in life and through such complex and often dramatic experiences as to be unteachable. One might be able to train a soldier to *manage* an army, to introduce a distinction we shall pursue later, but never to *lead* one. Moreover, leadership traits become such an integral part of a leader's being as to ensure that the person who has them will rise to the head of the pack in almost any circumstance. Had Margaret Thatcher gone into business rather than politics, she would have retired as chief executive officer of a major corporation instead of as prime minister of Great Britain. Had Pope John Paul II, as a young man, taken up machinist tools in the shipyards of Gdansk rather than holy orders in Krakow, his realm would be temporal now rather than spiritual, but a leader still he would be. Indeed,

for some trait theorists, history is written primarily by Great Men. There would now be no American union had there been no Abraham Lincoln to save it. Russia and China would have had no revolutions had V. I. Lenin and Mao Zedong never been born. And on a slightly less grand scale, Chrysler would have gone the way of Studebaker without Lee Iaccoca's leadership.

Not so fast, say situational theorists. The qualities that make a successful leader in one set of circumstances may make a dismal failure in another. Perhaps Lincoln was a great president. But is it clear that he would have made a great businessman? Is it even clear that he would have made a great president at any time other than the dark days of the mid-nineteenth century when the nation was hungry for a man of his particular courage, determination, and eloquence? How would his decidedly untelegenic mien and high-pitched voice have played on the evening news in 1990s America? One of his successors, Ulysses S. Grant, was, after all, widely considered to be as abject a failure in the White House as he was brilliant on the battlefield. What we consider greatness in a leader, argue the situationalists, is really a matter of being in the right place at the right time. A great man is not one who makes history but one whom history has made. Thus had Mao not been born in a tiny Hunan village in 1893, another young Chinese man or woman would have led the long march to Yunan. Had Lenin, like his brother, been arrested and executed by the Czar's secret police in 1887, another young Russian man or woman would have stepped off the train at St. Petersburg's Finland Station in April 1917 to ignite a revolution.

Arguments between these two schools are as fascinating as they are unresolvable. We will never know whether Abraham Lincoln would have been a good president in the 1990s, just as we will never know whether someone unnamed would have stepped forward to save the Union in the 1860s had Lincoln stayed in Illinois to practice law. It doesn't really matter, though, because most modern leadership research suggests that traits and situations are both significant. It is the interaction between the two that is critical. Personal traits associated with leadership are useless unless the situation allows them to be brought to bear. As Sidney Hook has pointed out, Napoleon banished to Elba had

---

[1]Warren Bennis and Burt Nanus, *Leaders* (New York: Harper & Row, 1985), p. 20.

[2]A difficult counterexample here is the young Arthur Wellesley, later to become, as the first Duke of Wellington, Napoleon's archnemesis; he was, by all accounts, a thoroughly dull lad who, far from dominating the playing fields of Eton, was removed from them for lack of promise.

choices and successfully plotted a return to power; Napoleon banished to St. Helena had none and died on that lonely South Atlantic island.[3] By the same token, we can all think of situations that cry out for leadership, some of them tragic, some that simply deteriorate—Bosnia, Kosovo, Somalia, and a million other places at home and abroad—because no one, seemingly, has the personal characteristics needed to take charge and to transform the situation for the better.

There are a myriad of such theories that stress the interaction between personal traits and situations, far too many to review here in any detail. We will concentrate on the views of just a few modern leadership theorists who have had a particular impact on public administration. The common thread in each set of theories is the observation that although there are leadership traits that can be identified, different situations require different traits.

One early version of this kind of leadership theory was presented in Robert Blake and Jane Mouton's "managerial grid."[4] According to this formulation, there are two major dimensions or axes on which we can assess managerial orientations or inclinations: (1) concern for people and (2) concern for production. Managers can rank anywhere from a low of 1 to a high of 9 on each dimension. Managers who rank low on both dimensions (1,1's in Blake and Mouton's terms) are exemplary of what they call "impoverished management," where the leader has only minimal concern for people and production and does the minimum required to hold the organization together. Managers who rank high on production, but low on people (9,1's) are termed "authority-obedience" types, noted for telling people exactly what to do and how to do it, concentrating on maximizing organizational output. Those at the opposite extreme, with a high concern for people and a low concern for production (1,9's) are "country-club" leaders, more interested in making employees feel good than in accomplishing goals. In

the middle (5,5's) are "organization men," managers, leaders who simply go along with the status quo to avoid rocking any boats. The best sort of managers in Blake and Mouton's view are those (9,9's) who are both people- and production-oriented, "team managers" who seek results through the commitment and involvement of all employees.

Where Blake and Mouton make the case for a nearly one-size-fits-all leadership style, others have argued that different situations call for distinctly different styles. Paul Hersey, Kenneth Blanchard, and Dewey Johnson, for instance, have proposed a "situational leadership" model.[5] In essence, this model states that a manager's style—ranging from directive ("telling," in their terms) to democratic ("delegating")—should be a function of his subordinates' "task-relevant maturity," which is a combination of ability, experience, motivation, self-esteem, and other variables. As an employee matures—gains ability, experience, confidence, and so forth—the manager should move from "telling" to "selling," and later from "selling" to "participating." Ultimately, when an employee is fully mature, the manager can adopt a leadership style of "delegating," in which the employee is largely self-directing. Taken together, these various managerial styles constitute what Hersey and Blanchard call a "Life Cycle Theory of Leadership."

Fred Fiedler's "contingency model" of leadership is similar in its emphasis on different styles for different situations.[6] The root of the Fiedler model is something called the "Least Preferred Coworker" (LPC) scale, which is a summary measure of a person's response to 16 pairs of traits (pleasantness/unpleasantness, friendliness/unfriendliness, cold/warm, boring/interesting, etc.) that might be used to describe the sort of employee that that person would like to work with. People who score high on the LPC scale are said to be "relationship-motivated"; people who score low are said to be "task-motivated." When is a task-motivated as opposed to relationship-motivated leadership style appropriate? This, Fiedler contends, depends on

[3]Sidney Hook, *The Hero in History* (New York: John Day, 1943), quoted in Bernard Bass, *Handbook of Leadership: Theory, Research, and Managerial Applications*, 3d ed. (New York: Free Press, 1990), p. 40.

[4]The latest version of this theory is elaborated in Robert R. Blake and Jane S. Mouton, *The Managerial Grid III* (Houston: Gulf Press, 1985).

[5]Paul Hersey, Kenneth H. Blanchard, and Dewey E. Johnson, *Management of Organizational Behavior*, 7th ed. (Upper Saddle River, N.J.: Prentice Hall, 1996).

[6]See Fred Fiedler, *New Approaches to Effective Leadership* (New York: Wiley, 1987).

"situational favorability." Situational favorability is a term Fiedler uses to summarize three other variables: leader-member relations, task structure, and leader "position power." When situational favorability is either very positive or very negative—that is, when leader-member relations are either very good or very bad, task structure is either very clear or very unclear, "position power" is either very obvious or entirely absent—a task-oriented leader is appropriate. By contrast, when situational favorability is somewhere in the middle—moderate leader-member relations, task structure, and position power—relationship-oriented leadership is in order.

It will perhaps not be surprising, given even this cursory introduction to leadership theory, to learn that there is little agreement even as to how to define leadership. Bennis and Nanus point to some 350 definitions. Bernard Bass, author of a nearly 1,200-page compendium of leadership theory and research, spends more than ten of those closely packed, double-column pages simply reviewing *categories* of definitions of leadership.[7] The problem is that it is practically impossible to define leadership theory without making judgments about how it operates. If we make our definition narrowly empirical—a leader is someone who has people following him—we are unable to distinguish some poor soul fleeing a mob from a great general rushing into battle at the head of his troops. To define leadership in a meaningful way is to get inside the heads of leaders and followers and understand intentions and motives. And to do that is to make a choice from among the welter of contending theories.

LESSONS FOR PUBLIC ADMINISTRATION

Does this mean that leadership theory has nothing to offer public administration? No, not at all. It does mean, though, that we need to be cautious in the theories we apply. It means, too, that it is not easy to generate a list of characteristics that describe an effective leader in public administration. Most attempts to do so look like nothing so much as the Boy Scout code, inventories of virtues—wisdom, strength, flexibility, honor, clarity, and so forth—that one would like to see in everyone, leaders and followers alike. Such lists also frequently resemble

[7]Bass, *Handbook of Leadership.*

what Herbert Simon once called the "proverbs of administration," where for "almost every principle one can find an equally plausible and acceptable contradictory principle."[8] In ordinary life, we tell one another "Look before you leap," as well as "He who hesitates is lost." In leadership theory, we confidently advise managers to "maintain a firm hold on the reins" while moving "carefully and democratically to secure consensus."[9]

These caveats notwithstanding, research in leadership theory does offer some insights that apply to public administration.

1. **Leadership can make a difference.** Organizations that are well led are more productive than those that are poorly led. At a time when public budgets are strained to the breaking point, it is important to recognize that more can be done with less.

2. **There is a difference between leadership and management.** Management is a linear process. It entails solving problems and overcoming obstacles by the workmanlike application of known techniques. Leadership is nonlinear. It involves redefining and rethinking problems in creative ways. Planning, organizing, staffing, and budgeting are management skills. Developing a vision of the future and motivating and inspiring people to achieve it are fundamental elements of leadership.[10] Public administration needs leaders *and* managers—but has more often cultivated only the latter.

3. **Leadership skills can be learned.** A large number of leadership training institutes have emerged in the past 20 years. The evidence indicates that, while not everyone can be transformed into a great leader, most administrators can learn some skills that can improve their leadership abilities.[11]

4. **There is no one "best" style of leadership.** Administrative leaders have to adapt to the particular circumstances of their agencies. Large

[8]Herbert Simon, *Administrative Behavior,* 3d ed. (New York: Free Press, 1976), p. 20
[9]These particular proverbs were found in a leading public administration textbook best left unidentified.
[10]See John P. Kotter, *A Force for Change: How Leadership Differs from Management* (New York: Free Press, 1990).
[11]See Jay A. Conger, *Learning to Lead: The Art of Transforming Managers into Leaders* (San Francisco: Jossey-Bass, 1992).

Box 1
Leadership Self-Assessment

Read each of the statements below, and rate yourself on a scale of 1 to 10 for each, depending on how strongly you agree with it.

1. I work well under pressure.
2. I am a team player.
3. I don't mind taking unpopular positions.
4. I am good at dealing with uncooperative people.
5. I am an effective communicator.
6. I have a strong set of values.
7. I am capable of motivating others.
8. I have a keen sense of humor.
9. I like challenges.
10. I listen well to others.

---

bureaucratic organizations immersed in routine operations in stable environments (such as the Social Security Administration) will probably benefit from a different leadership style than small collegial organizations doing creative work in unstable environments (such as the National Institutes of Health).

5. **The demand for leadership is increasing.** We live in a world of great change. Yesterday's solutions are not always adequate for today's problems, let alone tomorrow's. As Bennis and Nanus point out, the need for effective leadership has never been so great: "A chronic crisis of governance—that is, pervasive incapacity of organizations to cope with the expectations of their constituents—is now an overwhelming factor worldwide."[12]

FURTHER READING

Paul Hersey, Kenneth H. Blanchard, and Dewey E. Johnson, *Management of Organizational Behavior,* 7th ed. (Upper Saddle River, N.J.: Prentice Hall, 1996), provides a good overview of organization theory with an emphasis on leadership. The most comprehensive review of the leadership literature by far is Bernard Bass, *Handbook of Leadership: Theory, Research, and Managerial Applications,* 3d ed. (New York: Free Press, 1990). Though somewhat dense, this volume is especially valuable for the student who wishes to learn more about leadership theory.

Warren Bennis and Burt Nanus, *Leaders* (New York: Harper & Row, 1985), is a very well written, accessible example of the transformational leadership school. Jay Conger, *Learning to Lead: The Art of Transforming Managers into Leaders* (San Francisco: Jossey-Bass, 1992), provides an interesting personal account of various leadership training programs. Gary Wills, *Certain Trumpets* (New York: Simon & Schuster, 1994), is a collection of fascinating biographical essays on various types of leaders—military, political, religious, sports, and so forth—together with sketches of "anti-types" in each category.

Overview of Exercise

In this exercise, you will design and build paper airplanes. (That's right, paper airplanes!) The goal is to construct an airplane that flies as far and as accurately as possible and to manufacture it in quantity.

INSTRUCTIONS

Step One
Your instructor will announce the basic ground rules for this exercise: time available, permissible construction materials, venue, and so on.

Step Two
Develop and test various prototype paper airplanes. Seek to develop a plane that can achieve both accuracy and distance. To do this, imagine a rope stretching along the ground hundreds of feet into the distance. The winning airplane will be the one that launched from one end of the rope lands as close to the other end of the rope—and to the axis of the rope itself—as possible.

[12]Bennis and Nanus, *Leaders,* p. 2.

Step Three

Select one design as your entry.

Step Four

Manufacture as many copies of your design as possible in the time allowed.

Step Five

Your instructor will select at random one airplane from among the stock of those manufactured by each entrant. This is the plane that the entrant must use in the "fly-off." This rule is intended to prevent an entrant from making one really good example of a design and then padding inventory with a bunch of junky, knock-off copies.

Step Six

Participate in the fly-off.

Step Seven

The instructor will judge the fly-off according to the formula:

$$4a - b + c = d$$

where a is the absolute distance in feet from the starting line of the landing point of the plane

b is the distance in feet from the landing point of the plane to the imaginary rope

c is the number of copies of the plane manufactured by the entrant

d is the entrant's final score

Step Eight

Answer the questions posed by your instructor in the postflight debriefing. Note to instructors: The Instructor's Manual that accompanies *The Public Administration Workbook* provides a list of pertinent questions.

Exercise 5

Administrative Law

WHAT IS ADMINISTRATIVE LAW?

On the face of it, the question, "What is administrative law?" is a simple one: Administrative law is that body of law dealing with public administration. Unfortunately, that simple definition obscures a lot of complexity. In the United States, unlike many other countries, there is no single, codified set of laws dealing with public administration. You cannot, for instance, walk into a law library and expect to find on a shelf *The Administrative Laws of the United States* or *The Administrative Laws of California*. Instead, administrative law is tucked away in many different places—in federal and state constitutions, statutes, executive orders, regulations, treaties, and court decisions. All of these things taken together as they affect public administration constitute administrative law.

Thus if you challenge the right of your university to suspend you for violating a campus "speech code," you are dealing with a question of administrative law. So is a pilot who questions the authority of the Federal Aviation Administration to impose a mandatory retirement age of 60 or a computer technician who maintains that his employer has no right to insist on regular drug tests. Similarly, a major corporation that argues that a state environmental agency has exceeded its authority by requiring discharge permits is involved in a question of administrative law, as is a state welfare department that insists that mandates from the U.S. Department of Health and Human Services have impaired its autonomy. Administrative law, then, is engaged whenever questions arise about the powers that administrative agencies may lawfully exercise, the procedures they have used to make decisions, or the rights that employees and clients have in dealing with those agencies.

WHY IS ADMINISTRATIVE LAW IMPORTANT?

The traditional theory of public administration held that elected officials make policy and administrators implement it. Whether this neat distinction ever applied in practice is doubtful. Certainly it does not apply today. The scope of modern government is so vast and the issues government confronts are so technically complex that elected officials can attend directly only to a minute proportion of the items on the public agenda. Consequently, much of the day-to-day responsibility for making public policy is delegated—formally or informally—to public administrators. This is what is meant by the concept of the *administrative state*. Public administrators, not members of Congress, are the ones who determine safety standards for nuclear reactors, set the seasonal bag limits for hunters of migratory birds, decree who should be awarded broadcast licenses, and decide thousands of other questions, large and small.

The term we use to describe the exercise of this delegated power is *administrative discretion*. Administrative discretion is said to be *formal* whenever a legislative body explicitly grants decision-making authority to an administrative entity, as in the case of regulatory commissions. Discretion is considered *informal* whenever autonomous decision-making power arises naturally out of the structure of the situation. Police officers, for instance, exercise informal administration discretion constantly as they determine how to enforce the law in specific cases. Administrative discretion of either sort constitutes a serious theoretical challenge to representative democracy, the core assumption of which is that public officials must be held accountable to the public. How can we, the members of the public, ensure that the discretionary power wielded by unelected public administrators is exercised consistent with public purposes? Administrative law is one of several answers to this question. In effect, administrative law represents a check on administrative discretion.

STRUCTURES OF ADMINISTRATIVE LAW

Just as there is no single codified body of administrative law in the United States, there is no single set of actors and institutions—no administrative police or administrative courts (with certain exceptions)—to enforce it. Instead, agencies are expected, at least in the first instance, to uphold administrative law themselves, to interpret and follow guidance from the various sources of administrative law—constitutions, statutes, court decisions, and so forth. Some agencies have specialized, independent employees called Administrative Law Judges (ALJs) who serve as hearing officers and judges in disputes arising between an agency and its clients or employees (see box).

ALJ Facts

- The federal government employs approximately 1000 ALJs.
- Although many agencies use ALJs, most (around 60 percent) work for the Social Security Administration.
- Applicants for ALJ positions must be attorneys with at least seven years' experience practicing before federal courts or federal agencies.
- Once appointed, ALJs are relatively autonomous, insulated from direct agency control by civil service rules.

Certain agencies also have elaborate procedures for making decisions or promulgating rules and regulations, procedures that are intended to guarantee fairness and due process. This is especially true of regulatory agencies such as the Federal Trade Commission (FTC), Federal Communications Commission (FCC), Interstate Commerce Commission (ICC), and Securities and Exchange Commission (SEC), among others, which are charged with quasi-legislative or quasi-judicial functions.

Sometimes, of course, clients or employees or regulated industries are unsatisfied by their treatment at the hands of agency officials, even after going through several levels of internal appeal. In these circumstances, aggrieved parties may, depending on the circumstances, take their cases to specialized administrative agencies, such as the Equal Employment Opportunities Commission (EEOC) or the Merit Systems Protection Board (MSPB), two federal agencies responsible for various types of employment-related administrative law. Or they may seek relief directly through the courts. Indeed, state and federal courts are, in most instances, the final arbiters of administrative law disputes. Through a process known as judicial review, judges may review administrative actions and determine if they are lawful. Getting into court with a claim against an administrative agency is seldom easy, however. On the contrary, at least three major tests must be met for a court to exercise judicial review. First, the court in which a suit is brought must have *jurisdiction;* a federal district court will probably not entertain your claim against the Department of Motor Vehicles (DMV) for suspending your driver's license, for instance. Second, all administrative and lower court remedies must have been *exhausted;* even if a judge decides that she has jurisdiction, for example, she will not consider reinstating your driver's license until after you had gone through all DMV appeals procedures. Third, you must have *standing*—must demonstrate that you have been directly injured—to bring the suit; you cannot, in other words, sue the DMV to reinstate your roommate's license, even if he does drive you to work.

These tests exist both to avoid clogging the courts with frivolous cases and to avoid compromising administrative authority. After all, if anyone could sue any time he or she disliked something an agency did, public administration would be paralyzed. It is a basic rule of administrative law in the United States that courts shall refrain from substituting their substantive judgments for those of administrators, who are presumed to be experts in their domains. Courts instead limit themselves, at least in theory, to deciding whether administrators have remained within the confines of the law: Did they act within their authority, follow prescribed rules, observe due process, and so forth? So, for example, if you represent an environmental group that doesn't like where the Department of Transportation has decided to build a bypass, you probably won't get very far charging the DOT in court with having chosen an unwise site. Rather, you will need to demonstrate that the department violated some established administrative procedure—failed to hold public hearings, neglected to conduct a proper environmental impact statement, or the like—in making the decision if you expect to make any headway under judicial review provisions.

But while it is true that the principles of jurisdiction, exhaustion, and standing limit the applicability of judicial review in any particular case, it is equally true that court decisions have a major effect on public administration. Cases that do make it before the courts set precedents for the elaboration and interpretation of rules and procedures that are applied by all administrators in the course of their day-to-day work. Although you may not be able to sue to reinstate your roommate's driver's license, for instance, you can be sure that the operation of the Department of Motor Vehicles is very much constrained by a wide range of court decisions. All agencies, in fact, incorporate judicial decisions, directly or indirectly, into their standard operating procedures. Police departments design their investigation and arrest procedures to comply with Supreme Court interpretations of Fourth and Fifth Amendment protections; welfare agencies tailor their rules to match eligibility requirements that emerge from case law; colleges and universities establish or abolish affirmative action programs that reflect various judicial determinations about the meaning of the 1964 Civil Rights Act and related statutes. Law in the American system is largely judge-made law. Decisions made by judges in thousands and thousands of individual cases around the country constitute an important—if not always clear—element of the environment of American public administration.

THE ADMINISTRATIVE PROCEDURES ACT

One of our key points has been that American administrative law is not particularly well codified, that it is scattered across many different statutes, regulations, judicial interpretations, and so forth. Although this is certainly true overall, a major exception is the Administrative Procedures Act (APA), a statute that sets out general rules for federal administrative agencies. The APA provides guidelines for agency rule making and outlines the procedures that must be followed in administrative adjudicatory processes. It specifies, among other things, when agencies must hold hearings, how they should conduct those hearings, and what sort of evidence should be considered. The basic structure of the APA was set in 1946, but it has been amended several times since then. Two major amendments that you may be familiar with are the Freedom of Information Act and the Privacy Act. The Freedom of Information Act (section 552 of the APA) requires federal agencies to make various documents and records available to the public. The Privacy Act (section 552a of the APA) prohibits agencies from disclosing information about individuals without their consent and gives individuals the right to inspect records maintained on them. If you've ever asked a professor to fill out a letter of recommendation for you, you may have noticed a Privacy Act disclaimer—a place on the form that asks if you wish to waive your right of access to the letter so as to keep it confidential.

The heart of the APA, though, is the sections dealing with rule making and adjudication. A *rule* is an action taken by an administrative agency that resembles legislation. That is, it is (1) reasonably general and (2) aimed at prescribing future activity, not at judging something that has happened in the past. *Adjudication,* on the other hand, is an action taken by an administrative agency that resembles a judicial decision. It is specific to an individual or corporate entity and is directed at something that has already occurred. For example, the Federal Aviation Administration (FAA) has issued a rule if it adopts a policy requiring all aircraft flying within a certain distance of major airports (Class B airspace) to have onboard radio equipment (a Mode C transponder) that automatically provides air traffic controllers with information about aircraft altitude. The FAA is engaged in an adjudicatory action if it seeks to revoke the license of John Smith, a pilot who flew through the Philadelphia Class B airspace on April 15, 1999, without a Mode C transponder.

A full treatment of APA requirements for rule making and adjudication is beyond the scope of this chapter. Suffice it to say that the APA recognizes several different types of rules and rule making and a range of adjudicatory procedures. The most rigorous rule-making requirements are imposed on agencies that propose *substantive rules* under *formal rule-making procedures.* In these cases, agencies must follow very strict guidelines, hold formal hearings presided over by ALJs, hear testimony from all affected parties, and issue the rule based on "substantial evidence" in the written record. Fortunately, most agencies most of the time do not have to adhere to these procedures. Instead, they can rely on the informal "notice and comment" rule-making procedures outlined by the APA.

The same variation applies to adjudicatory procedures. Some actions simply require a notice of charges and an opportunity for the affected party to present his or her side of the story. Other actions require far more detailed safeguards of due process rights with the adjudicatory procedure resembling in its structure a full-blown trial complete with attorneys, cross-examination, rules of evidentiary disclosure, and so forth. What set of procedures must be followed depends, in general, on the nature of the interests involved and the costs of making a mistake. Courts have found that a student challenging a suspension from school is entitled to considerably less protection, for instance, than a person whose disability benefits are about to be terminated.

Although the provisions of the APA sound complex—and in many ways they are—the general principle of the statute is simple: If agencies follow correct procedures, the public interest will be protected. This process orientation reflects the belief, fundamental to American society in general and to American jurisprudence in particular, that if everyone's rights are respected and due process is observed, justice will have been done and outcomes will take care of themselves. The tricky part with respect to public administration is striking a balance between this precept and the need for administrative efficiency. Governance in the modern state without administrative discretion is inconceivable. Administrative discretion without constraint would be unbearable. Administrative law properly applied constrains administrative discretion without destroying it.

FURTHER READING

Good essays on some of the current issues in American administrative law can be found in Peter Schuck, ed., *Foundations of Administrative Law* (New York: Oxford University Press, 1994); Phillip J. Cooper and Chester A. Newland, eds., *Handbook of Public Law and Administration* (San Francisco: Jossey-Bass, 1997); and David Rosenbloom and Richard Schwartz, *Handbook of Regulation and Administrative Law* (New York: Dekker, 1994). A classic statement of the problem of administrative discretion—and a strong argument for increased rule making—is Kenneth Culp Davis, *Discretionary Justice* (Baton Rouge: Louisiana State University Press, 1969). Jerry Mashaw, *Due Process in the Administrative State* (New Haven, Conn.: Yale University Press, 1985), provides a detailed examination of due process questions in administrative law. State-level concerns—and an analysis of the Model State Administrative Procedures Act—form the core of Arthur Earl Bonfield, *State Administrative Rule Making* (Boston: Little, Brown, 1986). Two general texts, both somewhat dated but still useful as overviews of the field, are Florence Heffron and Neil McFeeley, *The Administrative Regulatory Process* (New York: Longman, 1983), and Phillip J. Cooper, *Public Law and Public Administration* (Palo Alto, Calif.: Mayfield, 1983).

A good, basic text used in law schools is William F. Fox, Jr, *Understanding Administrative Law,* 3rd ed. (N.Y.: Matthew Bender, 1997).

Overview of Exercise

In this exercise, you will review, argue, and decide a hypothetical case in administrative law that arises under the Americans with Disabilities Act of 1990. One team of students will act as plaintiff's attorneys and, based on facts presented in the exercise, prepare a complaint to be submitted to an arbitration panel, made up of a second team of students. A third team will act as defense attorneys for the plaintiff's agency and prepare a response to the complaint, also to be submitted to the arbitration panel.

INSTRUCTIONS

Step One
Your instructor will assign you to one of the following roles:

> Plaintiff's attorney
>
> Defense attorney
>
> Arbitrator

All participants should read the role information provided on Forms 18–20.

Step Two
All participants should read the background to the Americans with Disabilities Act presented on Form 21.

Step Three
All attorneys—plaintiff and defense—should read the fact pattern presented on Form 22.

Step Four
All participants should read the ADA legal tests and definitions presented on Form 23.

Step Five
Plaintiff's attorney should prepare a complaint using Form 24 and information gleaned from Forms 21–23. The "Statement of Claims" section of the complaint should list the facts, point by point, from the plaintiff's perspective, numbering each one. For instance, it might read: "(1) The plaintiff, Mary Smith, is a qualified individual with a disability . . . ; (2) The ADA requires that . . . ; (3) Despite a request for reasonable accommodation, the defendant . . . ";

and so forth. The idea is to list all the facts and allegations as clearly and systematically as possible. The "Relief Sought" section of the complaint should list, in the same manner, exactly what the plaintiff is seeking. For instance, it might begin: "(1) The plaintiff, Mary Smith, seeks reinstatement . . . ; (2) The plaintiff also seeks . . . "; and so forth. Copies of this complaint should be submitted simultaneously to the arbitration panel and to the defense attorneys.

Step Six
Upon receiving their copy of the claim form from the plaintiff's attorneys, defense attorneys should prepare a written response using Form 25 and information gleaned from Forms 21–23. The response may take any form the attorneys desire, though generally it will be a brief, point-by-point refutation of the allegations, with reference to appropriate statutory language. Copies of this response should be submitted simultaneously to the arbitration panel and to the plaintiff's attorneys.

Step Seven
Members of the arbitration panel, under the leadership of its designated chairperson, should familiarize themselves with the plaintiff's claim and the defense's response and convene a hearing, during which time attorneys for both sides will present their cases in full. The chairperson of the panel is charged with the responsibility for conducting this hearing in an orderly fashion and for following proper procedures. The plaintiff's case should be presented first, with the defense to follow.

Step Eight (Optional)
Plaintiff and defense attorneys may submit additional written evidence—medical records, statements from witnesses, performance evaluations, job descriptions, and so on—for the panel's consideration. Attorneys have a responsibility to inform opposing counsel of the nature of any evidence they plan to introduce far enough in advance that opposing counsel has time to ask to see it, consider it, and assemble evidence in rebuttal. Failure to observe this responsibility *may* be grounds for ruling evidence inadmissible.

Step Nine

During the hearing, arbitrators are encouraged to take an active role, within limits set by the chairperson, in questioning attorneys on the two sides. Attorneys should address themselves to the arbitrators, not to one another. Each side should be allowed a closing statement.

Step Ten

At the conclusion of the hearing, the arbitrators should retire to a private place, discuss the case among themselves, and reach a decision. Decisions should be written (use Form 26) and then formally read to assembled participants. Arbitration decisions in this case are based on majority vote. Arbitrators are empowered to find in favor of the plaintiff or in favor of the defense in whole or in part. If arbitrators accept one or more of the plaintiff's claims, remedies *may* include reinstatement, promotion, and awarding of back pay. Punitive damages are not permitted.

Role Information: Plaintiff's Attorney

Working with any other students assigned by the instructor to this role, as plaintiff's attorney you have two jobs in this simulation. First, you must prepare the formal complaint to be filed with the arbitration panel established by the State Human Rights Commission. To do this, you need to review carefully the ADA Legal Tests and Definitions (Form 23) and the Fact Pattern in this case (Form 22). It is essential that you understand both exactly what it takes to prove a case of discrimination under the ADA and what the issues are in the Mary Smith case. Use Form 24 to draft the actual complaint. If time allows and you have access to a law library, you may wish to do some research and cite cases that support your claim.

Your second task is to present your case before the arbitration panel. As part of this process, your instructor may allow you to include additional evidence as part of your case. If so, you may want to produce documents that help substantiate your case. What you produce will depend on exactly what sort of claim you are trying to prove. For instance, you might generate letters from physicians testifying to Mary Smith's disability or letters from coworkers that call into question management's responsiveness to disabled workers. Be creative. Remember, though, that you must give opposing counsel adequate notice of the nature of any evidence you plan to introduce and, if they ask, allow them to examine that evidence. Failure to observe this rule may lead to your evidence's being ruled inadmissible by the arbitrators. (Obviously, attorneys in the "real world" cannot manufacture evidence in this way. The point in doing it here is to encourage you to think about what sort of evidence would be useful in proving your claim.)

If your instructor chooses not to allow you to introduce additional evidence, simply be prepared to make a clear and convincing oral presentation of your claim to the arbitration panel. You must in any case be able to answer questions put to you by the panel and to rebut the case made by the defense. Your strategy must be to show by a preponderance of the evidence that the plaintiff meets all the tests set by the ADA.

Role Information: Defense Attorney

Working with any other students assigned by the instructor to this role, as a defense attorney you have two jobs in this simulation. First, you must prepare the agency's initial written response to the formal complaint filed by the plaintiff with the State Human Rights Commission. The plaintiff's attorney or attorneys will provide you with a copy of the complaint at the time of their filing. To prepare your response, you need to be thoroughly familiar with the ADA Legal Tests and Definitions (Form 23) and the Fact Pattern in this case (Form 22). It is essential that you understand both exactly what it takes to defend against a charge of discrimination under the ADA and what the issues are in the Mary Smith case. Use Form 25 to draft your written response to the complaint. Note that written responses to such complaints are generally brief; you will have the opportunity to elaborate later.

Your second task is to present your case before the arbitration panel. As part of this process, your instructor may allow you to include additional evidence as part of your case. If so, you may want to produce documents that help substantiate your case. What you produce will depend on exactly what sort of defense you are trying to mount. For instance, you might generate records of performance evaluations showing Mary Smith's low levels of productivity or letters from witnesses to objectionable behavior. Be creative. Remember that you have a duty to inform opposing counsel of the nature of any evidence you plan to introduce and to let them examine that evidence if they ask to see it. Failure to observe this procedure may lead the arbitrators to rule your evidence inadmissible. (Obviously, attorneys in the "real world" cannot manufacture evidence in this way. The point in doing it here is to encourage you to think about what sort of evidence would be useful in disputing this claim.)

If your instructor chooses not to allow you to introduce additional evidence, simply be prepared to make a clear and convincing defense of the agency's position to the arbitration panel. You must in any case be able to answer questions put to you by the panel and to rebut the claims made by the plaintiff. Your strategy must be to show how the plaintiff fails one or more of the legal tests set by the ADA.

Role Information: Arbitrator

Working with any other students who may be assigned to this role by the instructor, your job as arbitrator is to read the complaint and response filed, respectively, by the plaintiff and defense attorneys, to conduct a hearing at which the allegations can be fully aired by both sides, and, weighing all evidence, to make a judgment on the allegations. Be certain that you are fully familiar with the ADA Legal Tests and Definitions described on Form 23.

It is your responsibility as an arbitrator—to be exercised by the chairperson of the panel in particular—to ensure that proper procedures are followed and that evidence is presented fully and fairly. If your instructor permits additional evidence to be generated by the attorneys in this simulation, you have the right to rule on the admissibility of individual pieces of evidence in the hearing. In doing so, however, you should bear in mind that evidentiary rules are somewhat relaxed in administrative law cases, "hearsay" evidence, for instance, generally being allowed. In general, you should allow evidence to be presented if the attorneys introducing it have given adequate notice to opposing counsel.

It also your responsibility as an arbitrator to take an active role in the case, to probe and ask questions of the attorneys where appropriate.

The judgment you make in this case must be based on a "preponderance of the evidence." You have to be satisfied not "beyond a reasonable doubt" but merely that the greater weight of evidence is on one side rather than the other. Remember that your standard for judgment is *the law as it is written,* not some generalized sense of fairness or equity.

Background to the Americans with Disabilities Act

The Americans with Disabilities Act (ADA) of 1990 is one of the most significant and sweeping pieces of civil rights legislation passed in the past 30 years. Intended to "assure" disabled Americans of "equal opportunity, full participation, independent living, and economic self-sufficiency," the ADA obligates employers, enterprises offering public accommodations or engaged in public commerce, state and local governments, and providers of communications services to accommodate persons with physical and mental disabilities.[1] The implications of the ADA are far-reaching because it is estimated that some 43 million Americans—one out of every six citizens—suffers from a disability, "a physical or mental impairment that substantially limits one or more of the major activities of such individual."[2] Disabilities so defined may include psychological disorders, diseases, or conditions such as disfigurement, anatomical loss or dysfunction, as well as mental or psychological disorders including mental retardation, mental illness, and learning disabilities. The key test is whether any such disorder or condition in fact "substantially limits" a person's ability to carry on major life functions—walking, breathing, seeing, hearing, working, and so forth.

The legislation is organized into five major titles. Title I prohibits discrimination in employment and states that "no covered entity shall discriminate against a qualified individual with a disability because of the disability of such individual in regard to job application procedures, the hiring, advancement, or discharge of employees, employee compensation, job training, and other terms, conditions, and privileges of employment."[3] This title imposes on the employer an obligation to make "reasonable accommodations to the known physical or mental limitations" of otherwise qualified individuals, unless such accommodations would "impose an undue hardship" on the employer.[4] Title II prohibits discrimination by public authorities—state and local governments—in the provision of public services and states that "no qualified individual with a disability shall, by reason of such disability, be excluded from participation in or be denied the benefits of the services, programs, or activities of a public entity, or be subjected to discrimination by any such entity."[5] According to this title, all public services, programs, and activities—including public buildings and public transportation—must be accessible to individuals with disabilities. Title III extends Title II access and antidiscrimination provisions to private entities and specifies that "no individual shall be discriminated against on the basis of disability in the full and equal enjoyment of the goods, services, facilities, privileges, advantages, or accommodations of any place of public accommodation by any person who owns, leases (or leases to), or operates a place of public accommodation."[6] In effect, this title of the ADA requires private businesses to design and construct accessible facilities. Title IV deals specifically with telecommunications services and requires the Federal Communications Commission to ensure that telecommunications companies make provisions for individuals who are hearing-impaired or speech-impaired. Finally, Title V specifies a variety of miscellaneous provisions such as remedies and procedures and certain exemptions and exclusions to the ADA; for instance, although drug abuse is considered a disability, Title V states explicitly that individuals "cur-

---

[1]Sec. 2 (a) (8) [42 U.S.C. § 12101].
[2]Sec. 3 (2) [U.S.C. § 12102].
[3]Sec. 102. (a) [42 U.S.C. § 12112].

[4]Ibid., (b)(5)(A).
[5]Sec. 202 [42 U.S.C. § 12132].
[6]Sec. 302 (A) [42 U.S.C. § 12182].

rently engaging in the illegal use of drugs" are not per se protected by provisions of the act.[7]

All "covered entities"—for purposes of Title I, any state, local or private organization that employs more than 14 people—are expected to comply fully with the provisions of the ADA.[8] The law assumes that organizations will, on their own, take affirmative steps to accommodate disabled individuals. If an individual believes that his or her employer is not in compliance with the ADA and exhausts internal remedies—including arbitration, if it is specified in an employment contract—seeking to ameliorate the situation, the individual must look for outside relief. Adjudication of disputes that arise under Title I (Employment Discrimination) begin with a complaint filed with the federal Equal Employment Opportunities Commission, or with state or local agencies if they have similar jurisdiction under state law.[9] The EEOC or comparable state or local agency will conduct an investigation and issue a finding. If discrimination is found, the agency will seek conciliation—that is, it will request that the employer make reasonable accommodation. If conciliation fails, the EEOC or other enforcement agency may bring suit in court to force compliance and, if warranted, to seek damages. Even absent a finding of discrimination, individuals retain the right to bring suit in their own behalf once agency remedies have been exhausted.

[7] Sec. 510 (a) [42 U.S.C. § 12210].
[8] Definitions of "covered entities" vary for Titles II, III, and IV.

[9] The federal Departments of Justice and Transportation, Federal Communications Commission, and federal Architectural and Transportation Barriers Compliance Board share enforcement responsibilities for various aspects of Titles II, III, and IV.

Fact Pattern

The plaintiff, Mary Smith, was hired as a building inspector by the Polk County Department of Planning and Development (DPD) in 1993. Her primary responsibility was to ensure contractor compliance with building codes by inspecting residential and commercial building projects during various phases of construction. She received top performance evaluations from her supervisor until December 1997 when she suffered serious injuries in an automobile accident. Trauma to her neck and back left her partially paralyzed, requiring use of a wheelchair and walker. After 14 months of hospitalization and physical therapy, her physicians certified that she was capable of returning to work. In February 1999 Smith returned to the DPD and accepted an essentially clerical assignment that entailed reviewing and approving building permits, retaining her grade and pay as a building inspector. After two months, she expressed dissatisfaction with the assignment and asked to be allowed to resume her previous role as an inspector in the field. In May 1999, after consulting with Smith and her physicians, DPD management complied with this request, providing her with a car and driver to help her reach building sites. A review by her supervisor in August 1999 determined that Smith's performance in this capacity was substantively sound but at a low level of productivity. The average number of inspections carried out by DPD building inspectors was four per day; prior to her accident, Smith herself had averaged five to six inspections per day. Owing to her impaired mobility and neurological condition, Smith was now able to perform an average of two inspections per day.

Based on this review, Smith's supervisor suggested that she consider reassignment to office work, a recommendation that Smith declined. After lengthy discussion, it was agreed that Smith would continue in the field position and try to increase her productivity by 50 percent, a level that would still be less than that of the average inspector but one that the DPD would be willing to accept. Progress toward this goal would be assessed in a performance review in six months, in February 2000.

In the weeks following the August review, Smith sought to increase her productivity to the required level of three inspections per day but found it too taxing. She discussed the matter with her supervisor and in September 1999 asked to have an aide assigned to assist her mobility on the building sites. This accommodation was refused on the grounds that it created an unreasonable expense for the agency. Smith filed a complaint with the department's human resource manager, who investigated but found it baseless.

In October 1999, the position of chief building inspector became vacant. Smith applied, stating in her cover letter that not only was she well qualified by virtue of her education and long experience but that her impaired mobility would be less of a factor in this position. Because it is largely supervisory, she maintained, the average number of field inspections required, two per day, was the same as her demonstrated capability. Smith was interviewed for the position but did not get the job. In the letter of rejection, the DPD director stated that while Smith was in many respects qualified, her impaired mobility would interfere with essential job functions. Although the average number of inspections was, he noted, no greater than Smith's demonstrated capacity, they were different in kind, requiring greater speed and timeliness than Smith could ensure. Moreover, the additional administrative burdens of this position would mean that Smith would, in effect, have to be capable of performing more than two inspections per day in order to have the time necessary to complete other critical tasks.

In the weeks following her rejection, Smith became moody and despondent. Her productivity declined further. She argued frequently with her supervisor, gained a reputation among builders and contractors as someone who was "confrontational" and "unreliable," and complained regularly to coworkers about the "uncaring management" at DPD. At her scheduled performance review in February 2000, Smith accused her supervisor of being an "insensitive jerk" when he raised these issues and once again rejected her request for a mobility aide. The supervisor informed Smith that in view of her performance, he had no alternative but to reassign her to office duties. Smith refused and was told that she would therefore be terminated. The formal notice of termination cited as reasons "failure to perform assigned duties and insubordination."

Smith appealed her termination first to the DPD's human resource manager and then to the director of the DPD. Both dismissed her claim. In April 2000, Smith filed a formal complaint alleging bias in promotion and termination with the Employment Division of the State Human Rights Commission which, under a work-sharing agreement with the federal Equal Employment Opportunities Commission, was empowered to investigate and adjudicate, among other things, claims brought under the Americans with Disabilities Act of 1990. The matter is now to be heard by an arbitration panel assembled under the aegis of the Employment Division.

ADA Legal Tests and Definitions

For a person to prove that an employer has violated the provisions of the ADA, three basic legal tests must be met: The person must be (1) a qualified individual with (2) a disability who was (3) discriminated against because of that disability. Thus an employer can defend successfully against a charge of discrimination if he or she can prove that the individual bringing the action is not qualified for the position, does not have a covered disability, or was fired, not hired, or otherwise subjected to adverse personnel action for reasons unrelated to the disability.

The standard of proof used in these cases is "preponderance of evidence" (rather than "beyond a reasonable doubt," for instance). That is, the plaintiff must show, by greater weight of evidence, that he or she meets the tests described above.

Because definitional clarity is critical to proper consideration of ADA claims, several key terms are discussed here, with an emphasis on exact statutory or regulatory language. Be aware, however, that there are still ambiguities in these definitions. To some extent, these ambiguities, like those in any law, are being confronted and ultimately reduced through judicial interpretations of the statutes and regulations—that is to say, through court decisions. Were you actually to file, defend, or adjudicate a case under the ADA, you would have to become familiar with these decisions. Because there are hundreds of cases potentially relevant to an ADA claim, however, this is not a line of inquiry we can pursue in any detail here.

Qualified. A qualified individual is one who, "with or without reasonable accommodation, can perform the essential functions of the employment position that such individual holds or desires."[1]

Reasonable accommodation. Reasonable accommodation is defined as:

(A) making existing facilities used by employees readily accessible to and usable by individuals with disabilities; and

(B) job restructuring, part-time or modified work schedules, reassignment to a vacant position, acquisition or modification of equipment or devices, appropriate adjustment or modifications of examinations, training materials or policies, the provision of qualified readers or interpreters, and other similar accommodations for individuals with disabilities.[2]

Reasonable accommodation explicitly excludes anything that causes "undue hardship" to the employer or that would require the elimination of an "essential function" of the job, however.

Undue hardship. The ADA includes the following sections in an effort to clarify the meaning of "undue hardship":

(A) In general:

The term *undue hardship* means an action requiring significant difficulty or expense, when considered in light of the factors set forth in subparagraph (B).

(B) Factors to be considered:

In determining whether an accommodation would impose an undue hardship on a covered entity, factors to be considered include:

(i) the nature and cost of the accommodation needed under this Act;

(ii) the overall financial resources of the facility or facilities involved in the provision of the reasonable accommodation; the number of persons employed at such facility; the effect on expenses and resources, or the impact

[1] ADA § 101 (8), 42 U.S.C. § 12111 (8).

[2] ADA § 101 (9), 42 U.S.C. § 12111 (9).

otherwise of such accommodation upon the operation of the facility;

(iii) the overall financial resources of the covered entity; the overall size of the business of a covered entity with respect to the number of its employees; the number, type, and location of its facilities; and

(iv) the type of operation or operations of the covered entity including the composition, structure, and functions of the workforce of such entity; the geographic separateness, administrative, or fiscal relationship of the facility or facilities in question to the covered entity.[3]

Essential job functions. Essential job functions are *not* well defined in the statutory language, which simply says: "For the purposes of this title, consideration shall be given to the employer's judgment as to what functions of a job are essential, and if an employer has prepared a written job description before advertising or interviewing applicants for the job, this description shall be considered evidence of the essential functions of the job."[4]

Thus the statute gives the employer discretion to determine whether a job function is essential (i.e., the emphasis on "employer's judgment"). But at the same time, the statute places the burden of proof on the employer to demonstrate (e.g., through a previously written job description) that the function has been deemed essential. Moreover, it has become clear through case law that the mere existence of a function in a job description is, in itself, inadequate; requirements that are used only occasionally or that are in fact never applied cannot be construed as "essential job functions," even if they appear in a job description.[5]

Disability. The term *disability* means, with respect to an individual:

(A) a physical or mental impairment that substantially limits one or more of the major life activities of such individual;

(B) a record of such impairment; or

(C) being regarded as having such an impairment.[6]

The meaning of category A is obvious. Category B was included to protect from discrimination persons who have recovered from an impairment; category C seeks to protect persons who are perceived as disabled, even if they are not.

The statute does *not* list specific disabilities. The reason for this is that Congress recognized that no list could be exhaustive. Some guidance can be found in the legislative history, particularly in the Senate and House committee reports, which define physical and mental impairment as follows:

1. any physiological disorder or condition, cosmetic disfigurement, or anatomical loss affecting one or more of the following body systems: neurological; musculoskeletal; special sense organs; respiratory, including speech organs; cardiovascular; reproductive, digestive; genito-urinary; hemic and lymphatic; skin; and endocrine; or

2. any mental or psychological disorder such as mental retardation, organic brain syndrome, emotional or mental illness, and specific learning disabilities.[7]

In general, the ADA is meant to be inclusive, which is to say that any physical or mental disability, including contagious diseases, is covered unless specifically excepted. Statutory exceptions include homosexuality and bisexuality, transvestism, pedophilia, voyeurism and other sexual behavior disorders, compulsive gambling, kleptomania, pyromania, and substance abuse disorders resulting from current use of illegal drugs.[8]

Substantial limitation. According to EEOC regulations, persons with "substantial limitations" are those who are:

(i) Unable to perform a major life activity that the average person in the general population can perform; or

(ii) Significantly restricted as to the condition, manner or duration under which an individual can

---

[3]ADA § 101 (10), 42 U.S.C. § 12111 (10).
[4]ADA § 101 (8), 42 U.S.C. § 12111 (8).
[5]875 F. 2d 1073 (6th Cir. 1988); 815 F. 2d 571 (9th Cir. 1987).

[6]ADA § 3 (2), 42 U.S.C. § 12102 (Supp. II 1990).
[7]Quoted in Henry H. Perrit Jr., *Americans with Disabilities Act Handbook,* 2d ed. (New York: Wiley, 1991), p. 25.
[8]ADA § 511, 42 U.S.C. 12211.

perform a particular major life activity as compared to the condition, manner or duration under which the average person in the general population can perform that same major life activity.[9]

Discrimination. According to the ADA, discrimination means:

(1) limiting, segregating, or classifying a job applicant or employee in a way that adversely affects the opportunities or status of such applicant or employee because of the disability of such applicant or employee;

(2) participating in a contractual or other arrangement or relationship that has the effect of subjecting a covered entity's qualified applicant or employee with a disability to the discrimination prohibited by this title.

(3) utilizing standards, criteria, or methods of administration:

   (A) that have the effect of discrimination on the basis of disability; or

   (B) that perpetuate the discrimination of others who are subject to common administrative control;

(4) excluding or otherwise denying equal jobs or benefits to a qualified individual because of the known disability of an individual with whom the qualified individual is known to have a relationship or association;

(5) (A) not making reasonable accommodations to the known physical or mental limitations of an otherwise qualified individual with a disability who is an applicant or employee, unless such covered entity can demonstrate that the accommodation would impose an undue hardship on the operation of the business of such covered entity; or

   (B) denying employment opportunities to a job applicant or employee who is an otherwise qualified individual with a disability, if such denial is based on the need of such covered entity to make reasonable accommodation to the physical or mental impairments of the employee or applicant;

(6) using qualification standards, employment tests or other selection criteria that screen out or tend to screen out an individual with a disability or a class of individuals with disabilities unless the standard, test or other selection criteria, as used by the covered entity, is shown to be job-related for the position in question and is consistent with business necessity; and

(7) failing to select and administer tests concerning employment in the most effective manner to ensure that, when such test is administered to a job applicant or employee who has a disability that impairs sensory, manual, or speaking skills, such test results accurately reflect the skills, aptitude, or whatever other factor of such applicant or employee that such test purports to measure, rather than reflecting the impaired sensory, manual, or speaking skills of such employee or applicant (except where such skills are the factors that the test purports to measure).[10]

[9] 29 C.F.R. § 1630. 2(j)1(i) and (ii).

[10] ADA § 102 (b), 42 U.S.C. § 12112 (b).

Complaint

Name of Employee: _____

Name of Agency: _____

Statement of Claims: _____

_____

_____

_____

_____

_____

_____

_____

Relief Sought: _____

_____

_____

_____

_____

_____

_____

Response

Name of Employee: _____

Name of Agency: _____

Response to Claims: _____

_____

_____

_____

_____

_____

_____

_____

Arbitration Decision

Exercise 6

Administrative Ethics

ETHICS AND AMERICAN GOVERNMENT

Kickbacks, sleaze factors, revolving doors, secret bank accounts, phantom payrolls—the dispiriting shorthand of today's newspaper headlines suggests that American government has been beset by a veritable plague of dishonesty, corruption, and malfeasance. Between "this-scam" and "that-gate" it is little wonder that citizens' confidence and trust in government has plummeted over the past 20 years.

How much distrust is actually warranted is difficult to know, as bribes, payoffs, and other illicit behaviors are, by their nature, furtive. Though unethical behavior in government undoubtedly occurs—and likely always will, failing a basic change in human nature—much of what appears to be a wholesale decline in public morality in recent years is probably more a function of changed public expectations and heightened vigilance by the press and prosecutors than a real withering of our collective rectitude. It may also be noted, with some irony, that this apparent epidemic of unethical behavior has mostly involved elected officials and their political appointees. With relatively few exceptions, the millions of men and women who in recent years have been on the receiving end of politically motivated "bureaucrat bashing" continue to do their jobs with honesty and integrity.

This does not mean that we can safely forget about questions of administrative ethics. Even if we have not sunk into a national moral quagmire of historic proportions and even if administrators overall are an unusually honorable lot, there are at least three good reasons to pay attention to ethical issues. First, we owe it to ourselves as citizens of a republic to insist on exemplary conduct by our public officials; "relatively good" or "no worse than usual"

ought not to be considered acceptable when assessing the moral compasses of our political and administrative leaders. Second, even well-meaning public officials need guidance; clear-cut cases of theft and bribery excepted, there are very few simple "thou shalt" and "thou shalt not" rules in this arena. Finally, thinking systematically about ethics in government necessarily involves thinking about the role of government in society, and that is a useful and healthy thing to do.

WHAT ARE ETHICS?

The word *ethics* derives from *ethos,* the Greek term for the particular character or disposition of a people, society, or culture. In contemporary English usage, it refers, at least in the context that concerns us, to moral rules. To say that an act is ethical, therefore, is to say that it is morally defensible. In general, we make determinations about the morality of an act by holding it up to a general standard such as "Taking the life of another human being is wrong" or "You should never tell a lie." Some of these standards may be codified in civil or criminal law, in which case everyone in society is required to observe them. Other ethical standards may be rooted in general social mores, violations of which lead to disapprobation but not legal penalty. In American society, for instance, it is widely considered unethical to take advantage of someone in a business transaction, even when doing so is not strictly illegal. Still other ethical standards may pertain only to specific social groups; in some religious and moral traditions, for example, it is thought to be unethical to slaughter animals for food in other than a prescribed manner, while others disdain eating meat altogether.

Such group-specific ethics have also evolved in many established professions and occupations such as law, medicine, and journalism. Legal ethics, for instance, proscribe attorneys from representing someone involved in an adversarial proceeding with an individual who is already a client of that attorney. Medical ethics guide physicians' decisions on administering life-prolonging drugs to terminally ill patients. Professional ethics forbid journalists from revealing confidential news sources. In cases such as these, whatever sanctions there may be against violators of professional ethics are levied, at least in the first instance, by the profession itself.

Note that ethics and law are not identical. Although our public laws are, at least in theory, derived from general moral standards in society, many questions of ethics remain beyond the purview of the law, as clearly they must in a liberal, tolerant polity. This is an important point to remember, for in a society as law-oriented as ours, it is unfortunately easy to conclude, quite wrongly, that if something is legal, it must be ethical. Bear this warning in mind as you work through the case presented later in this exercise.

WHAT ARE ADMINISTRATIVE ETHICS?

When a highway administrator awards a paving contract in return for $10,000 in small, unmarked bills, most of us would agree that he has behaved unethically. So, too, would we think it unethical when the director of a state environmental agency puts her patently unqualified brother-in-law on the payroll for an essentially "no-show" job, uses public funds to build a new deck on her summer home, or runs up a fortune in personal overseas calls on the office phone. These are easy cases, involving at a minimum bribery, theft, and nepotism.

But how about the highway administrator who accepts an unpaid speaking engagement before the monthly dinner meeting of the local Highway Contractors Association, which reimburses him for his carfare and feeds him chicken à la king? What about the agency director who hires her patently qualified brother-in-law for a real job, uses public funds to cater a party at her summer home for a visiting delegation of foreign environmental officials, or charges the monthly rental on her cellular car phone, which she uses primarily for public busi-

ness, to her office account? These cases are less clear; certainly there appears to be no outright bribery or corruption involved. Any evaluation of the probity of these actions will probably start out with "Well, it depends. . . ." What are the agency rules about free meals from contractors? Was the brother-in-law the most qualified applicant? Was the catered party a matter of official business?

Even answers to questions like these do not always provide clear resolutions of ethical dilemmas in the public service. Knowing what is ethical is not always easy. To be ethical is to do the right thing. But what is the right thing? As with law, medicine, and other professions, public administration has developed ethical guidelines to help its practitioners deal with questions of this sort. One such set of guidelines is the code of ethics adopted by the American Society for Public Administration (ASPA) in 1981 (see box). As one would expect, the standards in this code stress the primacy of law, the importance of sound management, and the need to avoid conflicts of interest. The emphasis clearly reflects the traditional values of the profession and its historic sense of itself as a value-free instrument of public policy.

Yet ASPA's code also makes pointed references to concepts like "justice," "equity," "conscience," and "moral ambiguities" and gives a prominent place to the idea that public servants are responsible ultimately to the people. This suggests that ethical administrators sometimes have to make moral choices for themselves, that they cannot view themselves simply as order-taking technicians. And therein lies the major tension that underlies any discussion of ethics in public administration. How can a public administrator know what to do when ethical action is premised on both (1) subservience to the law and (2) a sense of individual conscience? What happens when obedience to those in lawfully authoritative positions requires actions that conflict with one's own reasoned estimate of the demands of equity, justice, and the public interest?

This is not simply a hypothetical academic quandary. It is a dilemma that virtually all administrators face at one time or another. What, for example, should the social worker do who believes deeply that public assistance programs for poor children are woefully inadequate but is bound by departmental regulations to report that a welfare mother has been earning $30 a week babysitting?

A Code of Ethics for Public Administration

The American Society for Public Administration exists to advance the science, processes, and art of public administration. The Society affirms its responsibility to develop the spirit of professionalism within its membership, and to increase public awareness of moral standards in public service by its example. To this end, we, the members of the Society, commit ourselves to the following principles:

1. Service to the public is beyond service to oneself.
2. The people are sovereign and those in public service are ultimately responsible to them.
3. Laws govern all actions of the public service. Where laws or regulations are ambiguous, leave discretion, or require change, we will seek to serve the best interests of the public.
4. Efficient and effective management is basic to public administration. Subversion through misuse of influence, fraud, waste, or abuse is intolerable. Employees who responsibly call attention to wrongdoing will be encouraged.
5. The merit system, equal opportunity, and affirmative action principles will be supported, implemented, and promoted.
6. Safeguarding the public trust is paramount. Conflicts of interest, bribes, gifts, or favors which subordinate public positions to private gains are unacceptable.
7. Service to the public creates demands for special sensitivity to the qualities of justice, courage, honesty, equity, competence and compassion. We esteem these qualities, and we will actively promote them.
8. Conscience performs a critical role in choosing among courses of action. It takes into account the moral ambiguities of life, and the necessity to examine value priorities: good ends never justify immoral means.
9. Public administrators are not engaged merely in preventing wrong, but in pursuing right through timely and energetic execution of their responsibilities.

Adopted by the National Council of the American Society for Public Administration on December 6, 1981.

How about the immigration official who has to decide whether to grant legal status to a refugee threatened by death squads in his war-torn country in the face of a federal policy that does not officially consider that country's regime repressive enough to warrant granting its citizens political asylum? What is the ethical course for a state environmental official who believes that his agency's recent grant of a discharge permit to a large factory will have a subtle, though substantial impact on groundwater pollution, and thereby increase cancer rates 10 or 20 years down the road? The examples of such dilemmas are endless, and they range from the mundane to the truly horrific.

Though we undoubtedly could resolve each of these predicaments on a case-by-case basis—albeit not to everyone's satisfaction—it is difficult to promulgate sensible general rules that anticipate future ethical dilemmas. Law and hierarchy are central to modern administration. A bureaucracy of men and women who act wholly according to the dictates of their own values is very nearly a contradiction in terms. Such a freewheeling system also makes a mockery of representative government, which rests on the idea that choices made by citizens through democratic processes will be translated reasonably faithfully into public policy. Yet it is at least as disturbing to contemplate a system that so emphasizes strict obedience to rules that administrators become amoral automatons. One need not even resort to extreme cases like Nazi Germany or the Soviet Union under Stalin to recognize that some laws, no matter how correct in form, are morally wrong and need to be disobeyed. This is one reason why codes of ethics, while helpful in some respects, cannot completely resolve ethical dilemmas for public administrators. If such codes accurately reflect, as they should, the fundamental values of the profession, they are bound to contain an internal tension between the need for organizational order and claims of individual moral judgment, for such is the nature of public administration.

There are other reasons that codes of ethics and other such guidelines cannot always help administrators "do the right thing." To begin with, although ethical rules are usually very clear when stated as general injunctions, they frequently become exceedingly vague when applied to specific circumstances. For instance, a common ethic among social service workers is to protect the interests of clients. While this seems unambiguous enough in the abstract, what does it mean in particular? What exactly is in the interest of an older person suffering from Alzheimer's disease? At what point are the benefits of independent living outweighed—in the client's own interests—by the risks of doing injury to himself or herself? The principle is intact, but it is not clear how it is to be applied.

An additional problem with ethical guidelines arises when principles remain intact only in the abstract. Consider this example: It is a widely accepted standard in public administration that it is unethical (as well as illegal) for an official to accept money or other gifts from individuals or groups who might materially benefit from a decision made by that official. Now, it is obvious that certain kinds of behaviors would clearly be out of bounds according to this rule. Certainly, an administrator would be in violation if he or she accepted, say, a gift box of gourmet coffee (much less $10,000 in small, unmarked bills) at Christmas from a contractor with whom he or she does business. But does that mean that the same administrator couldn't accept a cup or two of that same coffee from the contractor while visiting a job site? And if it is OK to accept the cup of coffee, what does that suggest about the principle? That it's all right to accept gifts as long as they have hot water added to them or are consumed immediately? Probably not. One could argue that what the principle really says is that an administrator shouldn't accept *valuable* gifts; that a cup of coffee worth 50 cents is allowable but a box of the beans from which the coffee is brewed is not. But then what is the cutoff in our definition of "valu-

able"? Would it be legitimate to accept a small packet of beans at Christmas worth 50 cents? Again, probably not, so maybe we can avoid the problem by saying that the cup of coffee is not really a gift, that it is instead a common courtesy extended in normal social interaction; such courtesies, we might argue, are OK. But what are the bounds of common courtesies? In some circles, providing limousine service or an evening's entertainment falls under this heading. If you think those sound excessive, where would you draw the line? And doesn't drawing a line just put you back in the business of trying to define "valuable"?

We might, of course, try to resolve the issue by saying, "Right, this is just too confusing. No one can accept any gift, no matter how small, under any circumstances. No coffee, brewed or otherwise. No limousine service. No anything." This resolution is clear enough. But is it practical? Supervising highway engineers are going to accept cups of coffee. Police officers are going to eat free donuts now and then. Almost everyone is going to take home a pencil from the office occasionally. If you brand common behaviors as unethical, what meaning does the word *ethical* have?

A final problem one must confront in trying to sort out ethical guidelines in the public sector—or anywhere else for that matter—is the fact that ethical principles sometimes simply conflict with one another or with other principles of good management. This is true even if we put aside the fundamental law-versus-conscience issue. To illustrate, consider two common principles in public administration: public disclosure and confidentiality. The first principle, buttressed by sunshine laws and the Freedom of Information Act, counsels administrators to eschew secrecy and to share as much information as possible with the public. The second principle, underpinned by the Privacy Act and related laws, warns the administrator not to disseminate information that might violate a citizen's right to privacy.[1] As few issues fail to engage both principles simultaneously, for the administrator this is a dilemma indeed.

In sum, ethical issues are an important problem in the public sector. Yet they admit no easy solu-

---

[1]See Herman Mertins, ed., *Professional Standards and Ethics: A Workbook for Public Administrators* (Washington, D.C.: American Society for Public Administration, 1979), pp. 19–20, for a discussion of this problem.

tions. Not only does the nature of modern bureaucracy leave little room for the maneuvering of individual conscience, but efforts to formulate general codes of ethics, however necessary and laudable, often run afoul of the difficulties of applying general rules to specific cases, countenancing unavoidable exceptions to absolute rules and reconciling irreconcilable principles. The question of administrative ethics must in the end remain open, subject to an ever-unfolding dialogue among administrators, political leaders, and citizens.

FURTHER READING

A good place to begin further reading in this field is with Stephen Bailey's classic article "Ethics and the Public Service," *Public Administration Review* 24 (November-December 1964). For important arguments on the relationship between constitutional values and administrative ethics, see two books by John Rohr: *Ethics for Bureaucrats: An Essay on Law and Values* (New York: Dekker, 1978) and *Public Service, Ethics, and Constitutional Practice* (Lawrence, Kansas: University Press of Kansas, 1998). Albert Hirschman provides an especially pithy summary of the choices facing an administrator caught in an ethical quandary in *Exit, Voice and Loyalty* (Cambridge, Mass.: Harvard University Press, 1970). A sophisticated case for personal responsibility in administration is presented in

Dennis F. Thompson, "Moral Responsibility of Public Officials: The Problem of Many Hands," *American Political Science Review* 74 (September 1980). In a 1980 article "Whistle-Blowing in the Public Sector: An Overview of the Issues," *Review of the Public Personnel Administration,* James Bowman reviews the history of whistle-blowing and the legal protections available to administrators who take this step.

Terry L. Cooper has done a great deal of interesting work in the field of administrative ethics. His edited *Handbook of Administrative Ethics* (New York: Dekker, 1994) contains 29 essays on the subject that range from philosophical inquiries to comparative analysis. His book *The Responsible Administrator,* 4th ed. (San Francisco: Jossey-Bass, 1998), discusses how people can remain ethical in an organizational environment. Cooper's related work, *An Ethic of Citizenship for Public Administration* (Englewood Cliffs, N.J.: Prentice Hall, 1991), attempts to describe the substance of appropriate ethics for public administration, based on the idea of citizenship.

Finally, you may wish to peruse a symposium on the topic "Ethics in the American Public Service" published in *Annals of the American Academy of Political and Social Science* (January 1995). Edited by Harry Reynolds Jr., this symposium consists of 12 original essays on such things as congressional ethics, the media and ethics, and the enforcement of administrative ethics.

Overview of Exercise

In this exercise, you will read a case study describing the ethical dilemma confronted by a middle manager in a county planning department. Your assignment will be to analyze the situation from the administrator's perspective and to outline what you would do if you found yourself in these circumstances.

INSTRUCTIONS

Step One
Carefully read the case material presented on Form 27.

Step Two
Prepare answers to the discussion questions on Form 28.

The Case

THE SETTING

Windham County is one of the most rapidly growing areas in the United States. By almost any measure—employment, housing starts, population increase—it has experienced extraordinary development in recent years. Although its economy, as in many similar areas along the eastern seaboard, was traditionally dependent on manufacturing, state and local officials worked hard to attract new service-based industries and have been successful in establishing Windham County as a major banking and insurance center. As a result, there has been a tremendous influx of white-collar workers, which has caused a boom in local residential and commercial construction. Consequently, pressures on Windham County's dwindling supply of vacant land are great. Roads that five years ago wound through quiet pastures and apple orchards are now clogged with cars making their way to and from the endless series of housing developments, shopping centers, and corporate plazas that line their tarmac. Demands for new water supplies, sewer lines, and other infrastructure improvements, as well as schools, medical facilities, and protective services, have multiplied apace. A Windham County version of Rip Van Winkle, awakening in the new millennium, would find his environs as foreign as the moon.

The entity mainly responsible for guiding this development is the county government. Although the county encompasses several small cities that bear responsibility for traditional urban services within their borders, most Windham County residents—and most of the county's land—are to be found in unincorporated areas. Thus the county is in the business of providing many primary services, including police and fire protection. Moreover, under state law, county government exercises many countywide functions, superseding the cities in such areas as transportation, libraries, health and social services, and land-use planning. Even schools are administered on a countywide basis, although through an independently elected school board.

Windham County government is organized on a strong executive-council model. A county executive is elected on a countywide basis for a term of four years; the executive is responsible for day-to-day administration, for appointing major administrative officers, and for preparing an annual budget. The county's legislative branch is a county council, the six members of which are elected by district; heading the council is an independent (countywide) council president. Elections to all county offices are partisan and are usually hotly contested, though campaigns and outcomes tend to turn more on personality and faction than ideology. Registration in the county is about evenly divided between Republicans and Democrats, and control of the executive and legislative offices has alternated between the two parties with considerable regularity.

Not surprisingly, development issues are central to county politics. In a jurisdiction where the names and faces of builders and bankers have become as famous—and occasionally infamous—as any politician's, candidates for office routinely stake out positions in favor of "responsible growth," suggesting vaguely that they will keep the fires of economic development stoked without buckling under to "undue pressures" from developers. The *Windham Journal*, the county's sole newspaper, regularly reports the development plans and deals, would-be and otherwise, that percolate through business and political circles and more than once has uncovered a distinctly malodorous transaction. Indeed, the whiff of corruption has never been far from development politics in Windham County, a fact that is not exactly dumbfounding given the tens of millions of dollars at stake in many of the deals. In the past 15 years, three elected officials have been indicted—two were convicted—for peddling their votes to developers. Two years ago, the director of planning resigned amid allegations that he had received consulting fees from an investment group with substantial land holdings in the county. Beyond these cases, if the rumor mills are to be believed, few top officials have maintained what one would consider a healthy distance between themselves and the contractors, builders, real estate moguls, and moneymen who have transformed the face of the county.

THE ISSUE

For the past few years, the biggest story in local development circles has been Bluestone Golf Course, a facility owned and operated by the county. Situated on 200 acres of gently rolling hills, Bluestone is the last green space of any size in northeastern Windham County, an area known locally as Volvo Valley. Bounded on the east by the Windham River and on the west by a major state highway, this corridor, with the golf course at its center, presents, from a developer's perspective, eye-popping demographics: Half the households within a 2-mile radius of the course have incomes of more than $90,000 a year; the average family consists of 1.8 professional wage earners and 1.1 children, owns 2.1 late-model foreign cars, and lives in an owner-occupied dwelling on 0.85 acres of land; moreover, 250,000 people live within a 15-minute drive of the golf course. What really makes the developers' pocket calculators smoke, though, is the fact that, as one put it, "the commercial potential of the corridor is underrealized." Roughly translated, this means that the upper-middle-class denizens of northeastern Windham County have to drive major distances to spend their money. Although the state highway that runs through the corridor, Windham Pike, is lined with seeming scores of strip developments, these are filled with grocery stores, insurance agencies, auto dealer-

ships, chiropractors' offices, and the usual jarring array of fast-food outlets, muffler shops, gas stations, and all-night "convenience marts." The region's only major shopping mall is located just off an interstate highway in the center of Windham County, 20 to 30 minutes by car from Volvo Valley.

Three years ago, acting on a recommendation from the County Office of Economic Development, the County Council approved in principle a plan to "swap" with a developer the Bluestone land for a yet-to-be-specified parcel elsewhere and a yet-to-be-specified amount of money. The theory was that both parties would profit handsomely from the exchange. The county would receive a significant amount of cash immediately, plus property and sales tax revenues that eventually would amount to $15 to $20 million per year; golfers would be mollified, it was hoped, by using the new parcel for another course with even more attractive facilities. The developer would receive 200 acres of extraordinarily prime land on which a new mall—with major department stores, restaurants, boutiques, and movie theaters—could be built.

Since the council's approval-in-principle of the exchange, a bewildering variety of proposals has been floated, sunk, and refloated. Initially, five major developers presented formal prospectuses to the county executive's office. Although the submissions were theoretically confidential—in part to protect all parties from speculative effects on land values, in part to help the county get the best deal possible—at least the rough outlines of all the proposals made it into the press in short order. The opportunities for leaks were manifold. The proposals were seen by the county executive and her immediate staff, the directors of planning and of the Office of Economic Development and their top staff, and all members of the council, who had resisted the suggestion that circulation of the proposals be restricted, for reasons of security, to a special committee. In any event, the net effect of the public disclosures was to make development politics in Windham County even more circuslike than usual. Citizen-action groups sprouted like dandelions to stake out positions on the issue: The Bluestone Golf Association lobbied furiously to protect its "historic links"; the Windham River Committee formed to press the county to keep the Bluestone land but convert it to a park and nature preserve; the Emergency Housing Action Coalition insisted that any development include "affordable housing" to accommodate Windham County's "growing low-income and homeless population"; a group calling itself Concerned Homeowners of Northeast Valley opposed any development that would threaten the "unique social and environmental character" of the area; the Small Merchants Association worried that a new mall would siphon off trade and benefit only "big-money investors in London, New York, and Tokyo." Meanwhile, major business and civic leaders scurried around the county, painting glowing pictures of new jobs and other economic benefits that would spin off from one proposal or another.

In this atmosphere, firm decisions proved elusive. Each time county officials seemed close to some agreement, a leak would produce a newspaper story, complete with maps and artists' sketches, followed by the mobilization of anyone and everyone who had a stake in the issue. Charges would inevitably be made about who contributed what to whose campaign or which spouse or brother-in-law worked for which developer. Indeed, it was in the midst of this free-for-all that one council member was indicted for trying to "rent" his vote to one of the developers with a Bluestone proposal pending. Although the vote in question involved rezoning of another property, and although the developer cooperated with the prosecutor's office and allowed himself to be "wired" during a meeting at which money was to change hands, the affair further tainted the whole Bluestone affair.

After three years of commotion and indecision, the county executive and council agreed six months ago on a process that would, they believed, bring the matter to closure. According to Resolution 252, a final set of sealed proposals was to be submitted to the Office of the County Executive on October 1. A small team of county officials—the county executive, the planning and development directors, and the council president—would review the proposals, consulting only with their senior staff, negotiate any

changes with the developers, and recommend one to the full council by November 1. The council would have two months to hold public hearings and vote the proposal up or down.

THE PROBLEM

You have been observing this extended dispute from the vantage point of a desk in the County Planning Office, where you have been employed for six years as a senior planning analyst. You report directly to the chief of the Planning Analysis and Administration Division, one of the office's two operating divisions, and supervise a staff of three entry-level planners. Your division, which employs eight professional staff members, is responsible for the development and administration of the county's long-range (20-year) land-use and transportation plan, the mid-range (five-year) capital development plan, the annual county profile (a snapshot of demographic trends), and any special planning projects. The other, slightly smaller division of the planning office, Planning Services, deals with day-to-day zoning and assessment questions.

Given your responsibilities, you have dealt with one facet or another of the Bluestone issue almost continuously, though not exclusively (you have too much else to do), for the past few years. As a consequence, you are about as well informed as anyone else in the county when it comes to the various plans for the property. And with your professional training and experience, you are well equipped to assess the costs and consequences of the various proposals. In general, you have grown weary of the whole affair. While you see genuine benefits accruing to the public if a Bluestone exchange goes through, you have begun to wonder whether development has gotten totally out of control in the county. Sometimes it seems that the 20-year plan might as well be written on an Etch-a-Sketch, the way planned green space regularly gets nibbled away in rezoning applications. It might not be so bad, you think, if the process were more orderly, if people stopped and thought about what they were doing and made more rational decisions. That's what you learned in your planning courses in graduate school. But that's not how the process works. There's too much money at stake. Otherwise sensible people start acting like hogs at a trough.

For years, though, you've stuck it out, keeping your head down and doing the best job you could. For various Bluestone schemes alone, you've dutifully supervised three transportation flow analyses, put together a county recreational needs assessment, and coordinated impact studies with the county's Water Resource Agency. Although you've gotten the impression that most of your work might as well have been chucked into a black hole—the politicians seem already to know the answers they want and are just looking for ways to rationalize them—you've always figured that your job was to analyze facts, not to set policy. No one—at least no one in a position of authority—has asked for your considered opinion about what to do with that golf course, and it's unlikely anyone will. Sure, you've heard the rumors about palms being greased and silent partnerships being arranged; no one who lives in Windham County, much less who works in the County Building, can avoid them. But you've never actually seen any hard evidence of corruption yourself, so you've decided to let the district attorney and the feds worry about it.

At least that was the situation until last week. On Wednesday, six days ago, your boss called you to his office and asked you to sit down. After a warm greeting and preliminary chitchat about your family, he indicated that the Bluestone Review Committee, as the small county team had become known, was nearing a decision on a development proposal. Although he (your boss) wasn't a member of the committee, he had, he said, been consulted frequently, particularly on technical planning questions. "Now we need your help," he smiled. He picked up a manila folder from his desk and withdrew a thin sheaf of papers that he passed across to you, indicating, with a wave of his hand, that you should look it over. You recognized it immediately as one of your transportation flow analyses—the one triggered by TriState's proposal for a sprawling, 200-store, multilevel mall at Bluestone. You flip through it perfunctorily and raise an eyebrow at

your boss, as if to say, What of it? This was an easy one as far as you were concerned. The study showed conclusively—more than a year ago—that even with improvements, Windham Pike could not begin to handle the volume of traffic generated by a project of that size; it wasn't even close. Why bring it up now, you wonder?

"There seems to be a problem with some of the numbers in that report," your boss continued, still smiling. "Nothing serious—and certainly no reflection on your work. It's just that the volume estimates are high and some of the destination data need cleaning up. I wonder if you could take a look at it this afternoon and fix it up. I've got to report back to the committee tomorrow."

You agree to check it over, although you doubt that there is anything wrong with it, and after a few more minutes of personal banter with your boss, you return to your office and pull out the files containing the supporting documentation for the report. After three hours of poring over the original demographic projections, trip studies, and transportation flow models, you lean back in your chair and rub your eyes. No errors here, you think. Sure, there's some room for judgment—after all, we're dealing with assumptions piled on top of assumptions. But how can we just reduce the volume estimates? And why should we? If anything, the new demographics bolster the original conclusions. You call your boss, but he's left for the day. So you position yourself in front of your computer and wearily peck out a brief memo that says, in essence, the report as written stands as far as you're concerned. After zapping it to his e-mail address, you grab your coat, head for home, and forget the whole thing.

Two days later, on Friday afternoon, you run into a casual acquaintance, an administrator from economic development, down by the vending machines in the basement. He gives you a playful poke in the ribs and says, "Hey, I hear it's gonna be TriState. You heard anything?"

"What?" you ask, never paying much attention to this fellow.

"You know, Bluestone. I hear the committee's coming out with an endorsement of the big TriState project. But it's still hush-hush. Keep it under your hat." He gives you a conspiratorial wink and walks away.

You're puzzled but are distracted enough by other problems not to give it too much thought. Later, though, your boss stops by the office and says something you find peculiar: "Sorry I didn't see you yesterday. I was tied up in meetings all day. You know, I think this Bluestone thing is finally going to be off our neck. I can't say anything more now, of course, but a deal is in the wind. Anyway, I got your note and wanted to let you know I appreciate the time you spent checking over that report. Some of the estimates were still a little off, but fortunately we got some revised numbers from Fogarty at State DOT. Listen, have a good weekend."

New numbers from Fogarty? What new numbers? Why would the transportation department have generated any new numbers? You make a note to call Fogarty on Monday.

MONDAY

Your call to Anne Fogarty has not been enlightening. Although you'd worked with her a fair amount in the past, today she seemed distant, even evasive. Yes, she said, her office had reassessed their flow projections in the northeastern corridor of Windham County. Just a routine adjustment based on some "revised assumptions." And no, she couldn't be more specific about the assumptions just now. She really didn't have the time today. There were a lot of things to wrap up around the office. You knew, didn't you, that she was leaving at the end of the week? Three weeks of accumulated vacation, then off to a new job in the private sector. Oh, really? With who? TriState Development, she said, and then rang off.

Now your stomach begins to hurt, and you really don't want to think about why. After staring out the window for half an hour, you decide to go down the hall and speak to your boss.

His office door is open. After he motions you in, his usual broad smile seems to fade a bit as you mention that you had been chatting with Fogarty. You are curious, you say, about the changed assumptions in the Windham Pike projections.

"Just a technical adjustment," he says. "DOT initiated it."

"But they don't seem to jibe with any of the other data we have," you point out.

"Look," says your boss. "You know how these things work. The assumptions in these models are always up for grabs, anybody's guess. DOT made the call; we accepted it. Now, I think it would be best if we didn't pursue this any further."

"I understand," you say. "But you know, I've heard some rumors that the TriState proposal is alive again. I know you can't talk about it, but . . ."

"That's right. I can't talk about it, and you shouldn't talk about it either."

"But just hypothetically . . . if those numbers are used . . ."

"Life is full of ifs," he says, cutting you off again. "Just like mathematical models." Then, with his smile completely gone, his eyes lock onto yours. "Let me be clear about this," he says. "This project has been in the works for three years. We've seen things get screwed up time and time again. Now it finally looks as if we're making progress. A lot of people have invested a lot of time and a lot of money. The political balance here is very delicate. No one is going to appreciate anyone who does anything to upset that balance. Your flow projections were estimates. DOT's flow projections were estimates. I have decided, and the rest of the committee has agreed, to go with the DOT's estimates. As an associate director of this office, that is my judgment to make. Now, do we understand each other?"

You nod your head vaguely and walk back to your office.

Questions

1. What should you, the young planner in this case, do now? Is it necessary or appropriate to report your suspicions to anyone? If so, to whom? Your supervisor's supervisor? The district attorney?

2. If you fail to report your suspicions in this case, are you guilty of an ethical violation? If so, why? Should a person who fails to report such information be subject to any sort of penalty? If you don't think that you, as the planner in this circumstance, have an obligation to pursue the matter, what are your reasons?

3. Would it be appropriate to say, in effect, "I don't want to get involved—but I also don't want any part of this situation either" and try to find another job? Why or why not?

4. What would the ASPA code of ethics advise you to do?

5. Assume that there is someone you trust at the *Windham Journal*. Would it be a good idea to leak your suspicions to the press and let them investigate? What would be the consequences?

6. Do you think you should be able to make a report about your suspicions—to anyone—anonymously?

7. Assuming that you decide to report something to someone, what exactly will you report? Would you say something just about your boss, just about Fogarty, or about both of them? Why?

8. What do you think that most people would do if they were confronted with the planner's dilemma?

9. Let us suppose that while neither you nor anyone else can find evidence of any criminal wrongdoing in this case, some ethical questions remain. Should a local chapter of ASPA, or some other professional public administration group, have the responsibility to police the ethics of its members?

10. Is there anything that can be done to avoid, or at least minimize, unethical behavior in public administration in general? How about in this case in particular?

PART TWO

Public Personnel Administration

WHAT IS PUBLIC PERSONNEL ADMINISTRATION?

The heart of any government agency, or any organization for that matter, is its personnel. How effectively an agency accomplishes its mission is heavily determined by the skill, determination, and morale of its employees. These are the central concerns of public personnel administration, a subfield of public administration sometimes more descriptively known as "human resource management." The main job of the personnel administrator is to make sure that an agency has working for it the most capable people possible. This means not only hiring the best candidates for each job to begin with but also ensuring that the people who already work for any agency have the requisite knowledge, skills, and abilities to perform their jobs effectively. Thus personnel administration involves all of the following administrative processes: candidate recruitment, testing and selection, performance evaluation, training, career development, and compensation and pay administration. The five exercises in Part Two are designed to give you an opportunity to learn at first hand some of the techniques used by personnel administrators.

RANK-IN-JOB VERSUS RANK-IN-PERSON

Before we learn specific techniques, however, we would do well to consider some general theory. The foundation of American public personnel administration, the wellspring from which all the techniques flow, is the idea of the *job*. Recruitment, training, compensation, evaluation, and so forth are all rooted in this very basic construct. This may seem perfectly obvious, but it really isn't. What it means

is that in the minds of personnel administrators, all government agencies—or almost all—are conceived of as sets of jobs, not as collections of people. In fact, we might say that the first law of American public personnel administration is that *jobs exist independent of their occupants.* Strictly speaking, an employee or a prospective employee is treated not as a unique, individual person but as a set of knowledge, skills, and abilities that may or may not fit a particular job.

The name given to this theory that underlies American public personnel administration is *position classification,* also known as the *rank-in-job* system. Position classification entails two related assumptions. First, the only things relevant to a personnel decision are the knowledge, skills, and abilities that a person brings to a job; all else is ignored. Second, the status and compensation an employee receives are solely a function of the job the person holds. This means that if I want a job as a carpenter, only my carpentry skills will be considered; moreover, even if I have a degree in analytical chemistry, speak seven languages fluently, and am an accomplished concert pianist, I will be treated and paid as a carpenter (assuming I get the job).

Contrast this, for a moment, with the major alternative system of personnel administration, known as *rank classification* or *rank-in-person.* In this system, which is used by most countries in the world, narrowly defined jobs are not nearly so determining. Although an effort is made to match a person's skills to a job, far more attention is paid to the general qualifications and assets a person represents. Given a certain level of education, skill, or experience, a person is assigned a rank, which is held regardless of the particular job that person is performing.

Not all organizations in the United States use the rank-in-job system, but most do. Noting the few exceptions may help explain the differences between the two systems: The military, the teaching profession, and the foreign service are prominent examples. Whether one works in the motor pool or as a clerk in a company headquarters, a private is a private; whether one teaches "Introduction to American Government" or a graduate seminar in political theory, an assistant professor is still an assistant professor; and whether one approves visas in our embassy in Cairo or analyzes political developments from a desk in the State Department, an FSO-8 is still an FSO-8. In all these cases, pay and status go with the rank a person holds, not the job he or she performs.

WHY RANK-IN-JOB?

Again, these are exceptions in the United States. Most personnel systems here are based on the rank-in-job concept. Our emphasis on jobs rather than human beings in this country may seem odd, given the people-oriented nature of public personnel administration, but it has deep historical roots. One reason for this emphasis derives from Frederick Taylor and the impact of Scientific Management theories on public administration: Taylor and his disciples saw government as a machine to accomplish particular purposes. Just as an engineer designs and assembles separate components to create a complex mechanical device, so a builder of organizations stitches together jobs to create a network of activity to accomplish some broader purpose. In both cases, the parts—mechanical components or jobs—are important only insofar as they contribute to the efficient functioning of the whole machine.

A second historical reason for personnel administration's focus on jobs rather than people was the battle waged by civil service reformers against the spoils system in the late nineteenth century. By forcing government employers to pay attention only to job-related characteristics of potential employees, reformers felt that they could exclude partisan political considerations from personnel decisions. If you are hiring a typist, they argued, you should pay attention only to how well applicants type, not to whether they are Republicans or Democrats. Performance, not politics, should be the criterion for selection.

Although these arguments may seem a little dated, their logic, bolstered by more modern problems and concerns, continues to structure American public personnel administration. Efforts to reduce artificial barriers to employment based on race or sex, consistent with affirmative action policies, for instance, have used job-based techniques to assess the discriminatory impact of various hiring and promotional criteria (see Exercise 9). The most important explanation for the persistence of the emphasis on jobs in American personnel administration, however, may be the nature of American democracy: By construing public employees as cogs in the machine, to use a Taylorist phrase, American personnel managers help maintain the distinction (a polite fiction, some would say) between politics and administration, a distinction that allows citizens to believe that they, through their elected representatives, are still in charge of the bureaucrats.

Does all this mean that American personnel administrators are heartless automatons who are unconcerned with people? Of course not. It does mean, though, that personnel administrators make a deliberate effort to ignore individual characteristics that are not job-related. In fact, this is the major lesson that you should learn from the first exercise in Part Two. Only by focusing on the job and its requirements, it is argued, can we ensure high quality for an agency and fair treatment for its employees.

FURTHER READING

Good, comprehensive overviews of public personnel administration in the United States may be found in any one of a number of personnel management textbooks. Two of the most useful ones are Dennis L. Dresang, *Public Personnel Management and Public Policy,* 3d ed. (New York: Addison Wesley Longman, 1999), and Lloyd G. Nigro and Felix A. Nigro, *The New Public Personnel Administration,* 4th ed. (Itasca, Ill.: Peacock, 1995). Three good collections of readings in the field may be found in Steven W. Hays and Richard C. Kearney, eds., *Public Personnel Administration: Problems and Prospects,* 3d ed. (Englewood Cliffs, N.J.: Prentice Hall, 1995), Jack Rabin, ed., *Handbook of Public Personnel Administration* (New York: Marcel Dekker, 1994), and Frank J. Thompson, ed., *Classics of Public Personnel Policy,* 2d ed. (Pacific Grove, Calif.: Brooks/Cole, 1991).

Exercise 7

Job Analysis and the Job Description

A SHORT FABLE

Imagine for a moment that you are T. R. Hardy, head of a medium-size regulatory agency in a midwestern state. You are working quietly at your desk late one Friday afternoon, trying to get some paperwork finished before the weekend. Suddenly, there is a knock at your door, and before you can even say, "Come in," Frank Johnson, your agency personnel director, rushes into your office. "T. R.," he says, "we've got a problem. I've just heard that most of the clericals are threatening to sue us for sex discrimination. They claim that the only reason they're getting paid less than the maintenance staff is because they're women. I tried to tell them how silly . . ."

"T. R.? Listen, I need to talk to you. Oh, sorry, Frank. I didn't know you were in here." The source of this latest interruption is Sonia Fletcher, chief economist in the agency's rate division. "I hope I'm not interrupting anything important. But this really can't wait," she continues, with only a glance at a clearly perturbed Frank Johnson. "One of my senior economists is threatening to quit. He says he didn't get as big a merit increase as he thought he should. I tried to explain that I didn't feel he was working up to standard, but he . . ."

"Frank? Sonia? I didn't know we were having a staff meeting this afternoon." Alan Bateson, the agency's Equal Employment Opportunity (EEO) officer, moves quickly into the room. "Well, anyway, I guess it's just as well we're all here. Remember our last round of recruitment for junior rate analysts? I've just learned that one of the unsuccessful applicants is going to challenge the process. Maybe even

go to court. He maintains that we had no business demanding advanced degrees for these positions, that this requirement wasn't related to the job and . . ."

"Excuse me, Alan, but I hadn't finished," interjects Sonia.

"*You* weren't finished!" says Frank, raising his voice. "I was here first and you interrupted me."

As the voices of your three aides merge in a cacophonous babble, you sit back, close your eyes, and try to concentrate. Sex discrimination? Unfair evaluation? Unreasonable hiring standards? What to do? The promise of a quiet, relaxing weekend seems very far away.

THE MORAL

We may justly sympathize with T. R. Hardy. None of these problems will be simple to resolve. But if T. R. is a perceptive manager and thinks carefully about these questions, a useful lesson that may forestall future difficulties can be learned. Although each problem is different, a common thread runs throughout, a thread that may well reflect a fundamental gap in the agency's personnel structure. Note that each dispute involves disagreements about the nature of the job in question. The clerical workers are arguing that their jobs are undervalued by the agency, at least in comparison with the maintenance workers'; Frank Johnson disagrees. The senior economist believes that his job performance has not been assessed properly; Sonia Fletcher disagrees. The unsuccessful applicant for the job of junior rate analyst feels that the requirement for an

115

advanced degree is unreasonable; whoever set the job criteria disagreed. In each case, there is disagreement about what a particular job requires, either in terms of qualifications needed (the junior rate analyst), behaviors expected (the senior economist), or the level and value of effort exerted (the clericals). One thing this may indicate is that the agency has not adequately analyzed its jobs. That is, it has not systematically identified all the tasks that an employee occupying each position must perform. If we can't identify job tasks systematically, we don't have much to go by, either as managers or as employees. We certainly can't evaluate someone's performance fairly, for we don't have any standards that are clearly related to the job itself. We can't decide what level of compensation is equitable, for we aren't really sure what one class of jobs involves in comparison with another. Nor are we able to set appropriate qualifications to use for recruitment; without knowledge of day-to-day job requirements, how is one to say whether a Ph.D. rather than a high school diploma is needed?

WHAT IS JOB ANALYSIS?

Job analysis may be formally defined as the collection and collation of information regarding the tasks performed in various positions in an organization and assessments of the knowledge, skills, and abilities necessary to perform those tasks successfully. To state it more simply, job analysis means figuring out what a particular job involves and what qualifications someone needs to do that job. Job analyses are important, as our story about T. R. Hardy makes clear, because almost all other personnel processes depend on them.

HOW ARE JOB ANALYSES DONE?

There are many different ways to conduct job analyses. Some techniques are quantitative and involve evaluating the tasks performed by a worker (the *job incumbent*) against a preset general checklist of job tasks. Other techniques rely on relatively unstructured interviews with job incumbents and their supervisors to try to get a picture of what a job

involves. Whether quantitative and structured or nonquantitative and unstructured, all thorough job analyses require the person doing the analysis to become as familiar as possible with the job being studied. This often involves observation of the work itself, reading technical literature pertinent to the occupation, and becoming acquainted with organization charts and statements of organizational purpose; a review of old job descriptions also is useful. For many jobs, a good starting point is the *Dictionary of Occupational Titles,* published by the U.S. Department of Labor; this volume provides general descriptions of more than 20,000 jobs. Extensive background research is essential for a sound job analysis, for the analyst must try to describe not just what an incumbent does but what he or she should be doing in terms of organizational goals and professional requirements. In other words, a job description derived wholly from observing a typist who types only 15 words a minute would probably not suffice.

FURTHER READING

The literature on job analysis and position classification is generally fairly technical. Good overviews may be found in the personnel administration textbooks cited in the introduction to Part Two. The near-official handbook for position classifiers is Harold D. Suskin, ed., *Job Evaluation and Pay Administration in the Public Sector* (Washington, D.C.: International Personnel Management Association, 1977). This volume contains many useful articles on the subject but is quite technical in orientation. Although somewhat dated, Jay M. Shafritz's *Position Classification: A Behavioral Analysis for the Public Service* (New York: Praeger, 1973) is still useful. This empirical analysis of the effects of position classification reminds us that techniques do not always work out as planned.

Finally, you may find it useful to put the American system of position classification in comparative perspective by considering its major alternative, rank classification. Ferrel Heady, *Public Administration: A Comparative Perspective,* 5th ed. (New York: Dekker, 1995), provides an excellent introduction to alternative personnel systems.

Overview of Exercise

In this exercise, you will conduct a job analysis and write a job description. Several members of your class who actually hold jobs will be designated "job incumbents."[1] The remaining members of your class will be designated "job analysts." Working in small groups, job analysts will interview a single job incumbent and complete Form 30, "Job Analysis Questionnaire." Each job analyst will then prepare a Job Description (Form 33) for the job analyzed.

Note that this exercise is an abbreviated version of job analysis, as it is based mainly on a single interview with a job incumbent. You are not required to observe the job incumbent's work or to talk with his or her supervisors and coworkers, although your instructor may ask you to do some background library research on the occupation being analyzed. Remember that if you were working as a professional personnel administrator, you would need to take all these additional steps to conduct a sound job analysis and prepare a valid job description. Moreover, unless you were taking part in a wholesale classification survey, you would likely be working alone, rather than as a member of a job analysis team.

INSTRUCTIONS

Step One

Your instructor will select members of the class who actually hold jobs to play the roles of job incum-

bents. Remaining members of the class will play the roles of job analysts.

Step Two

Job analysts should read Form 29, "Instructions for Job Analysts," carefully and familiarize themselves with the items on Form 30.

Step Three

A team of job analysts should be assigned to each job incumbent. Analysts should interview the incumbent to whom they have been assigned and complete Form 30.

Step Four

Job analysts should read Form 31, "Instructions for Writing Job Descriptions," and review the sample job description on Form 32. (If you are a job incumbent, your instructor may ask you to step out of your role at this point, obtain a completed copy of Form 30 either for your job or for another incumbent's, and complete a job description.)

Step Five

Each job analyst should complete Form 33, "Job Description," for the job that he or she has analyzed.

Step Six

Answer the questions on Form 34.

---

[1]Your instructor may ask you to go to a public agency and analyze the position of an actual job incumbent. If so, your instructor will modify the instructions accordingly.

Instructions For Job Analysts

The major tasks of a job analyst are to describe as accurately and thoroughly as possible the duties performed by a job incumbent and to assess the skills, knowledge, and abilities necessary to perform those duties satisfactorily. Form 30, which should be completed during your interview with the job incumbent, will help you do this by directing your attention to the key elements of the job being analyzed. The following detailed instructions explain how to complete Form 30.

A. *General Information:* Fill in agency name, job title, and job incumbent's name.

B. *Job Duties:* List each discrete job duty separately, and estimate the amount of time the job incumbent spends on each duty. Be as specific as possible in identifying job duties, focusing on actual job behaviors. For instance, job duties of a secretary might include "types correspondence and reports; answers telephone; operates photocopy machine; operates fax machine."

C. *Job Relationships*
  1. *Supervision Received:* Provide the name(s) of the job incumbent's immediate supervisor(s) and describe how closely the job incumbent is supervised; that is, how much autonomy, or independence, does the job incumbent have in performing his or her work?
  2. *Supervision Given:* Provide the title(s) of employees supervised by the job incumbent and the total number supervised.
  3. *Other Job Relationships:* Describe any significant nonsupervisory interactions the job incumbent has with other employees or with clients in performing his or her job duties. For instance, do the incumbent's duties require extensive cooperation with other workers? Does the incumbent have extensive contact with the public?

D. *Job Qualifications*
  1. *Knowledge, Skills, and Abilities Required:* Describe the knowledge, skills, and abilities required to perform each of the job duties identified in part B, including, where possible, acceptable levels of performance. To use the secretarial example, a job incumbent might need the ability to type 65 words per minute, to respond knowledgeably and pleasantly to telephone inquiries, and to operate basic office machinery. Note that where specific duties require the same underlying skills ("operate photocopy machine" and "operate fax machine"), the skill or skills need be mentioned only once ("operate basic office machinery").
  2. *Education or Training Required:* Describe here the level of education (e.g., high school diploma, civil engineering B.S., chemistry Ph.D.) or type of training (vocational courses in laboratory technology, secretarial school, etc.) required to perform the job duties. Make sure that whatever education or training you specify is in fact job-related; unjustified educational or training requirements may constitute discriminatory and thus illegal barriers to employment. Also specify here any training or education that may be possible after a person has been hired to fill the job (e.g., "on-the-job training provided").
  3. *Experience Required:* Describe any previous work (or nonwork) experiences necessary to perform the job duties (e.g., "three years' accountancy experience required"). As with education and training, be sure that any experience you specify is in fact job-related.
  4. *Other Requirements:* Describe any additional requirements necessary to perform the job duties. These might include such things as holding certain licenses or permits, willingness to relocate, or owning an automobile.

Job Analysis Questionnaire

A. GENERAL INFORMATION

    1. Agency/Organization Name _____

    2. Job Title _____

    3. Job Incumbent Name _____

B. JOB DUTIES

                Duty   *Percent of Time Devoted to Duty*

    1.

    2.

    3.

    4.

    5.

    6.

    7.

    8.

C. JOB RELATIONSHIPS

    1. Supervision Received:

        a. Title of Supervisor(s):

        b. Extent of Supervision:

    2. Supervision Given:

        a. Titles of Employees Supervised:

            i.

            ii.

   iii.

   iv.

   v.

  b. Total Number of Employees Supervised:

 3. Other Job Relationships:

D. JOB QUALIFICATIONS

 1. Knowledge, Skills, and Abilities Required:

  a.

  b.

  c.

  d.

  e.

  f.

  g.

  h.

 2. Education or Training Required:

 3. Experience Required:

 4. Other Requirements:

Submitted by: _____

         Name of Job Analyst

Instructions For Writing Job Descriptions

As noted earlier, a job description is a narrative summary of a particular job's duties and responsibilities, together with a statement of qualifications necessary to perform the job satisfactorily. Job descriptions provide the foundation for a myriad of personnel processes, including recruitment, performance evaluation, and compensation.

Since job descriptions are based on job analyses, you might ask what the difference is between a job description and the completed version of Form 30. In this exercise, the difference is chiefly one of how the material is organized and written; substantively, they will be very similar. Remember, though, that a full job analysis would probably require interviewing or observing the work of several people holding the same type of job as well as discussing the job with the incumbent's supervisors and coworkers. A job description thus usually summarizes a great deal of information. It is the job description, not the pile of paperwork generated during a job analysis, that constitutes the real currency of personnel administration. Consequently, it is worth learning how to write one clearly, accurately, and succinctly.

Although there is no one right form for a job description, you should observe the following general rules:

1. Begin with a general statement of job duties and responsibilities that encompasses job relationships. See the statement of "General Responsibilities" in the example on Form 32.

2. List the major duties of the job, in descending order of importance, together with any relevant performance standards. See "Major Duties" in the example on Form 32.

3. Identify the relevant knowledge, skills, and abilities required. See the corresponding section in the example on Form 32.

4. Specify the levels of education, training, and experience required for appointment. Note on-the-job training if relevant. Be sure that the qualifications specified are appropriate to the job.

5. Keep the description as concise as possible by avoiding unnecessary words. Use a "telegraphic" writing style: The subject of the description, the job incumbent, is assumed; thus a simple verb-object form (e.g., "Analyzes financial data," "Supervises three-person maintenance staff") can be used.

Sample Job Description

Job Title:	Budget Analyst I

General Responsibilities: Under the supervision of an Assistant Budget Director, reviews annual budget requests of state agencies, analyzes legislation prior to action of Governor, and undertakes program analyses and evaluations.

Major Duties:

1. Reviews annual budget requests from one or more state agencies.
2. Recommends agency budget figures to Assistant Budget Director.
3. Analyzes legislation prior to action of Governor.
4. Evaluates effectiveness of agency programs.

Required Knowledge, Skills, and Abilities: Knowledge of budget formats and statutes governing state budget procedures; ability to perform statistical analyses, including multiple regression; working knowledge of standard accounting procedures; ability to write clearly; good interpersonal skills.

Qualifications: Master's degree in Public Administration or related field or Bachelor's degree with three years of experience in budgeting and financial administration.

Job Description

Job Title:

Responsibilities:

Major Duties:

Required Knowledge,
Skills, and Abilities:

Qualifications:

Questions

1. Why is it important to be as precise as possible in identifying specific job duties when conducting job analyses and writing job descriptions?

2. What drawbacks, if any, do you see with efforts to define jobs in this way? Is it really possible—or desirable—to ignore the individuals who occupy the jobs?

3. Would you rather work for an organization that defined your job very carefully in writing or for one that left things more open?

Exercise 8

Performance Evaluation

PERFORMANCE EVALUATION: WHAT, WHY, AND HOW?

Most members of organizations—employers and employees—embrace performance evaluation with all the enthusiasm usually shown a bad case of the flu. Few people enjoy having their work evaluated, especially when they think their pay, promotion chances, or their very jobs depend on the outcomes. Probably not many more enjoy evaluating the work of others; even if you think you know what other employees are doing wrong, and even if you have supervisory responsibility for their work, it is seldom easy to summon the courage to tell them, no matter how constructive the criticism. A major reason for the dread most people experience in the face of performance evaluation is that organizations are more than the cool lines of authority and neat boxes that appear on organizational charts. In organizations, social relationships develop quickly; informal norms of interaction become established, often cemented by close working relationships and even friendships that pull at formal organizational roles.

Yet performance evaluation is unavoidable. As long as personnel decisions have to be made—that is, as long as choices have to be made about whom to promote or to whom to give a merit raise or whom to fire—assessments of work have to be undertaken.

In fact, the only sort of organization that could avoid performance evaluation completely would be one that made all personnel decisions randomly or by reference to some arbitrary rule unrelated to quality of work. As most of us prefer not to work in organizations where decisions are made by pulling names or numbers out of a hat, we make some effort to measure one another's performance.

The key phrase here is "some effort." Although almost all organizations evaluate their employees' performances, relatively few do so in a systematic and conscientious manner. Valid performance evaluations require hard work and a heavy commitment of the organization's time and resources. Managers must be convinced that the results of the evaluations will be useful for achieving organizational goals; employees must believe that the method of evaluation is fair and unbiased.

What exactly do we mean by "systematic performance evaluation"? What distinguishes sound from unsound methods of evaluating employee performance? While no one method will be right for every job in every organization, all systems of performance evaluation worthy of the name are distinguished by one central idea: Those employee traits or behaviors—and only those employee traits and behaviors—directly related to the performance of job duties are measured. For the evaluator, this requires two kinds of information. First, he or she needs to understand the exact nature of the job; second, he or she needs to have accurate knowledge of what the job incumbent has actually been doing. The first requirement should be familiar to anyone who completed the preceding exercise. It is by reading a valid job description, based on a thorough job analysis, that evaluators know the nature of a job. More precisely, job descriptions provide detailed specifications of job duties. Each of these job duties, which in the language of performance evaluation are called *job dimensions,* can be used as a yardstick against which to measure the actual performance of job incumbents.

The nature of the yardstick varies widely, however. In fact, we may identify three broad types of performance appraisal systems, each of which focuses on very different measures of performance.

THREE APPROACHES TO PERFORMANCE EVALUATION

The first approach focuses on employee *traits.* Trait-rating systems, though declining in popularity, are still widely used, mainly because they are easy and inexpensive to administer. With trait-based systems, certain traits or personality characteristics—"initiative," "promptness," "courtesy, "perseverance"—are identified as essential to acceptable job performance. Supervisors then rate employees on these traits, making a check in an appropriate column—average, good, excellent—for each item; usually there is also space on a form of this type for the supervisor to make free-form narrative comments about the employee ("Fred has had an unusually productive year and played a key role in the preparation of our annual report"). You are probably familiar with this sort of evaluative instrument, for this is the format that most law schools and other graduate programs (as well as many employers) use on the standard letters of recommendation they require from applicants.

Although they are simple to devise and use, trait-based evaluation systems present serious problems. Even for psychologists, personality traits are slippery commodities. To ask a general manager not only to assess someone's personality but also to make inferences about the effect of that personality on job performance is to invite criticism that the system is invalid, that it doesn't measure what it purports to measure.

Moreover, because personality is, by definition, neither a transient nor an easily manipulated behavior, the prescriptive implications of a trait-based system are unclear at best. When personality is identified—rightly or wrongly—as the cause of an employee's performance problem, what are we supposed to do about it? Employers and employees alike are left with no constructive suggestions for performance improvement.

The second approach seeks to avoid some of these shortcomings by focusing narrowly on employee *behaviors.* Here we evaluate not the person, but what the person does (a distinction that owes much to child psychology: "Johnny isn't a bad boy," his mother notes as she surveys the smoking ruins of her house; "he just exhibits bad behaviors"). In the most popular of the behavioral systems—Behaviorally Anchored Rating Scales, or BARS—for each of the job dimensions identified in

a job analysis, one generates a series of statements that describe the behavior—from excellent to execrable—of hypothetical job incumbents. If we were to develop BARS for the secretarial job discussed in Exercise 7, we would have to write "anchor" statements for the three job dimensions of typing correspondence and reports, answering the telephone, and operating office machinery. Some examples for the typing dimension would be "uses proper form in typing business letters," "fails to retain copies of correspondence for office files," and "frequently misspells words."

Once arrayed on weighted scales, the statements provide relatively objective points of comparison in the evaluation process. A supervisor simply reads the statements and decides which set best describes the behavior of the employee in question. It is easy to quantify BARS evaluations, with a certain number of points awarded for each level of performance (e.g., 5 for "excellent," 4 for "good," with each dimension subject to some multiplier that reflects the relative importance of the dimension to the job); once each employee is evaluated on each dimension, a total performance score can easily be determined.

Proponents of the behavioral approach cite not only its relative objectivity but its instructional character as well. By looking at a BARS form or similar instrument, an employee can learn exactly what behaviors are expected and change his or her own conduct accordingly. Because trait-based systems of performance evaluation usually focus on immutable facets of people's personalities, they cannot serve this function.

Still, behavioral approaches are not without weaknesses. They are, to begin with, time-consuming and expensive to design. A good BARS system requires the generation of scores of anchor statements for each job, each of which needs to be carefully validated. And every job class requires a new set of scales: Sets of anchor statements developed for a secretarial job cannot be used to evaluate a welder. Some critics also argue that behavioral systems are too rigid and directive. Not only do jobs change from year to year (even day to day), but seldom is there one "best" way to do a job, as such approaches seem to assume. The corollary assumption, that what is important is how a job gets done, not what is actually accomplished, clearly misses the point, critics argue.

The final approach to performance evaluation responds to these criticisms, at least in part, by focusing on *results.* Here attention shifts away from the behaviors in which employees engage to the things that they accomplish. Instead of specifying how a salesperson makes contacts with potential customers ("always shines shoes and wears clean shirt," "seldom returns phone calls," "keeps accurate records of visits made"), we would simply ask, "How many widgets did Zander sell last quarter?" If Zander sells a lot of widgets, we are not likely to care much about his sales "behavior": He is welcome to wear a gorilla suit, speak in limericks, and ride to appointments on a unicycle, as long as sales volume stays high.

The most popular and best known of these results-oriented systems is Management by Objectives (MBO). Although MBO may take various forms, differing in degree of formality, most MBO systems consist of three basic steps:

1. Setting goals and objectives
2. Working toward the goals and objectives
3. Reviewing performance

Although MBO does not logically require heavy employee participation in goal setting, most systems rely on it on the assumption that employees need to "buy in" psychologically. Indeed, heightened motivation and creativity through employee participation and "empowerment" are usually cited as the chief benefits of results-oriented systems like MBO.

Like trait and behavior approaches, result-based systems have problems. Depending on the design of the system, it may be difficult to compare the performance of employees on a common metric. Objectives, after all, will vary with the employee. Therefore, it may be hard to link evaluations to pay and promotion decisions—at least in any way that is perceived as fair. Furthermore, an overemphasis on results may lead to employee confusion and uncertainty about the hows of getting the job done. Worse, it may lead to an "anything goes" philosophy in which ethics and legality are skirted as long as the objective is achieved. Also, results-based systems require special efforts on the part of raters to weigh and filter out extraneous factors—factors beyond the control of the employee—in writing evaluations.

FURTHER READING

One of the classic statements on the problems of performance evaluation, with particular emphasis on the importance of employee participation, is Douglas McGregor, "An Uneasy Look at Performance Appraisal," *Harvard Business Review* (May-June 1957). For a more recent textbook overview of performance appraisal systems, consult Gary Latham and Kenneth Wexley, *Increasing Productivity Through Performance Appraisal* (Reading, Mass.: Addison-Wesley, 1994). Also of interest are William Swan and Phillip Margulies, *How to Do a Superior Performance Appraisal* (New York: Wiley, 1991); William J. Bruns, Jr., *Performance Measurement, Evaluation and Incentives* (New York: McGraw Hill, 1992); and Jacky Holloway, Jenny Lewis, and Geoff Mallory, *Performance Measurement and Evaluation* (Newbury Parks, Calif.: Sage, 1995). More information on BARS can be found in R. S. Atkins and E. T. Conlon, "Behaviorally Anchored Rating Scales: Some Theoretical Issues," *Academy of Management Review* 3 (January 1978); and D. P. Schwab et al., "Behaviorally Anchored Rating Scales: A Review of the Literature," *Personnel Psychology* 28 (Winter 1975).

Overview of Exercise

In this exercise, you will construct a performance evaluation system for the job you analyzed and described in Exercise 7. Because you will not have the opportunity to observe employee performance, your task is to *create* the evaluation instrument, not apply it.

INSTRUCTIONS

Step One
Review the job description you prepared for Exercise 7. If you played the role of job incumbent and did not write a job description, obtain com-

pleted copies of Forms 30 and 33 from one of your classmates who served as a job analyst.

Step Two

Decide which approach to performance evaluation—trait-based, behavior-based, or results-based—you wish to take in designing an appraisal instrument for this job. Remember, there is no right answer to this question. You will need to weigh a variety of factors—some inherent in the approach, some peculiar to the job in question—in making your choice. Think about the advantages and disadvantages of each approach discussed in the introduction to this exercise.

If you decide to use a *trait-based system,* review Form 35.

If you decide to use a *behavior-based system,* review Form 37.

If you decide to use a *results-based system,* review Form 39.

You may, if you like, use some combination of these systems, in which case you will probably want to review all of these forms before you design your own evaluation form from scratch.

Step Three

Use the appropriate worksheet (Form 36, 38, or 40) to design your appraisal form.

Step Four

Answer the questions on Form 41.

Designing a Trait-Based System

This form describes how to create a trait-based evaluation system.

1. Read through your job analysis and job description and identify the major job dimensions.

2. For each job dimension, decide which characteristics or traits—such as honesty, courtesy, or maturity—are required for the successful performance of the job. Some characteristics or traits may apply to more than one job dimension.

3. Arrange the traits you have selected on Form 36 or some similar form of your own devising such that you, or some other evaluator, would be able to rate the performance of the job incumbent.

4. Consider augmenting your evaluation form (either Form 36 or your own version) with one or more open-ended statements, such as "Describe any outstanding achievements or contributions by this employee this year."

Trait-Based Evaluation Worksheet (Model)

Job Title: _____

Incumbent: _____

Trait	Excellent	Very Good	Average	Fair	Poor	Unacceptable

Designing a Behavior-Based System

This form describes how to implement an abbreviated version of Behaviorally Anchored Rating Scales (BARS), which is the most common example of a behavior-based performance evaluation system.

1. Read through your job analysis and job description and identify the major job dimensions.

2. Make a judgment about the relative importance of each job dimension and express it as a percentage. For instance, if the three job dimensions of secretary are typing, photocopying, and telephone answering, after reading the job analysis we might decide to weight them as follows: typing, 60 percent; telephone answering, 30 percent; and photocopying, 10 percent.

3. *For each job dimension,* create one copy of Form 38 (or another like it of your own design). If you are working with five job dimensions, you need to create five blank forms; if you are working with three job dimensions, you need to create three blank forms. It doesn't matter whether you use photocopies, copies torn out of workbooks, or handwritten versions.

4. Fill in the appropriate information at the top of each copy of Form 38 that you made: Indicate the job title, the job dimension, and the factor weight (from step 2).

5. Write a series of statements that describe a range—from excellent to unacceptable—of behaviors for each job dimension. Be creative and make them up. For instance, if you are generating statements for the job of waiter (for the job dimension "food service"), you might write statements like "frequently spills food on customers" and "always remembers to mention special menu items." The main idea is to compose statements that would describe real, observable behaviors of someone doing that job (not necessarily the person you used for the job analysis—*any* person who might hold that job).

6. Arrange the statements you wrote in step 5 in the corresponding blank spaces on the various versions of Form 38 that you copied. Clipped or stapled together, these scales constitute your completed performance evaluation form.

Behavior-Based Evaluation Worksheet (Model)

Incumbent: _____

Job Title: _____

Job Dimension: _____

Factor Weight: _____

5. Excellent _____

_____

4. Good _____

_____

3. Fair _____

_____

2. Poor _____

_____

1. Unacceptable _____

_____

Designing a Results-Based System

This form explains how to design an MBO-style, results-oriented performance evaluation system.

1. Read through your job analysis and job description and identify the major job dimensions.

2. Generate one or more measurable performance goals for each of the major job dimensions, and write the goals in the appropriate spaces on Form 40 (or another form of your devising). The goals should be directly related to the job dimension and must be measurable in objective, quantifiable terms. For the job of secretary, for instance, with its job dimensions of typing, photocopying, and telephone answering, we would generate such goals as "type final drafts of technical reports at an average rate of one page every four minutes" or "provide average turnaround of less than one hour on top-priority photocopy requests."

3. If possible, discuss the goals with the job incumbent (the person who provided the basis for the job analysis). The performance level expected should be *reasonable* from the perspective of both the individual and the organization.

Results-Based Evaluation Worksheet (Model)

MBO WORKSHEET

Incumbent: _____

Job Title: _____

Performance Evaluation					
Performance Goal	Goal Weight (%)	Superlative	Successful	Marginal	Not Acceptable

Questions

1. If you applied the evaluation form you developed in this exercise to the behavior of a job incumbent, do you think you would produce a fair and accurate evaluation? Why or why not?

2. How do you suppose the job incumbent would react to your instrument or to the evaluation method that you chose? Do you think he or she would cooperate willingly with the evaluation?

3. How would you feel about having your own work (perhaps even your work as a student) evaluated in this way?

4. What are the strengths and weaknesses of the various methods of performance evaluation discussed in this exercise? Are there any approaches that you can think of that might be better? If so, what makes them better?

Exercise 9

Recruitment and Selection

ANGST AND THE JOB INTERVIEW: A ONE-HALF-ACT PLAY

THE TIME: The not-too-distant future
THE SCENE: A college placement office

You have shined your shoes, combed your hair, and donned a freshly pressed suit. You now sit nervously in the placement office, waiting for your name to be called, eyes scanning for the hundredth time a résumé you're convinced is too thin. I really want this job, you think. What will they ask me? Are my grades high enough? Why did they pick me for this interview, anyway? Do I have any skills I can offer this organization?

Relax. A little anxiety in the face of a job interview is to be expected. You wouldn't be sitting there if there weren't some evidence to suggest that you were qualified for the job. In any event, consider how the world must look from the perspective of the person on the other side of the interview table: How can we get the best person to fill this position? What sorts of questions should I ask to make sure I really get to know this candidate? Will I be able to avoid making judgments on superficial characteristics that have nothing to do with the job? If I focus too much on grade-point averages and standardized test scores, will I be screening people out who might well be perfect for our organization?

Recruiting and selecting candidates for employment is not easy for the candidates or the employer. Although both parties have a common interest in making a good match, the information needed to do that is often difficult to obtain. As was noted in the introduction to Part Two, the merit principle states that personnel decisions should be guided solely by reference to a person's qualifications. Specifically, it tells us to ask whether the knowledge, skills, and abilities required for a job are matched by the knowledge, skills, and abilities embodied in a candidate. If we have done a sound job analysis, we know what knowledge, skills, and abilities a job requires. Our problem now is to address the other half of the equation: How do we assess a candidate's qualifications?

TYPES OF SELECTION DEVICES

Employers use a wide variety of techniques to assess the qualifications of prospective employees and to help them make hiring decisions. Which device or set of devices any particular agency adopts will depend on the size and sophistication of the organization, any general personnel rules that govern the jurisdiction, and the nature of the job being filled.

For most organizations, the first cut through a pool of candidates is made by a review of *job applications.* Typically, job applications ask candidates for general identity information, education and employment histories, and references. Although some agencies use very general application forms to cover a wide range of positions, the most useful forms are those designed especially for particular job categories. When seeking to fill the position of accountant, for instance, an organization would be well advised to ask a series of questions specific to accounting skills and qualifications. These questions can (and should) be derived from a thorough job analysis.

Some organizations request *résumés* instead of or in addition to job applications. Résumés usually provide the same general information as an application form but are written by candidates rather than employers. Because they are not standardized, it is more difficult to make systematic comparisons among candidates with résumés than it is with job applications. The use of résumés rather than applications may be appropriate, however, when attempting to fill high-level (e.g., city manager, county budget director) or unique (e.g., limnologist, utilities economist) positions.

Regardless of whether applications or résumés or both are used, however, it is important that the individuals reviewing them take care to apply appropriate standards when making judgments about the suitability of candidates. A concerted effort must be made to ensure that the criteria applied are (1) job-related and (2) the same for all candidates. One way to do this is to develop a written scoring system, again derived from a job analysis, that can be applied to the applications or résumés. It might be determined, for instance, that each year of experience is worth 5 points or that demonstrated mastery of a particular skill is worth 10 points. Such a system helps guard against bias in the initial stages of the selection process.

Once preliminary selection decisions have been made and the pool of eligible candidates has been narrowed, many organizations choose to *interview* a small number of finalists. Oral interviews, either in person or over the telephone, have the advantage of flexibility and allow employers to ask more subtle and detailed questions than applications usually permit. Interviews also provide the opportunity to assess candidates' personal characteristics and social skills. But these advantages must be treated cautiously. Interviews can easily be abused to the detriment of candidate and employer alike. Unless interviews focus only on issues directly related to the job, they may discriminate, intentionally or unintentionally, against worthy job seekers. The most useful interviews are usually those based on carefully prepared questions that can be scored as described earlier.

Many organizations use some form of paper-and-pencil *test* as part of their selection process. This technique can be used as an initial screening device (all applicants take the test) or can be restricted to a later stage of the process. Depending on the nature of the job, tests may be aimed at assessing either achievement (how much do you already know about this field?) or aptitude (how likely are you to be able to learn?). Because of the time and expense

involved in validating tests of this sort, they are usually adopted only by large organizations that plan to use them to fill multiple positions.

In addition to standardized tests, other forms of examination are available. *Work sampling* and *assessment centers* are two of the most popular. Work sampling requires that the applicant actually perform some of the tasks used on the job—typing is a common example. Assessment centers are simulated work experiences. Depending on the job in question, candidates are required to make decisions about complex, hypothetical problems, demonstrate an ability to budget their time, and interact effectively with other people.

THE IMPORTANCE OF JOB-RELATEDNESS AND VALIDATION

By now it should be clear that the answer to the question "How do we assess a candidate's qualifications?" involves more than simply gathering all the information about the candidate that we can. Our task is not just to gather information; it is to gather *job-related* information. This is a point that must constantly be borne in mind, regardless of the selection device used. It is as important in conducting an interview as it is in designing a test. In practical terms, it means that a good application is not necessarily one that generates three thick file folders of information about a candidate. Instead, a good application is one that asks specific questions about job-related qualifications.

The reasons for the focus on job-relatedness should also be clear: It ensures a certain level of fairness to the prospective employee and helps the employer choose the person who will make the best contribution to the mission of the organization. This is the essence of the merit principle. Without this sort of standard to sift and winnow facts about candidates, an employer could easily be overwhelmed by even the minimal amounts of information presented on typical résumés. When this happens, it is not unusual to become distracted and swayed by extraneous considerations. You may unconsciously overstress the fact that one candidate attended your alma mater or was active in the college sailing club. This phenomenon is especially problematic in interviews that have not been well planned and are not based on questions directly tied to the job; considerations of personal appearance and deportment can quickly grow out of all proportion to their real importance. This doesn't mean that a candidate's personal appearance or extracurricular activities should necessarily be ignored. The question is, are they related to the job? If you are hiring someone to sell sailboats, membership in the college sailing club should be a plus. If you are hiring a social worker for the county welfare department, it should not.

When a personnel selection device such as an application, test, or interview has been carefully designed so that it elicits information that is truly job-related, we say that it has *validity*. Stated more generally, an instrument is *valid* if it measures when it is supposed to measure. The concept of validity is important because in personnel management, as in other endeavors including the natural sciences, many of the things we are interested in knowing about cannot be seen directly; we can only make inferences about them based on observations of things we can see. In personnel administration, for instance, we cannot see knowledge, skills, or abilities directly; they are, after all, only abstract intellectual categories. As a result, we try to measure them indirectly, using instruments like tests and interviews. A test is not knowledge; it is at best only a measure of knowledge. But if we think it measures knowledge well, we call it a valid test. Similarly, a scientist may be interested in knowing the temperature of the air. As temperature cannot be seen directly (it, too, is an abstraction), he or she must rely on observing the volume of mercury in one of those small glass cylinders we call thermometers. A thermometer is considered a valid instrument for this purpose precisely because we know that there is a direct correspondence between changes in the volume of mercury and changes in temperature; indeed, we have come, by convention, to equate temperature with the volume of contained mercury. Any scientist who tried to use, say, a compass to measure temperature would not get very far, for the instrument is invalid for the purpose.

MODELS OF VALIDITY

How do we know when an instrument is valid? How do we decide whether a test or an interview measures what it is supposed to measure? Four basic techniques, called validity models, are avail-

able to help us make the determination. The most rigorous is the *predictive validity model*. To apply this model, a personnel manager must (1) administer a particular selection instrument, such as a test, to a pool of applicants; (2) hire candidates randomly or according to some criterion other than test results; (3) evaluate employee performance on the job; and (4) correlate initial test results with performance evaluations. If there is a strong relationship between test results and job performance, we may say that the test has predictive validity. We could then use the test with confidence in filling future positions. Although this method of validation is very accurate, it is difficult, if not impossible, to apply in most personnel management situations. Not only do merit system rules usually prohibit step (2), but most organizations would find it expensive (in many senses) to hire a large number of potentially unqualified people for the sake of validating a test.

The second method, the *concurrent validity model*, is less rigorous, though more manageable. With this approach, a personnel specialist administers a test or other selection device to a group of current employees. The resultant rankings then are correlated with performance evaluations. As with the first model, a strong association between the two variables indicates validity. In this case, we will have somewhat less confidence in the validity of our selection device, as chances for bias are greater. As the concurrent model relies on the scores of current employees, we have no way of knowing whether test results (or interview results) are a function of knowledge and skills learned on the job or knowledge and skills held before entry. If the knowledge and skills were acquired on the job, the test will not be a proper instrument for assessing the qualifications of *prospective* employees.

The third model of validity is termed *content validity*. Unlike the first two, which are often referred to as empirical validity models, content validity is based on logical, nonempirical analysis; hence it is called a *logical model of validity*. The content validity method requires the personnel administrator to compare systematically the content of the selection device with the content of the job. If the two are very similar, we would say that the selection device has content validity. A typing test is a good example of a selection device that has content validity when used to assess the abilities of prospective typists. The test itself is virtually the same as the job. Unfortunately, not all jobs lend themselves this easily to selection devices that have such clear content validity. Where jobs require particular intellectual or interpersonal skills that are less directly observable than typing, assessment centers or simulations may provide useful selection devices with content validity. These approaches have candidates participate in extended problem-solving sessions, sometimes lasting several days; their behavior is observed and scored by trained personnel specialists. If the situations and problems the candidates confront are similar to those they would face on the job, a case could be made that the selection device has content validity. To meet the requirements of content validity, a selection procedure need not have a behavioral content, however. We often use the content validity model to validate application forms or interview questions. The essential element in content validation is the logical link between the content of the selection device and the content of the job, as measured by job analysis.

The final model of validity is called *construct validity;* like content validity, it is a logical or non-empirical model. This technique assumes that some general personality trait or ability, such as intelligence, acute hearing, or creativity, is central to the job in question. Although it may occasionally be possible to make a persuasive case for a selection device based on construct validity (e.g., fighter pilots need sharp, uncorrected vision), the relationship between various general traits and most jobs is generally tenuous at best; moreover, there are serious questions concerning our ability to measure many so-called traits, such as intelligence. As a result, construct validity is considered the weakest form of validation available.

Good personnel practice obviously requires that all selection devices—from applications and interviews through assessment centers and paper-and-pencil tests—be valid. As has been noted repeatedly, validity and the merit principle go hand in hand. But while it is clear that valid selection devices are useful to organizations, it should be pointed out that many organizations have been slow in recognizing their value. Indeed, the major spur to increased validation in recent years has come from outside personnel administration, specifically from Congress, the courts, and regulatory agencies. A series of major Supreme Court decisions, beginning with *Griggs* v. *Duke Power* in 1971, coupled with the Civil Rights Act of 1964 (especially Title VII), the 1972 Equal Employment Opportunity Act, the Americans with Disabilities Act, and rules promulgated by the Equal Employment Opportunity Commission, have sought to combat race, sex, age, and disabilities discrimination in employment by insisting that selection criteria be job-related. These mandates have been clear and persistent. They have moved employers, public and private, closer to an approximation of the merit principle by insisting that artificial barriers to employment be removed. This means that employers must be able to justify (validate) their selection devices whenever the devices have an adverse impact on minorities. Thus if a paper-and-pencil test has produced a pass rate among blacks that is only half that of whites, the organization administering the test must be able to show that the test is indeed valid. Twenty years ago, the federal Office of Personnel Management chose (under duress) to withdraw the Professional and Administrative Career Examination (PACE) because it could not be validated in the face of such discriminatory impact.

FURTHER READING

The literature in the field of personnel selection and test validation is more technical and specialized than that in most other areas of public personnel administration, and much of it is concerned with fairly arcane questions of personnel psychology and statistical analysis. Although not recommended for the casual reader, perhaps the most authoritative guide to this subject is *Principles for the Validation and Use of Personnel Selection Procedures,* 2d ed. (Berkeley, Calif.: American Psychological Association, 1980). A more accessible treatment can be found in John Hamman and Uday Desai, "Current Issues and Challenges in Recruitment and Selection," in Steven W. Hays and Richard C. Kearney, eds., *Public Personnel Administration: Problems and Prospects,* 3d ed. (Englewood Cliffs, N.J.: Prentice Hall, 1995).

As noted in the text, court cases have figured prominently in the evolution of personnel selection techniques. One of the most important was *Griggs v. Duke Power* (1971). This has been reprinted in Frank J. Thompson, ed., *Classics of Personnel Policy*, 2d ed. (Pacific Grove, Calif.: Brooks/Cole, 1991).

Also available in the Thompson volume is a copy of Title VII of the Civil Rights Act of 1964, as amended by the Equal Employment Opportunity Act of 1972; this law has had a sweeping impact on the practice of personnel administration in America and is worth reading.

Overview of Exercise

In this exercise, you will first devise and discuss a selection strategy for the job you analyzed in Exercise 7. You will then simulate a selection process by reviewing résumés and interviewing job applicants.

INSTRUCTIONS

Step One
Review the job analysis and job description you completed for Exercise 7. Assume that this position is vacant and you have been put in charge of filling it. Use Form 42 to outline and justify the set of selection procedures you plan to use.

Step Two
Review the job description provided on Form 43 *or* the job description selected by your instructor. Assume that this position is vacant and you are responsible for filling it. At your instructor's option, you will choose either from among the three hypothetical applicants whose résumés have been provided on Forms 44–46, or from among actual résumés submitted by your classmates. Review the résumés as directed by your instructor, and make your selection.

Step Three
Refamiliarize yourself with the job description chosen by your instructor. Assume that you have decided that you need to interview the applicants before you can make a final selection. Working in small groups as directed by your instructor, prepare a series of questions appropriate to an interview for this position. Your questions should be aimed at eliciting information—and only that information—that is job-relevant.

Step Four
Interview each of the candidates for the position, as directed by your instructor. Discuss the results of your interviews with other members of your group, and make your selection.

Step Five
Answer the questions on Form 47.

Employee Selection Strategy

Job Title: _____

1. What selection devices will be appropriate in screening candidates for this position?

2. Assuming that you decide to use job applications, résumés, interviews, or some combination of these, how will you weight the information you receive? Will you assign point values to different qualifications or attributes? Provide some specific examples of how you will weight information from applications or résumés, and where appropriate, list some questions you will pose in an interview.

3. What means will you use to validate the selection devices you have chosen?

Job Description

Job Title:	**Budget Analyst I**

General Responsibilities: Under the supervision of an Assistant Budget Director, reviews annual budget requests of state agencies, analyzes legislation prior to action of Governor, and undertakes program analyses and evaluations.

Major Duties:
1. Reviews annual budget requests from one or more state agencies.
2. Recommends agency budget figures to Assistant Budget Director.
3. Analyzes legislation prior to action of Governor.
4. Evaluates effectiveness of agency programs.

Required Knowledge, Skills, and Abilities: Knowledge of budget formats and statutes governing state budget procedures; ability to perform statistical analyses, including multiple regression; working knowledge of standard accounting procedures; ability to write clearly; good interpersonal skills.

Qualifications: Master's degree in Public Administration or related field or Bachelor's degree with three years of experience in budgeting and financial administration.

Marty Smith
123 Pleasant Lane
Anytown, US 45678

Education: W. T. Grant High School
Backhome, US
Graduated (honors): June 1994

State College
College Center, US
B.A., History (June 1998)

Union University
M.P.A. (expected: June 2001)

Experience: Bartleby's Tavern
Cook
(Summers, 1994–1996)

Senator Bill Good
U.S. Senate
Intern (Summer 1997)

Tatters Clothing
Manager
August 1995–December 1998

City of Anytown
Finance Department
Analyst
September 1998–present

Interests: Sailing and reading

Alex Jones
8 Butterworth Circle
Upper Anytown, US 45679

CAREER GOAL: To obtain a position of managerial responsibility in the area of finance and budgeting

WORK EXPERIENCE: Senior analyst, State Forestry Service, 1996–present. Responsible for designing and implementing resource use studies. Supervise one employee.

Junior analyst, State Forestry Service, 1995–1996. Wrote major studies of state fishery resources.

Management Intern, Closynuph Accounting, 1994–1995. Rotated through all major departments of large accounting firm.

EDUCATION: M.B.A., Cash University, 1997
B.S., Accounting, Cash University, 1994

PUBLICATIONS: "Deep Water for State Fisheries" (State Occasional Paper, 1996)

HOBBIES: Personal computers

Name:	Cat Peters
Address:	P.O. Box 333 East Anytown, US 45677
Accomplishments:	Designed and flew experimental aircraft; finished in top 200 in 1997 Boston Marathon; written and produced documentary video based on travel in East Asia.
Education:	Ph.D., Policy Studies, Turnover U.; M.A., Political Science, Lower Sussex College, England; B.A., Liberal Studies, State College.
Experience:	Community development worker for Peace Corps in North Africa (2 years); staff assistant to Anytown Community College President (3 years); freelance editor and financial consultant (5 years).
References:	Available on request

Questions

1. To what extent have the employers for whom you've worked (or sought to work), including summer or part-time jobs, used valid selection devices? Did their selection procedures have any noticeable effects on the quality of their employees (yourself excluded, of course!)?

2. Looking ahead to jobs you may apply for in the future, what selection procedures do you hope will be used? Are there particular devices you consider particularly fair or unfair?

3. Some seasoned managers believe that their subjective judgments about people are a better guide to their personnel decisions than any formal system of testing or quantitative scoring. Do you think this view has any merit? Is it always important to develop systematic and "valid" selection devices? Why or why not?

Exercise 10

Job Evaluation

PAY AND THE PUBLIC SECTOR

How much should a librarian be paid? Should a social worker earn more than a police officer? Is the job of custodian worth more or less than the job of file clerk?

If you find these questions perplexing, do not despair. Determining wage and salary levels is a complex and often controversial process, one that engages profound philosophical issues. Some would argue, for instance, that large differentials in salary cannot be justified in a democratic society or that at the very least our current predisposition to value intellectual work much more highly than manual labor is inequitable. Others would maintain that work has no value in itself; only market forces can accurately and fairly determine the worth of various jobs.

A lack of social consensus over these kinds of issues is reflected in the field of public administration. Traditionally, wage and salary levels in the public sector have been set more or less in accordance with the principle of comparability. That is to say, most governmental jurisdictions have sought to pay accountants salaries roughly equivalent to those earned by accountants in the private sector. But this statement has to be qualified by the phrase "more or less" for at least two reasons. First, many jobs (librarian, police officer, firefighter, and so on) have no true private sector equivalents; hence alternative methods have to be found to set compensation levels for these types of jobs. Second, most public jurisdictions, including the federal government, have shown a marked reluctance to apply the comparability principle to all levels of jobs, particularly at upper managerial levels. It is not unusual—indeed, it is the norm—for a top public administra-

tor with responsibility for a large organization, hundreds of employees, and a huge budget to be paid at a level associated with a mid-level private sector manager. The reason for this is primarily political: The legislators who must ultimately approve pay packages fear that their constituents will not tolerate high salaries for bureaucrats, especially if it means increased taxes.

WHAT IS JOB EVALUATION?

Job evaluation is the process of assessing the value of various jobs to an organization through a systematic comparison of job demands, responsibilities, and working conditions. Job evaluations are intended to deal specifically with the "apples and oranges" problem: All jobs in an organization, regardless of their titles, are assumed to be comprised of certain general dimensions. The dimensions of each job can be measured, weighed, and compared to the dimensions of every other job in the organization, with salary differentials based on the observed differences in job dimensions.

HOW ARE JOB EVALUATIONS DONE?

There are many different techniques of job evaluation. Most of them, however, can be placed in one of four categories: the ranking method, the classification method, the factor comparison method, and the point method.

The *ranking method* is the simplest. With this method, a team of evaluators reads a set of job descriptions and ranks each relative to the others, from highest to lowest, in terms of the job's worth to the organization. If ten jobs are being evaluated, the result will be a list ranked from 1 to 10. When evaluators disagree about the rankings—and they often do—results can be averaged, much as with a national poll of coaches to determine college football rankings.

The *classification method,* used widely in government, is similar to the ranking method in that evaluators typically assess the worth of the job as a whole when they make comparisons (which is why they are often called *whole-job* methods of job evaluation). The difference here is that there is a preestablished system of job grades into which each job is placed. For instance, a jurisdiction might decide that all civil service jobs will be classified in 12 separate levels. Each grade is defined by a certain level of responsibility or skill (necessarily stated in very general terms) to which evaluators refer when deciding how to classify a position. Although the classification method can be made more sophisticated by having evaluators look more at separate job dimensions than at the job as a whole, most jurisdictions seem to prefer the simplicity of whole-job classification. The problem with this approach, as with the ranking method, is that there is considerable leeway for subjectivity in the evaluation process.

The *factor comparison method,* though relatively complex, reduces bias and subjectivity. First, evaluators identify certain key jobs, which are assumed to be compensated at appropriate levels. Next, they assess how much of the salary for each of the key jobs is attributable to each of several predetermined factors, such as responsibility and skill. Third, all other jobs in the organization are compared, factor by factor, to the key jobs, producing a set of rankings that orders each of the jobs on each of the factors. Because each factor in the key job has a dollar amount attached to it (from step 2), evaluators can assign dollar values to the factors of the other jobs in accordance with their places in the rankings. The final step is to add the dollars attached to each factor for each job to arrive at an overall wage or salary figure.

The fourth type of job evaluation technique, the *point method,* is similar to the factor comparison method in its focus on specific job dimensions. Job evaluators first draw up a list of factors or criteria that may be used to assess all jobs in a jurisdiction. One popular scheme, for instance, identifies four key factors: know-how, problem solving, accountability, and working conditions. The federal government uses nine separate factors, including knowledge required by the job, physical demands of the job, and supervision exercised and received. Although the specific factors vary from jurisdiction to jurisdiction, the underlying idea is always the same: Generate a list of job dimensions that can be used to measure many different jobs.

The second step in the point system is to assign numerical weights to the factors. This is usually done using a base of 100 points, although one could just as well use a base of any other number. To use a simple example, let us say that a jurisdiction has decided to use four factors for its job evaluation system: knowledge required, autonomy, significance of tasks, and working conditions. Job evaluators might decide to assign 25 points to each of these factors (for a total of 100 possible points). Alternatively, they might decide to weight the first factor, knowledge required, more heavily and assign it 40 points, allocating 20 points to each of the remaining factors (still for a total of 100 points). There is no one best way to allocate points among factors. How it is done depends entirely on the professional judgment of the individuals conducting the job evaluation. The only rule is that the weights should be a reasonable reflection of the importance of the factors. For example, it wouldn't make much sense to allocate 97 points to autonomy and only 1 point each to knowledge required, significance of tasks, and working conditions. But beyond such extreme cases, there are few guidelines. To help control for subjectivity, the weighting process is sometimes guided by collective bargaining agreements, task forces, or representative committees balanced to include men, women, minorities, managers, employees, and others.

As the third step in the point system of job evaluation, each factor is broken into degree or quality levels, with some proportion of the factor's points allocated to each degree. We might, for instance, decide to break our "knowledge required" factor into three degree levels: (1) high degree of professional training and experience, (2) some technical skill, and (3) unskilled. Had we allocated 40 points, to this factor, we might assign 40 points to the first degree, 20 to the second, and zero to the third. As in assigning total points to factors, there is no hard and fast rule for how many points each degree should receive, other than that the top degree level should be assigned a number of points equal to the total for that factor; judgment must be exercised in assigning points to subordinate degrees.

Once degrees have been established for each factor, with points allocated to each degree, the point system itself is complete. The job evaluator then looks at each job in the organization and decides how to rate it. If he or she determines that the job of budget analyst requires a "high degree of professional training and experience" in terms of knowledge required, 40 points are assigned to the job. After similar judgments are made about the job for each of the other factors, it will have a point total that reflects its overall worth, at least in terms of the established point system. When every job has been rated on every factor, there will be a hierarchical ordering of jobs, ranging in this case from zero to 100, although ties in ranking are certainly possible. If the point system was sound, the final ranking should appear sensible, with high-skill, high-responsibility jobs at the top and low-skill, low-responsibility jobs at the bottom. It all depends, of course, on how the factors and degrees were weighted in the first place. If the evaluator had chosen to assign a great deal of weight to working conditions and very little weight to knowledge and responsibility, it would be possible to wind up with custodial employees ranked far above agency managers. Although this could conceivably be an appropriate outcome, a wise job evaluator would probably go back and revise factor weights.

The final step in the point method of job evaluation is to attach dollar figures (actually pay ranges) to each job. This is done first by determining the market value of certain benchmark jobs. The evaluator would conduct a salary survey to find out how much accountants, for instance, are paid in the region. Once this is done for several jobs, all other jobs can be assigned pay levels commensurate with their relative point totals. Say that we conducted salary surveys for three benchmark jobs: accountants, custodians, and computer programmers.[1] We find that depending on years of experience, accoun-

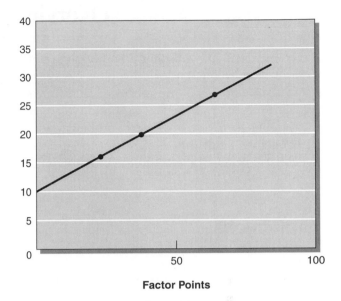

Figure 10.1
Extrapolation of Pay Ranges

tants are paid on average $25,000 to $28,000 a year, custodians $16,000 to $18,000, and computer programmers $19,000 to $21,000. Let's also say that the application of our point system indicated that the job of accountant was worth 64 points, the job of custodian was worth 21 points, and the job of computer programmer was worth 37 points. We could then produce something like the graph in Figure 10.1. By finding where the point total for each remaining job (using the horizontal axis) intersects the diagonal line, we can read across to see what the approximate pay range should be (on the vertical line).

Note that the job evaluation process is used to determine *pay ranges* rather than specific salary figures. The reason is simply that an employee's compensation is usually intended to reflect some degree of individual effort and experience. By setting a range, job evaluators leave room for merit increases, productivity bonuses, and seniority increments.

FURTHER READING

As was the case for job analysis and position classification, the single most useful reference work for job evaluation and compensation problems is Harold D. Suskin, ed., *Job Evaluation and Pay Administration in the Public Sector* (Washington, D.C.: International Personnel Management Association, 1977).

---

[1] If the job evaluation process is being used to address sex-biased pay equity questions, it is obviously important to select benchmark jobs that do not smuggle sex bias into the calculations. We would have to be careful, therefore, about using female-dominated professions (like secretaries) for this purpose.

Overview of Exercise

In this exercise, you will devise and apply a point system of job evaluation for a hypothetical organization that includes all the jobs analyzed by your class in Exercise 7. After choosing and weighing a set of job factors, you will determine degree levels for each job factor and make appropriate point assignments. You will then read the job descriptions carefully, rate each job, and produce a ranked list.

INSTRUCTIONS

Step One

Decide on a list of job factors. You may use some of the factors discussed in the text (responsibility, knowledge, autonomy, etc.) or devise your own categories. Make sure your final set of factors is *inclusive* (i.e., it includes factors that tap all relevant job dimensions) and does not overlap (i.e., you don't have two or three factors that measure the same thing); this is important because any overlap of factors produces an overweighting of a job dimension. Write the names of your factors in the spaces available on Forms 48a–f.

Step Two

Using a base of 100 points, weight each of your job factors. Write the number of points you have assigned each factor in the spaces on Forms 48a–f. Remember, the total for all factors should equal 100.

Step Three

Identify degree or quality levels for each factor, and assign the number of points you think appropriate to each, writing the information in the spaces on Forms 48a–f. Try to identify at least three or four quality levels for each factor. Remember that the highest level should be assigned the full point value for that factor; for lower levels, use your best judgment.

Step Four

Read the description of each of the jobs your class has analyzed; your instructor will make copies available to you. Rate each job according to the point system you have developed, using Form 49 to record your ratings.

Step Five

Answer the questions on Form 50.

Factors and Degrees for Job Evaluation

Factor 1 _____   Weight _____

Degrees   Point Value

a. _____   _____

_____

_____

b. _____   _____

_____

_____

c. _____   _____

_____

_____   _____

d. _____   _____

_____

_____

Factors and Degrees for Job Evaluation

Factor 2 _____   Weight _____

	Degrees	*Point Value*
a.	_____	_____
	_____	
	_____	
b.	_____	_____
	_____	
	_____	
c.	_____	_____
	_____	
	_____	_____
d.	_____	_____
	_____	
	_____	

Factors and Degrees for Job Evaluation

Factor 3 _____   Weight _____

Degrees   Point Value

a. _____   _____
   _____
   _____

b. _____   _____
   _____
   _____

c. _____   _____
   _____
   _____   _____

d. _____   _____
   _____
   _____

Factors and Degrees for Job Evaluation

Factor 4 _____   Weight _____

	Degrees	*Point Value*
a.	_____	_____
	_____	
	_____	
b.	_____	_____
	_____	
	_____	
c.	_____	_____
	_____	
	_____	_____
d.	_____	_____
	_____	
	_____	

Factors and Degrees for Job Evaluation

Factor 5 _____   Weight _____

	Degrees	*Point Value*

a. _____   _____

_____

_____

b. _____   _____

_____

_____

c. _____   _____

_____

_____   _____

d. _____   _____

_____

_____

Factors and Degrees for Job Evaluation

Factor 6 _____   Weight _____

Degrees   Point Value

a. _____   _____
_____
_____

b. _____   _____
_____
_____

c. _____   _____
_____
_____   _____

d. _____   _____
_____
_____

Job Rating Worksheet

Degree Points*

Job Title	F1	F2	F3	F4	F5	F6	Total Points

*F = Factor.

Questions

1. Do the point totals you produced on Form 49 seem reasonable? That is, do higher-rated jobs seem, in commonsense terms, worth more than lower-ranked jobs?

2. How easy do you think it would be to reweight factors to produce a different ordering of jobs? Would any reweighting be fair? Are factor weights entirely subjective and arbitrary, or do they have some objective basis?

3. Discuss the wages and salaries actually earned by the people who hold these jobs. To what extent are wage and salary differentials reflected in the ranking you produced? If actual wages and salaries do not follow the pattern of your ranking, how would you account for it? In your opinion, how are these variations influenced, if at all, by the fact that the jobs are not really in the same organization? Should this make a difference?

4. To what extent do you think job evaluation provides a useful and equitable means of determining levels of compensation? What are its strengths and weaknesses? Would you prefer to work in an organization that used some form of job evaluation to set compensation levels or one that used an alternative method, such as collective bargaining?

Exercise 11

Collective Bargaining

BILATERALISM AND PUBLIC MANAGEMENT

Students who have completed the preceding four exercises may have come away with the impression that public personnel administration is an activity dominated by white-collar managers in business suits who, after careful and dispassionate analysis, issue edicts that determine the shape and structure of an organization's personnel system. Although there is perhaps some truth to this picture, there is considerably less now than there was 20 or 25 years ago. Public personnel management is no longer unilateral management. That is, no longer (or at least less often) can personnel managers simply write rules and regulations, set compensation levels, or make other significant decisions that affect public employees without considerable consultation with those employees. The extent of such consultation varies widely from jurisdiction to jurisdiction, to be sure. But as a general rule, public workers across the nation have become well organized and have forced public employers to recognize their rights and interests as employees.

This is not, by any means, to suggest that the tools and techniques of public personnel administration discussed earlier, such as job analysis, performance evaluation, and job evaluation, have been rendered outdated or unnecessary by the advent of public employee unionization and collective bargaining. Rather, it is to say that the manner in which these tools and techniques are used in particular situations may be subject to collective negotiations with employees. Some jurisdictions, for instance, allow employees to bargain over the process of position classification; others permit bargaining about the system of performance evaluation to be used. Most jurisdictions, of course, allow employees to bargain over wages, salaries, and fringe benefits (the federal government is a significant exception). Other items that often fall within the scope of bargaining agreements are work schedules, disciplinary procedures, grievance processes, training and promotion opportunities, and union security provisions (dues checkoff, exclusive representation rights, use of public facilities for union activities, etc.). Thus, personnel administrators and other public managers increasingly need to recognize that they work in a complex environment of bilateral authority. The tools and techniques of personnel administration must be adapted to this environment.

THE RISE OF PUBLIC EMPLOYEE UNIONS

Although public employee unions have been in existence in the United States for well over 100 years, they did not begin to have a serious and continuing impact on public personnel administration until the middle of the twentieth century. One reason was that state and federal governments either ignored public employee unions or placed heavy restrictions on their activities. It was not until 1959, for example, that Wisconsin became the first state to pass a law requiring its municipalities to bargain with their public employees. And despite a series of executive orders dating to 1962 that conferred limited bargaining rights on federal workers, the federal government did not enact a statute protecting the bargaining rights of its employees until 1978.

These obstacles notwithstanding, public employee unionization has grown at a rapid pace in recent years. All but a few states have now passed laws authorizing some sort of collective bargaining with public employees. In fact, the great majority of municipal employees today are covered by union contracts, as are most state and federal workers. This trend is especially remarkable because it has occurred amid a precipitous decline in union membership in the private sector. Indeed, despite the late start for public sector unions, a far higher percentage of public than private sector workers are now organized.

THE BARGAINING PROCESS

It is difficult to make generalizations about the process of public sector collective bargaining in the United States because each state (and the federal government) has its own peculiar set of laws and administrative regulations governing labor relations. A practice permitted in one state may be explicitly prohibited in another; the range of bargainable items, the kind of recognition granted to unions, and the rights of employees to engage in strikes or other job actions are examples of the types of provisions that vary widely from jurisdiction to jurisdiction.

Recognizing that there will be exceptions, however, we can make a few general observations about how collective bargaining proceeds in the public sector. To begin with, public sector bargaining, like private sector collective bargaining, is intendedly *bilateral*. This means that there are two distinct parties, employers and employees, involved in the bargaining, each of which has a separate and opposing set of interests. Hard, good-faith bargaining between the two sides should produce an agreement, or a contract, at the point of equilibrium of their interests. Note, however, the use of the term *intendedly* as a modifier of *bilateral*. This is to underscore the fact that public sector managers, especially elected officials and their appointees, may not always view union members as adversaries. After all, union members vote; this creates a complication that doesn't arise in the private sector. Although some jurisdictions try to inject a "multilateral" element into bargaining by making provisions for citizen participation, the bilateral model is the norm.

The first step in the bargaining process involves identifying the parties. In effect, it is necessary to answer the question "Who's going to be doing the bargaining for whom?" This is done by defining the *bargaining unit*. In some cases, all employees in an agency are lumped together in a single bargaining unit; in other cases, employees are grouped by occupation or position (clerical workers, technicians, etc.). Once bargaining units are defined, employees are allowed to vote on whether they want to be represented by a union and if so, which one. Called a *certification election,* this process is usually overseen by a special state or federal agency charged with ensuring fair labor practices. Once a union is certified as the bargaining agent for the employees in a unit, it may, again depending on the laws of the jurisdiction, be allowed to collect dues or a "fair share" of representation costs from all employees in the unit.

Following certification, *contract negotiations* can begin. Typically, the union will assemble a negotiating team, drawn from specially elected (or selected) rank-and-file union members, union officers, and occasionally professional negotiators from the state or national union of which the local union is an affiliate. The union team will put together a list of contract proposals or demands and will meet with a corresponding team from management, which will have its own set of proposals. The management team may consist of top agency officials, labor relations administrators from specialized agencies, or combinations thereof. Through a series of face-to-face bargaining sessions, interspersed with private discussions within each team, the two parties seek to reach accord and to agree on the language of a contract. Once the parties have produced a tentative contract, each side must seek the formal approval of its constituency—the full union membership or a legislative body.

IMPASSE RESOLUTION PROCEDURES

Bargaining does not always produce contracts, of course, at least not in such a straightforward manner. Occasionally, the two parties are simply unable to come to terms. Such a stalemate is called an *impasse.* When an impasse is reached, several things can happen. First, employees may decide to strike or to take some other job action (work slowdowns, "sick-outs," "working to rule," etc.). Although strikes by public employees are illegal in most jurisdictions, they are hardly uncommon.

More often, attempts are made to resolve the impasse through *third-party intervention*. This refers to the intercession of a neutral and independent person into the stalemated bilateral negotiations. There are three main types of third-party intervention. The first and least intrusive of the three is *mediation*. The job of a mediator is to try to convince both parties to be more flexible and to return to serious bargaining. Lacking the formal power to impose a settlement, a mediator must rely solely on persuasion and his or her reputation as a fair and unbiased individual. Often a mediator will arrange to sit in on renewed talks in an effort to bring the two sides together.

The second type of third-party intervention, sometimes used when mediation fails, is called *fact-finding*. Like a mediator, a fact-finder is a neutral, disinterested person called in to help resolve an impasse. A fact-finder takes a more active and assertive role than a mediator, however. Usually, a fact-finder holds a formal hearing and otherwise gathers information pertinent to the questions in the negotiation. He or she then issues a public report containing a recommended settlement of the disputed provisions in the contract. Although this report is not binding on either party, it often serves to pressure the two sides to accept compromises and thus resolve the impasse.

The third type of third-party intervention is *arbitration*. Arbitration differs significantly from both mediation and fact-finding in that an arbitrator has legal authority to break an impasse and *impose* a settlement. Actually, there are several varieties of arbitration. The first, often termed *general binding arbitration,* permits an arbitrator to review the proposals of both sides and then pick and choose among the positions of labor and management to create a contract the arbitrator considers fair. The arbitrator may, if he or she deems it necessary, write new provisions or even draft a new contract.

The second type of arbitration, *final offer arbitration (item selection),* limits the power of the arbitrator in an important way: Though he or she can still impose a settlement, the contract must be constructed from provisions actually proposed by one side or the other; the arbitrator may not exercise creativity and draft wholly new or compromised provisions. Many people believe that this limitation on the power of the arbitrator encourages labor and management to submit more reasonable and tem-

perate proposals, for they will fear that anything less than reasonable and temperate will drive the arbitrator to the position of the other side.

The third type of arbitration is a variation on the second. Its name—*final offer arbitration (package selection)*—effectively summarizes the difference. In this type of arbitration, the arbitrator must choose, without modification, either the entire package submitted as a last, best offer by management or the entire package submitted as a last, best offer by labor. This type of arbitration creates a high-stakes game for the original parties. Even more than with the item selection variety, each side knows that it must submit a moderate and reasonable last, best offer to the arbitrator. Anything less than that is likely to produce an unalloyed victory for the other side.

Sentiment is strong among labor relations specialists in favor of bilateral negotiations. Third-party intervention is viewed as a last resort, something to be used only when labor and management are truly stalemated. Similarly, once it is determined that a third party must be called in to break an impasse, there is a bias in favor of the least intrusive intervention. One major reason is that labor and management, whatever their fundamental differences, share a long-term interest in coexistence. It is better for them to work things out for themselves than to rely on an outside referee; after all, there won't be a referee around on a day-to-day basis as the work of the organization proceeds through the year. And it is certainly better for labor and management to bargain their way to a contract, even if they have to use a mediator or a fact-finder, than it is to have one imposed by an arbitrator. Most people involved in labor relations believe that arbitration is useful only for preventing strikes. And even then, some would argue that strikes are to be preferred.

FURTHER READING

The literature on public sector labor relations is vast and varied. A good place to begin is Richard C. Kearney's *Labor Relations in the Public Sector,* 2d ed. (New York: Dekker, 1992), which provides a textbook overview of the major issues in the field. Also good as an introduction is Charles J. Coleman, *Managing Labor Relations in the Public Sector* (San Francisco: Jossey-Bass, 1990).

Four excellent edited volumes that treat the full range of public sector labor relations concerns are David Lewin et al., eds, *Public Sector Labor Relations: Analysis and Readings* (Lexington, Mass.: Lexington Books, 1988); Benjamin Aaron et al., eds., *Public Sector Bargaining,* 2d ed. (Washington, D.C.: Bureau of National Affairs, 1988); Richard Freeman and Casey Ichniowski, eds., *When Public Sector Workers Unionize* (Chicago: University of Chicago Press, 1988); and Jack Rabin, ed., *Handbook of Public Sector Labor Relations* (New York: Marcel Dekker, 1994).

For a detailed look at municipal labor relations, with an emphasis on very practical questions of determining bargaining units, selecting representatives, assessing unfair labor practices, and so forth, see Joan E. Pynes and Joan M. Lafferty, *Local Government Labor Relations: A Guide for Public Administrators* (Westport, Conn.: Quorum Books, 1993).

Federal labor relations are the focus of a 1993 special issue (volume 16, number 6) of the *International Journal of Public Administration,* edited by Richard Kearney.

Overview of Exercise

This exercise simulates a round of collective bargaining between the City of Barnswallow and the Barnswallow chapter of the International Federation of Firefighters (IFF). Playing the role of a member of the city's bargaining team, the union's bargaining team, or a neutral third-party mediator or arbitrator, you use the current contract between the city and the union as a baseline and attempt to negotiate a new agreement.

INSTRUCTIONS

Step One
Your instructor will assign to you one of the following roles in this exercise:

H. Rodriguez, Mayor of Barnswallow

J. Symes, City Personnel Director

N. Rich, City Budget Director

D. Raucher, Fire Commissioner

T. Sweeney, IFF Local 492 President

P. Jeffries, Union Bargaining Team Member

G. Rank, Union Bargaining Team Member

F. Martin, IFF Representative

I. M. Fair, Mediator

B. Just, Arbitrator

Classes larger than ten students will subdivide into two or more sets of bargaining teams. Read the information about your role provided on Forms

51a–j. Use the information provided as a general guide to behavior throughout the exercise. Feel free, however, to embellish your role as you see fit. Use your imagination!

Step Two
Read through the provisions of the current contract (Form 52) and familiarize yourself with the characteristics of the City of Barnswallow, IFF Local 492, and the other background information provided on Form 53.

Step Three
Meet with the other members of your bargaining team and establish an initial bargaining position. Decide which provisions of the current contract should remain intact, which should be altered, and which should be thrown out. You may, if you like, propose entirely new provisions or even draft a wholly different contract. Each member of the bargaining team will probably have slightly different perspectives on what items to stress, what positions to take, and what overall strategy to adopt in dealing with the opposing bargaining team. Try to work out reasonable compromises. Students playing the role of mediator or arbitrator should await further directions from the course instructor.

Step Four
Arrange a face-to-face bargaining session with the opposing bargaining team. Each side should present its demands and receive reactions from the other side.

Step Five

Review the proposals submitted by the opposing team in a private session with your bargaining team. Reformulate your positions as you deem appropriate.

Step Six

Arrange further bargaining sessions and conduct private meetings with your team as needed. Work to produce a new contract satisfactory to your team.

Step Seven

Once agreement between the two sides has been reached on all provisions of a new contract, each side should complete Form 54, "Outline of the Contract Between the City of Barnswallow and the International Federation of Firefighters, Barnswallow Chapter." Obtain appropriate signatures on Form 54 and present it to the instructor.

Step Eight

In the event that agreement between the two sides on all provisions of a new contract cannot be reached by the time specified by your instructor, an impasse will be declared. At this time, the two parties to your negotiation will be subject to one of several impasse resolution procedures (mediation, general binding arbitration, final offer arbitration with package selection, or final offer arbitration with item selection)—your instructor will inform you at the outset of the exercise which impasse resolution procedure governs your negotiations. Parties governed by mediation will return to bargaining with the intervention and assistance of a neutral mediator; bargaining will continue until a contract has been negotiated or time ends, whichever comes first. If a contract is successfully negotiated, complete Form 54, obtaining the required signatures. Parties governed by arbitration should read and follow Steps Nine and Ten.

Step Nine

If an impasse has been declared and your parties are governed by any form of arbitration, each bargaining team is to complete Form 54 independently. This form now represents the final, best offer your team is willing to make with respect to each of the provisions under negotiation. Be sure to complete this form fully and carefully, especially the final section that allows you to add provisions or provide the full text of any altered provisions; you need not obtain signatures from the opposing team for this step. Upon completing the form, submit it to the arbitrator designated by your instructor.

Step Ten

After reviewing the submissions from both parties, the arbitrator will hold a hearing at a time designated by the instructor. At this hearing, the arbitrator will take testimony from both parties regarding their submissions. The arbitrator may raise any questions he or she likes about the submissions. Following the hearing, the arbitrator will review all materials, complete and sign a clean copy of Form 54 summarizing his or her judgment, and at a time set by the instructor, announce this judgment. Representatives of both parties will then sign the arbitrated version of Form 54.

Step Eleven

Answer the questions on Form 55.

ROLE:
Mayor H. Rodriguez

Mayor Rodriguez believes that continued economic prosperity in Barnswallow depends on creating a hospitable tax environment for businesses and citizens. To that end, the mayor has instructed city administrative officers to pare spending wherever possible. While recognizing the importance of first-rate fire protection, Rodriguez believes that the current fire department is too large and that Barnswallow firefighters already receive more than generous compensation. The mayor's major goal in the present round of negotiations is to see at least a modest decrease in the fire department's operating budget. Although Rodriguez does not participate in direct, face-to-face negotiations with union representatives, the mayor's approval is required before any contract proposals can be formally offered to the other side.

ROLE:
J. Symes, City Personnel Director

J. Symes has worked for the City of Barnswallow for almost 30 years and has spent the last 15 years as city personnel director. Symes grew up with a personnel system that was heavily management-oriented and has never completely adjusted to the complexities of collective bargaining. Consequently, Symes is very sensitive to the management rights and prerogatives covered by the contract and believes that the city has given up too much of its authority to set policy without union "interference." Symes is especially interested in revising the grievance procedure to make it more difficult for firefighters to challenge departmental decisions. Symes would also like to see a two- or three-year contract negotiated, rather than another one-year contract, and is in favor of abolishing across-the-board salary increases in favor of a pure merit pay system.

ROLE:
N. Rich, City Budget Director

N. Rich, like J. Symes, is a professional public administrator, although Rich is considerably younger and does not share Symes's thinly veiled hostility toward the city's unions. Rich is interested only in the "bottom line." The budget director's goal, like the mayor's, is to hold down costs. With an eye toward the city's long-term financial health, Rich is especially interested in excising "time bombs"—items that aren't expensive now but whose costs will explode later on—from Barnswallow's labor contracts. Hence the budget director worries about total staffing levels and pension rights, as well as short-term wage and benefit expenses. Rich would like to cut at least 25 positions from the department. Like Symes, Rich is in favor of longer-term contracts; the budget director believes that the longer the contract, the greater the savings for the city.

ROLE:
D. Raucher, Fire Commissioner

D. Raucher has been commissioner of the Barnswallow Fire Department for four years. Most of his/her career was spent as a firefighter and officer in a large city in a nearby state. Although Raucher feels considerable empathy for the men and women of the department and indeed was once active in another IFF local, he/she recognizes the commissioner's role as a member of the city's management team. As top administrative officer of the department, Raucher's main goal is to increase managerial autonomy and especially to enhance the authority of departmental officers to establish work rotations and effect transfers as they deem necessary. Moreover, Raucher has been promised by the mayor, off the record, that any savings in the department's operating budget will be rewarded by support for new capital expenditures in new firefighting equipment, including new pumper and ladder trucks. Raucher thus has considerable interest in holding down contract costs as well.

ROLE:
T. Sweeney, IFF Local 492 President

T. Sweeney is serving a third two-year term as president of the Barnswallow chapter (Local 492) of the IFF. Although he/she is interested in running for a fourth term, Sweeney is being pressured by a group of younger, more militant firefighters (Sweeney is 57) to step aside at the end of the current negotiations. Sweeney's major goal is to shore up support among union members by negotiating a contract with substantial wage and benefit increases.

ROLE
P. Jeffries, Union Bargaining Team Member

P. Jeffries is a 58-year-old engineer who entered the department the same year as T. Sweeney and who has remained a close friend and supporter of Sweeney. Jeffries was very active in the old Barnswallow Firefighters Association (the predecessor of the union) but has not taken a leading role in the activities of the local since the advent of collective bargaining. Jeffries has publicly bemoaned the "lack of cooperation" between the city and the IFF in various union meetings, although a recent dispute over sick pay with an assistant chief, which led to Jeffries's filing a grievance, has softened his/her attitude toward the union and its role. Jeffries agreed to run for a seat on the bargaining team at Sweeney's request. Jeffries's main goal is to improve the provision of the contract dealing with pensions and press for improved insurance coverage for retired employees. Jeffries is also sensitive to problems in the grievance procedure and is supportive of higher pay.

ROLE:
G. Rank, Union Bargaining Team Member

G. Rank is a 27-year-old firefighter who has worked for the Barnswallow Fire Department for five years. Rank is one of the leading "young turks" who has been pressuring President Sweeney to step down. Rank has been mentioned prominently as a candidate for the job of union president in the next election. Rank's major goal in the negotiations is to press for increased fringe benefits, especially in the area of job training and education. Rank also supports a substantial increase in wages and salaries and is sympathetic to the demands of F. Martin, the IFF representative. Rank is opposed to any contract that runs more than one year unless specific cost-of-living adjustment (COLA) provisions are negotiated.

ROLE:
F. Martin, IFF Representative

F. Martin is a professional union negotiator employed by the national office of the IFF. Martin's job is to assist local chapters, such as Barnswallow's, in contract negotiations and other proceedings affecting IFF members. Martin has a reputation as a tough, no-nonsense negotiator and has been accused by municipal officials elsewhere of being an instigator of strikes and other illegal job actions. Martin's goal is to strengthen virtually all contract provisions, especially those dealing with union rights and grievance procedures. Martin would like to restrict management prerogatives to transfer workers from one fire station to another without their consent, replace discretionary merit raises with across-the-board increases, require strict adherence to seniority in promotion decisions, and mandate a four-platoon work rotation system (24 hours on, 72 hours off). Martin insists that the union refuse to accept a contract that runs for more than one year, arguing that any step-up of inflation would lock workers into low wage scales.

ROLE:
I.M. Fair, Mediator

Fair's job is to act as a neutral third party and try to persuade union and management to compromise and come to terms when an impasse has been reached. Fair has no authority to impose a settlement but must instead rely on his/her skills of persuasion. Once an impasse has been declared, Fair may be as active as he/she wishes; that is, Fair may propose contract provisions to each side that he/she feels will garner agreement or may simply act as a go-between in stalemated discussions.

ROLE:
B. Just, Arbitrator

Once an impasse has been declared, Just's job is to receive the final contract proposals from each side and to reach a fair and reasonable judgment regarding a new contract. Just's precise powers as arbitrator will be determined in advance by the instructor. Just may have virtually unlimited power to write a new contract (general binding arbitration) or may be limited to either accepting, as a whole, the set of proposals of one side or the other (final offer arbitration with package selection) or choosing among the various provisions proposed by each side (final offer arbitration with item selection). In any event, Just should use the arbitration hearings to gather as much information as possible to reach an equitable settlement.

Agreement Between the City of Barnswallow and the International Federation of Firefighters, Barnswallow Chapter

Effective January 1, 2000–December 31, 2000

ARTICLE I
AGREEMENT

This agreement is made and entered into this 22nd day of December, 1999, by and between the City of Barnswallow, hereinafter referred to as the "City," and the Barnswallow Chapter of the International Federation of Firefighters, hereinafter referred to as the "Union" or the "IFF."

ARTICLE II
RECOGNITION

The City recognizes the IFF (Barnswallow Chapter) as the sole and exclusive bargaining representative as certified by the State Department of Labor in respect to matters concerning wages, salaries, hours, vacations, sick leave, grievance procedures, and other terms and conditions of employment as specifically set forth in this Agreement, for all employees of the City in the collective bargaining unit designated by that certification dated April 23, 1971, as follows: All employees of the Barnswallow Fire Department in the job classes Firefighter, Hose Operator, Engineer, and Driver.

Excluded from the collective bargaining unit are all administrative and line officers of the Barnswallow Fire Department, including all Battalion Chiefs, Captains, and Lieutenants.

ARTICLE III
UNION DUES

During the term of this Agreement, the City agrees to deduct monthly membership dues, proportionately each pay period, from the wages and salaries due all members who individually and voluntarily give the City written authorization to do so. The City shall forward such dues for the previous month's salaries to the Treasurer of the Union on or before the tenth day of each month. The Union assumes full responsibility for the disposition of monies so deducted once they have been remitted to the Treasurer.

ARTICLE IV
MANAGEMENT RIGHTS

The Union recognizes that, except as hereinafter specifically provided, the operations and administration of the Barnswallow Fire Department, including, but not limited to, the right to make rules and regulations pertaining thereto, shall be fully vested in the Commissioner of the Barnswallow Fire Department and his/her designees, as the executive agent of the City of Barnswallow. Except as hereinafter specifically provided, nothing herein stated shall be construed as a delegation or waiver of any powers or duties vested in the Commissioner of the Barnswallow Fire Department, the Mayor of the City of Barnswallow, or any administrative official or their designees by virtue of any provision of the laws and ordinances of the State or the City of Barnswallow.

ARTICLE V
UNION REPRESENTATIVES AND PRIVILEGES

5.1 The Union, its officers and members, shall not engage in union activities, hold meetings on City property, or utilize City facilities in any way that interferes with or interrupts normal City operations or the obligations and duties of Union members as employees.

5.2 The Union shall have the right to make reasonable use of City space, facilities, and equipment for proper activities related to its position as the recognized representative of Department employees.

5.3 The Union shall have the right to post at appropriate locations in City fire stations bulletins and notices relevant to official Union business.

ARTICLE VI
GRIEVANCE PROCEDURE

6.1 A grievance is defined as any dispute or difference concerning the interpretation, application, or claimed violation of any provision of this Agreement.

6.2 Every attempt will be made to resolve any grievance speedily and informally by meetings between affected parties.

6.3 In the event that informal resolution procedures fail to satisfy the aggrieved party, the following formal procedure is to be followed:

Step 1.

An aggrieved member of the bargaining unit (hereafter called "the appellant") shall present an appeal in writing and signed by the appellant in the first instance to the Company Captain. The Captain shall discuss the grievance with the appellant. The Union will be notified by the Captain and may send representatives to all meetings where the grievance is discussed with the appellant. The Captain shall consider the appeal and reply in writing within seven (7) workdays after receipt of the appeal. For the purposes of this procedure, Saturdays and Sundays shall not be counted as workdays.

Step 2.

If the matter is not resolved, the appellant shall file a written appeal to the Battalion Chief within seven (7) workdays after receipt of the Step 1 decision, with copies to the Captain and the Union. The Battalion Chief shall discuss the appeal with the Captain and the appellant. The Union will be notified by the Battalion Chief and may send representatives to all meetings where the grievance is discussed with the appellant. The Battalion Chief shall consider the appeal and reply in writing within ten (10) workdays after receipt of the appeal.

Step 3.

If the matter is not resolved, the appellant may appeal in writing to the Commissioner of the Barnswallow Fire Department within fifteen (15) workdays after receipt of the Step 2 decision. The Commissioner of the Barnswallow Fire Department, sitting with a panel composed of one member from the City of Barnswallow Personnel Department and two members designated by the Union, shall conduct a hearing within fifteen (15) workdays after receipt of the appeal. Such hearing shall be conducted with concern for due process. The appellant shall have the right to testify, introduce documentary evidence, and present witnesses on his/her behalf. The Commissioner of the Barnswallow Fire Department shall render a decision on the appeal, in writing, within ten (10) workdays after the hearing, with copies to the appellant and Union. The other members of the hearing panel may state their views in separate opinions, which shall be appended to the decision of the Commissioner of the Barnswallow Fire Department. Said separate opinions are advisory only and are not to be construed as binding on the City of Barnswallow or the appellant.

Step 4.

If the matter is not resolved, the Union, acting on behalf of the appellant, may file a written appeal within seven (7) workdays to the American Arbitration Association (AAA) for binding arbitration under its rules. The arbitration shall be by a neutral arbitrator selected under AAA rules, and the decision of the arbitrator shall be final and binding. The costs of arbitration shall be borne equally by the parties.

ARTICLE VII
NO STRIKES OR LOCKOUTS

The Union and the City subscribe to the principle that any and all differences under this Agreement be resolved by peaceful and legal means without interruption of City services. The Union therefore agrees that neither it nor any of its officers, agents, employees, or members will instigate, engage in, support, or condone any strike, work stoppage, or other concerted refusal to perform work by any employees in the bargaining unit during the life of this Agreement. The City agrees that there shall be no lockout during the life of this Agreement.

ARTICLE VIII
WAGES AND BENEFITS

8.1 For the period January 1, 2000, through December 31, 2000, *salaries* of members of the bargaining unit shall be adjusted in the following manner:

a. Each member of the bargaining unit shall have his/her salary increased by an amount equal to 2% of his/her base salary for the period January 1, 1999, through December 31, 1999.

b. In addition, an amount equal to 1% of the base salaries for January 1, 1999, to December 31, 1999, of all employees in the bargaining unit shall be allocated to a special merit pool. This pool shall be used to provide additional salary increments to members of the bargaining unit. Decisions about allocation of merit money rest solely with the Commissioner of the Barnswallow Fire Department, who will seek the advice of his/her subordinate line officers.

8.2 Employees shall be required to work no more than four (4) of the following nine (9) holidays:

New Year's Day   Independence Day
Thanksgiving   Good Friday   Christmas
Easter   Labor Day   New Year's Eve
Memorial Day

Decisions as to which holidays an employee shall work are to be understood as a prerogative of management. When required to work on one of the holidays designated above, employees shall be compensated at one and one-half times their normal hourly rate.

8.3 Employees shall receive paid vacation according to the following schedule:

1st year through 5th year	2 weeks
6th year through 10th year	3 weeks
11th year through 15th year	4 weeks
16th and later years	5 weeks

8.4 Employees are responsible for purchasing and maintaining their own uniforms and personal equipment. The City shall, however, provide an annual *uniform allowance* of $400 to all uniformed personnel to defray purchase and maintenance costs.

8.5 Employees required to report for duty at times other than their regularly scheduled rotations shall receive *overtime pay* of one and one-half times their normal hourly rate.

8.6 The City agrees to pay one-half the *tuition and fee expenses,* up to a total of $1,000 per employee per year, of any employee enrolled in an approved course of study related to firefighting or fire safety. Approval of the course of study rests solely with the Commissioner of the Barnswallow Fire Department or his/her designees.

8.7 The City shall pay the entire cost of the employee's *Blue Cross Blue Shield Major Medical coverage.* Should the employee elect family coverage, the employee shall pay a monthly contribution of $200.

8.8 The City shall pay the entire cost of a group *disability insurance* policy for each employee. Said policy, to be selected by the City of Barnswallow, shall provide benefits of not less than $2,000 per month to any disabled employee.

8.9 The City shall provide *term life insurance* at no cost to the employee in the amount of two times the annual salary of the employee. Choice of a policy and insurance company rests solely with the City of Barnswallow.

8.10 *Paid sick leave* accrues to employees at the rate of five (5) days per year for the first year of employment and ten (10) days per year for each succeeding year. Sick leave may not be carried over from one year to the next.

ARTICLE IX
PENSION RIGHTS

The City shall contribute an amount equal to 5% of each employee's salary to the State Employees Pension Fund on behalf of the employee. Each employee shall contribute a minimum of 5% and a maximum of 10% to said Fund. Full pension rights are available at age 60 or following 30 years of employment, whichever comes first.

ARTICLE X
MAINTENANCE OF PRACTICES

The parties agree that there is a body of written policies and of practices and interpretations of those policies that govern administrative decisions concerning wages, salaries, hours, workload, sick leave, vacations, grievance procedures, transfers, suspension, and dismissal not explicitly covered in this Agreement. Such policies and practices shall be continued for the life of this Agreement. An administrative action not in accordance with the past application or interpretation of the above policies shall be grievable.

ARTICLE XI
NONDISCRIMINATION

The City and the Union, to the extent of their respective authority, agree not to discriminate against a Union member with respect to the application of the provisions of this Agreement because of race, creed, color, sex, religion, national origin, veteran or handicapped status, or membership or nonmembership in the Union.

ARTICLE XII
CONTRACT PERIOD AND FURTHER NEGOTIATIONS

This agreement shall be binding on both parties for the period January 1, 2000, through December 31, 2000. Both parties agree that negotiations to extend or modify this contract for any period beyond December 31, 2000, should commence no later than August 1, 2000.

Background Information

THE CITY

Barnswallow is a medium-size city (population 350,000) in a Middle Atlantic state. Although city finances are now fairly stable, like many older cities in the Northeast, Barnswallow experienced considerable economic distress from the mid-1960s through the late 1980s as large numbers of middle-class whites moved to the suburbs, causing a serious erosion of Barnswallow's tax base. Deteriorating neighborhoods, increases in the city's crime rate, including rates of arson, and rising joblessness, placed great strains on city services.

By the mid-1990s, things began to turn around for Barnswallow. An energetic young lawyer, H. Rodriguez, defeated the candidate of the city's political machine for mayor. Rodriguez assembled a small team of able, professional administrators and, often with intense opposition from the city council, began to reform Barnswallow's administrative apparatus: Budgeting procedures were rationalized, a thorough merit system was installed for city workers, and procurement practices were modernized. Through these reforms, and by discharging almost 200 city workers, Rodriguez managed to balance the city's budget and improve its bond rating. Barnswallow's fiscal health was also assisted considerably by a general increase in economic prosperity and by an influx of young, well-to-do professionals back into the city. In a recent interview with the *Barnswallow Evening Chronicle*, Rodriguez hinted that next year's city budget would include a significant reduction in the property tax rate. Knowledgeable observers are convinced that Rodriguez will announce a reelection bid shortly.

THE UNION

Local 492 is an affiliate of the International Federation of Firefighters (IFF), one of the largest unions of firefighters in America. Although Barnswallow's firefighters have been organized for nearly 50 years, collective negotiations with the city have taken place only since the early 1970s, following a change in state law authorizing bargaining with uniformed municipal employees. Prior to this time, the Barnswallow Firefighters Association, the predecessor of Local 492, acted largely as a social organization and as an informal lobby for fire safety and other firefighter concerns in the city. The union today represents 296 people at 18 fire stations. Support for the union among members is high, although there is a growing rift between older and younger firefighters: The younger members have been pressing the union leadership to take a hard line against the Rodriguez administration's budget policies and have advocated militant job actions, including strikes, in dealing with the city.

CITY-UNION RELATIONS

Relations between the city and the union were relatively harmonious during the first 25 years of collective bargaining. Support for Barnswallow's political machine by union members was rewarded with generous contracts. Agreements were negotiated promptly and smoothly, with no serious threats of disruptions in city services. With the advent of the Rodriguez administration, relations took a turn for the worse. Negotiations on the 1997–1999 (two-year) contract were marked by acrimony and distrust on both sides, with the union charging that the Rodriguez administration was trying to "balance the city budget on the backs of its employees." A strike (still illegal under state law) by firefighters was threatened in 1997 when the city refused to budge from its proposal to close three fire stations and eliminate 37 jobs. The 2000 contract (one-year) was finally settled when the State Public Employee Relations Board intervened and brought the case to an arbitrator.

BARNSWALLOW FIRE DEPARTMENT: ORGANIZATION AND STAFFING

The head of the Barnswallow Fire Department is the fire commissioner, an official appointed by the mayor and confirmed by the city council; the fire commissioner is responsible for planning and coordinating the work of the department. Directly below and responsible to the commissioner are a series of professional fire administrators who are in charge, respectively, of fire prevention, fire extinguishment, finance and budgeting, training, equipment, and personnel. The most important of these administrators is the chief fire marshall, the official responsible for the Division of Fire Extinguishment. The chief fire marshall is the principal "firefighter" of the department, in direct command of Barnswallow's firefighting and rescue operations. Reporting to the fire marshall are five battalion fire chiefs, who in turn supervise the city's 34 fire captains. Each captain commands a fire company; the city's 34 fire companies are deployed at 18 separate fire stations.

The 296 men and women represented by IFF Local 492 are organized into specialized companies (pumper, hose, ladder, rescue, etc.) attached to the fire stations. Depending on the size of the area it serves, each fire station has from one to four companies. Four job classes form the basis of Local 492: firefighter, engineer, hose operator, and driver. Table 11.1 provides a breakdown of the numbers of people filling each job class, together with their average annual salaries.

CURRENT CONTRACT COSTS

Basic salary costs of the Barnswallow Fire Department can be estimated from the data provided in Table 11.1. Additional information that may be used to gauge the cost of the 2000 contract as well as proposals under negotiation is as follows:

1. Under current department procedures, each fire company is organized into three platoons, designated A, B, and C. Each platoon works a 24-hour shift and is then off for 48 hours. Overtime rates apply whenever an employee is required to work more than 24 hours in any 72-hour period. Employees are typically required to work an average of 60 hours of overtime pay per year.

Table 11.1 Distribution and Salaries of Local 492 Members

Job Class	Number of Employees	Average Salary (1999)
Firefighter	127	$33,000
Engineer	40	35,500
Hose operator	74	34,000
Driver	55	36,000

2. An average of 42 employees per year have taken advantage of the contract provision providing tuition assistance. Of these, 34 receive the $1,000 maximum grant, as their costs equal or exceed the limit set by the contract. The eight remaining employees have been granted an average of $475 each.

3. Individual Blue Cross Blue Shield major medical coverage costs the city $4,000 per year per employee. Blue Cross Blue Shield family coverage costs $7,000 per year (see contract provision 8.7). Currently, 210 employees opt for family coverage.

4. The city's current disability policy costs $150 per year per employee. Each $100-per-month increase in benefits adds $15 to the cost of the yearly premium.

5. The city's term life insurance policy costs $100 per year per employee given the current benefit structure (see contract provision 8.9). There is a direct relationship between the annual premium per employee and the projected average benefit, such that an increase in benefits to three times annual salary would raise the premium to $150 per employee; an increase to four times salary would cost $200 per employee.

6. For the purposes of this exercise, the inflation rate and other aggregate indicators of national economic well-being are assumed to be the same as those actually prevailing at the time the exercise is conducted. Although this information has no direct bearing on the costs of the 2000 contract, it may influence the course of negotiations on a new agreement.

Outline of the Contract Between the City of Barnswallow
and
the International Federation of Firefighters, Barnswallow Chapter

Instructions: This form provides a skeletal outline of the current (2000) contract between the City of Barnswallow and IFF Local 492. Each number on this form corresponds to a provision in the current contract. In the space provided after each number, write "retain," "delete," or "alter," depending on how the new contract you have just negotiated (or are submitting for arbitration) differs from the 2000 contract. Wherever you write "alter" (that is, whenever a new provision differs from a previous provision), provide a brief summary of the changes. Enter the complete text of the altered provisions as well as any completely new provisions you may negotiate (or propose) at the end of this form. Obtain signatures as required.

I. AGREEMENT _____

_____

II. RECOGNITION _____

_____

III. UNION DUES _____

_____

IV. MANAGEMENT RIGHTS _____

_____

V. UNION REPRESENTATIVES AND PRIVILEGES _____

_____

VI. GRIEVANCE PROCEDURE _____

_____

VII. NO STRIKES OR LOCKOUTS _____

_____

VIII. WAGES AND BENEFITS _____

_____

_____

_____

IX. PENSION RIGHTS _____

_____

X. MAINTENANCE OF PRACTICES _____

_____

XI. NONDISCRIMINATION _____

_____

XII. CONTRACT PERIOD AND FURTHER NEGOTIATIONS _____

_____

ADDITIONAL PROVISIONS AND/OR TEXT OF ALTERED PROVISIONS

SIGNATURES

The undersigned are duly authorized representatives of the City of Barnswallow and the Barnswallow Chapter (Local 492) of the International Federation of Firefighters.
IN WITNESS WHEREOF THE PARTIES HERETO HAVE SET THEIR HANDS AND SEALS ON THIS ___ DAY OF _____, 20_____:

For the City   *For the Union*

_____   _____
J. Symes   T. Sweeney

_____   _____
N. Rich   P. Jeffries

_____   _____
D. Raucher   G. Rank

                                                               _____
                                                               F. Martin

---

For Cases That Go to Arbitration Only

The undersigned, being a duly authorized representative of the State Public Employee Relations Board and a certified arbitrator empowered by Section 317.6(a) of State Statutes to resolve impasses in labor disputes, does hereby warrant that the attached is a fair and legal contract binding the two parties for the period specified.

_____
B. Just

Questions

1. How effective was your bargaining team? Did you achieve any or all of your aims in the contract? To what do you attribute your success or failure?

2. Assuming that more than one set of bargaining teams was operating in your class, what were the major differences in the contracts that were negotiated? Did the method of impasse resolution used (if any) have any systematic effect on outcomes?

3. What types of third-party intervention, if any, do you think are most appropriate to resolve impasses? Would you support the use of any type of arbitration?

4. Do you think public employees should be allowed to strike? If you think strikes by public employees should be illegal, what would you do as a public administrator if your employees struck anyway?

PART THREE

Public Budgeting

WHAT IS A BUDGET?

A budget is a document that sets forth how money is to be spent. Although budgets come in a bewildering variety of shapes and sizes, all budgets—personal, corporate, and governmental—have one central and simple element in common: They tell us what we are buying and how much it costs.

Budgets are usually written for a fixed period of time called a *fiscal year*, which is any consecutive 12-month period that an organization uses to plan its expenditures. Of course, budget administrators are always interested in shorter and longer periods of time as well—Is there enough left in the budget to buy a new computer? What is the implication of this expenditure for the next five years?—but use the fiscal year as the basic unit of time for casting a budget. The fiscal year for the federal government is October 1 to September 30. Many states and localities operate on a July 1 to June 30 fiscal year.

WHY DO WE BUDGET?

If we had all the money we wanted, we probably wouldn't need to write budgets. Given a limitless checking account, for instance, you wouldn't have to worry about setting aside enough to pay the telephone bill at the end of the month. The fact is, however, that there is never enough money to do everything we want to do. Money is scarce. As a result, we must forgo some things we want in favor of other things we must have. Even national governments, with their access to printing presses, have to make choices about what to buy and what not to buy. This is where budgets come in. By listing clearly and systematically all the things we plan to

buy, we can make sure we make our purchases sensibly so that there is money left at the end of the month to pay that phone bill.

Guarding against financial imprudence is not the only reason to budget, however. A second reason governments budget is to ensure that money is spent only in accordance with specified public purposes. That is, budgets provide the means for citizens and public officials to control or account for the expenditure of public funds. Instead of just sending truckloads of cash from the Treasury to government offices at the beginning of each fiscal year and saying, "Go administer," we draw up a budget that specifies in detail what things should be purchased and how much should be spent on them. Then we say, "Go administer." But we add, "And we want to see the receipts!"

As several of the exercises in Part Three make clear, budgets are useful for a third reason as well: They help us make decisions. By classifying alternative expenditures in ways that allow systematic comparison, we can make informed choices about which investments of public funds promise the best return. It is possible to devise budget systems that help officials weigh the relative merits of two different job training schemes, for instance, or decide whether building a new state park is worth its cost.

HOW DO WE BUDGET?

There are as many different ways to construct budgets as there are organizations that seek to do so. Fortunately for the student of budgeting, however, the thousands of different specific approaches used by various units of government are really variations on a few simple themes. This set of exercises introduces the four fundamental approaches that constitute the building blocks of all budget systems. Once the logic of these systems is mastered, one can understand and reproduce virtually any budgetary system; it is necessary only to take an organizing pinch from one and add a conceptual dash or two from another. There are four basic budget systems:

Line-item budgeting

Performance budgeting

Program budgeting

Zero-base budgeting

The four represent a historical progression in ideas about budgeting, with line-item budgeting the earliest and zero-base budgeting the most recent. This is not to say that later ideas have displaced earlier ideas, at least not completely. Line-item budgeting is still an integral part of virtually all public budgeting systems, just as many of the concepts of performance and program budgeting are widely used today. The point is that new techniques or formats have been developed as demands on budget systems have changed. Generally speaking, the line of progression has been from less complex to more complex, as we have asked our budgeting systems to undertake more and more tasks.

FURTHER READING

A useful overview of public budgeting in the United States is Donald Axelrod, *Budgeting for Modern Government,* 2d ed. (New York: St. Martin's Press, 1995). Also good as introductions are Thomas Lynch, *Public Budgeting in America,* 4th ed. (Englewood Cliffs, N.J.: Prentice Hall, 1994); Robert Lee, Jr. and Ronald W. Johnson, *Public Budgeting Systems,* 6th ed. (Gaithersburg, MD: Aspen Publishers, 1998); and Irene S. Rubin, *The Politics of Public Budgeting* (Chatham, N.J.: Chatham House, 1997).

Exercise 12

Line-Item Budgeting

BUDGETING FOR CONTROL

Line-item budgeting is the oldest and most ubiquitous form of budgeting. So widely used is this technique, in fact, that to most people a budget *is* a line-item budget, even if they've never heard the term.

Table 12.1 is an example of a line-item budget. Note that it contains two basic elements: a *commodity to be purchased* (personal services, office supplies, telephone, etc.) and a *cost.* Although line-item budgets can be organized in many different ways, similar commodities are usually classified together. This makes it easier for the budget to be read and interpreted.

Some line-item budgets are more detailed and include more information than others. For instance, the "Office Supplies" category in this Department of Parks and Recreation budget might, in another organization's budget, be broken down into "pencils," "paper clips," "staples," and so forth. The amount of detail in a line-item budget is a function of the

Table 12.1 Budget Request Form: Department of Parks and Recreation

Item	FY 1999–2000	FY 2000–2001 (Request)
PERSONAL SERVICE		
Classified positions		
Administrative	$84,000	$92,000
Secretarial	32,000	34,000
Maintenance	53,000	56,500
Nonclassified positions		
Seasonal recreation	23,600	25,300
Seasonal maintenance	17,000	19,400
TOTAL PERSONAL SERVICE	209,600	227,200
OTHER OPERATING EXPENSES		
Telephone	3,600	4,000
Postage	1,750	2,200
Printing and advertising	12,300	14,000
Office supplies	2,600	3,250
Equipment maintenance	4,350	5,300
Grass seed, fertilizer	1,500	1,750
Contingencies	3,700	4,800
TOTAL OTHER OPERATING EXPENSES	29,800	35,300
TOTAL DEPARTMENTAL EXPENSES	$239,400	$262,500

amount of control that central budget administrators wish to extend over their operating units. The more autonomy and discretion granted, the less detailed the line-item budget. The idea of control is central to line-item budgeting. Line-item budgets were developed initially and have retained their popularity precisely because they provide such an effective means of controlling public expenditures. The information that a line-item budget offers can also be expanded by providing extra data on costs or expenditures. The budget in Table 12.1 shows actual expenditures for FY 1999–2000, as well as the FY 2000–2001 request. Some line-item budgets require the organization to show expenditures in earlier years (e.g., FY 1998–1999) or to provide a column of figures that show the percentage change from one year's expenditure to the next. Information of this kind is often used by public officials, especially legislators, to help them decide whether to grant a budget request.

FURTHER READING

Technical accounting treatises aside, the literature on line-item budgeting is relatively sparse. Allen Schick's *Budget Innovation in the States* (Washington, D.C.: Brookings Institution, 1971) contains some useful material. Two dated but still interesting accounts are William F. Willoughby, *The Movement for Budgetary Reform in the States* (New York: Appleton, 1918), and Frederick A. Cleveland and Arthur E. Buck, *The Budget and Responsible Government* (New York: Macmillan, 1920).

Especially enterprising students may wish to read through the report of the Taft Commission of 1912 and the Budget and Accounting Act of 1921. These two documents, which had formative effects on budgeting in the federal government, are presented in Albert C. Hyde and Jay M. Shafritz, eds., *Government Budgeting: Theory, Process, Politics* (Oak Park, Ill.: Moore, 1978).

Overview of Exercise

The Adams County Board of Supervisors has recently approved a plan to consolidate library services in the county. In an effort to cut costs and improve services next year, the public libraries from the county's six incorporated towns, four villages, and one city are to be merged and operated as one system. Complicated negotiations by county officials, municipal officials, and representatives of two public employee unions have produced an agreement for a single new organizational structure known as the Adams County Library.

As deputy county budget director, it is your responsibility to prepare an initial line-item budget for the new library system. Your task is complicated because there is no single budget base on which to build. Because the system is new, you basically have to start from scratch. You do have two sources of information to guide your efforts, however. The first is a memorandum from the budget director outlining her expectations and those of the supervisors with respect to the new library system. Second, you have the results of a budget survey you conducted that summarizes the operating expenses of the 11 units to be consolidated.

INSTRUCTIONS

Step One
Read the memo from the budget director (Form 56) and review your budget survey data (Forms 57a–k). You may fill in the date on her memo with the current year.

Step Two
Use Budget Request Form 58 to construct a line-item budget for the new Adams County Library. Although you may organize the budget in any way you see fit, make sure you take Budget Director Johnson's directives into account. Note that the designation "FY 1" is used on Form 58 rather than a specific year (or pair of years); this convention is used throughout these budget exercises to avoid assigning particular dates that may not correspond to the year you are actually completing them. To add a touch of realism, you may substitute the appropriate upcoming fiscal year (assume a July 1 to June 30 fiscal year) in place of FY 1.

IT Option
- Download the Excel file **LineItem** from www.awlonline.com/huddleston. This contains all of

the information found on Forms 57a–k and will allow you to manipulate the data in a spreadsheet.

- Create a consolidated spreadsheet—in effect an electronic template for the final budget you must present on Form 58. This will allow you to experiment with changing different numbers without having to worry about complicated calculations and recalculations.

Step Three

Answer the questions on Form 59.

14 October 20 __

TO: A. C. Andrews
Deputy Budget Director

FROM: Sarah T. Johnson
Budget Director

RE: Library Budget

As you know, the supervisors voted last night to approve the consolidation plan for the county library system. I'd like you to take charge of putting together a preliminary first-year budget for the board's review.

Your budget should take the following points into consideration:

1. All existing public libraries in the county, including the branches in the city of Waynesfield, are to remain open.
2. The county's cost-sharing agreement with the municipalities assumes that there will be an overall savings of three percent (3%) from the aggregate of the existing library budgets.
3. No cuts are to be made in any full-time library employees. Cuts may be proposed in other categories.
4. As per the county's agreement with the public employee unions, salary scales within job classifications are to be standardized at the highest levels currently paid by any of the newly consolidated units.
5. All township and village librarians previously designated "head librarians" (full- or part-time) are to be redesignated "branch librarians" and are to be compensated accordingly.
6. The position of head librarian for the city of Waynesfield is to be eliminated. A new position, director of county libraries, is to be created, budgeted at $45,000.

As the start-up date for the new system is July 1, we'll include this in our regular budget cycle. Please have all documentation completed by December 15.

Library Budget Survey

Municipality ___City of Waynesfield___

	Job Title	Salary	Number or Hours	Cost
PROFESSIONAL STAFF				
Full-time	Head librarian	$40,000	1	$ 40,000
	Branch librarian	34,000	6	204,000
	Reference librarian	32,000	5	160,000
	Assistant librarian	29,000	9	261,000
Part-time	Reference librarian	15,500	2	31,000
	Assistant librarian	13,375	3	40,125
OTHER STAFF				
Full-time	Administrative assistant	22,000	1	22,000
	Circulation clerk	20,000	8	160,000
	Secretary	19,500	2	39,000
	Maintenance worker	16,000	4	64,000
	Page	15,000	3	45,000
Part-time	Circulation clerk	$6.00/hr.	7,020 hrs.	42,120
	Maintenance worker	5.75/hr.	2,000 hrs.	11,500
	Page	5.00/hr.	13,260 hrs.	66,300

OTHER ANNUAL OPERATING EXPENSES

Acquisitions	$275,000
Supplies	110,000
Utilities	96,700
Maintenance	32,600
Other (please specify)	43,000*

*Includes $21,000 for bookmobile services, $11,000 for in-school programs, $6,500 for summer children's programs, and $4,500 for travel.

FORM 57b

Library Budget Survey

Municipality _____Village of Clear Creek_____

	Job Title	Salary	Number or Hours	Cost
PROFESSIONAL STAFF				
Full-time	Head librarian	$25,000	1	$25,000
Part-time				
OTHER STAFF				
Full-time				
Part-time	Maintenance worker	$5.45/hr.	780 hrs.	4,251

OTHER ANNUAL OPERATING EXPENSES

Acquisitions	$2,500
Supplies	750
Utilities	3,600
Maintenance	1,260
Other (please specify)	—

Library Budget Survey

Municipality ____Village of Woolford____

	Job Title	Salary	Number or Hours	Cost
PROFESSIONAL STAFF				
Full-time	Head librarian	$27,500	1	$27,500
	Assistant librarian	24,000	2	48,000
Part-time				
OTHER STAFF				
Full-time	Circulation clerk	14,000	1	14,000
	Maintenance worker	14,500	1	14,500
Part-time	Page	$5.25/hr.	1,040 hrs.	5,460

OTHER ANNUAL OPERATING EXPENSES

Acquisitions	$12,500
Supplies	2,450
Utilities	4,200
Maintenance	3,500
Other (please specify)	—

FORM 57d

Library Budget Survey

Municipality ___Village of East Woolford___

	Job Title	Salary	Number or Hours	Cost
PROFESSIONAL STAFF				
Full-time	Head librarian	$25,500	1	$25,500
	Assistant librarian	22,750	1	22,750
Part-time				
OTHER STAFF				
Full-time	Circulation clerk	14,500	1	14,500
	Maintenance worker	13,500	1	13,500
Part-time	Circulation clerk	$5.25/hr.	800 hrs.	4,200

OTHER ANNUAL OPERATING EXPENSES

Acquisitions	$17,000
Supplies	3,400
Utilities	4,700
Maintenance	2,000
Other (please specify)	—

Library Budget Survey

Municipality ___Village of Glenridge___

	Job Title	Salary	Number or Hours	Cost
PROFESSIONAL STAFF				
Full-time	Head librarian	$24,750	1	$24,750
Part-time				
OTHER STAFF				
Full-time				
Part-time	Maintenance worker	$5.25/hr.	520 hrs.	2,730

OTHER ANNUAL OPERATING EXPENSES

Acquisitions	$1,350
Supplies	600
Utilities	2,500
Maintenance	275
Other (please specify)	—

Library Budget Survey

Municipality <u>Town of Littleton</u>

	Job Title	Salary	Number or Hours	Cost
PROFESSIONAL STAFF				
Full-time	Head librarian	$31,150	1	$31,150
	Reference librarian	26,500	1	26,500
	Assistant librarian	25,000	2	50,000
Part-time	Assistant librarian	12,000	1	12,000
OTHER STAFF				
Full-time	Circulation clerk	17,500	4	70,000
	Maintenance worker	14,500	1	14,500
	Page	12,000	1	12,000
Part-time	Circulation clerk	$5.25/hr.	520	2,730
	Page	5.00/hr.	1,560	7,800

OTHER ANNUAL OPERATING EXPENSES
Acquisitions $25,700
Supplies   6,425
Utilities   5,300
Maintenance   2,675
Other (please specify)   1,300*

*Senior Center outreach program.

Library Budget Survey

Municipality ___Town of Keeler___

	Job Title	Salary	Number or Hours	Cost
PROFESSIONAL STAFF				
Full-time	Head librarian	$24,000	1	$24,000
Part-time				
OTHER STAFF				
Full-time				
Part-time	Circulation clerk	$5.25/hr.	1,200 hrs.	6,300

OTHER ANNUAL OPERATING EXPENSES
Acquisitions $1,400
Supplies   200
Utilities   2,100
Maintenance   —
Other (please specify)   —

Library Budget Survey

Municipality __Town of Mt. Tom__

	Job Title	Salary	Number or Hours	Cost
PROFESSIONAL STAFF Full-time				
Part-time	Head librarian	$14,000	1	$14,000
OTHER STAFF Full-time				
Part-time	Page	$5.25/hr.	520 hrs.	2,730

OTHER ANNUAL OPERATING EXPENSES
Acquisitions   —
Supplies $300
Utilities   1,700
Maintenance   —
Other (please specify)   500*

*To organize the annual Mt. Tom book drive, the main source of book donations for the Mt. Tom library.

Library Budget Survey

Municipality ___Town of Warren___

	Job Title	Salary	Number or Hours	Cost
PROFESSIONAL STAFF				
Full-time	Head librarian	$26,500	1	$26,500
Part-time	Assistant librarian	$13,000	1	$13,000
OTHER STAFF				
Full-time	Circulation clerk	14,000	1	14,000
Part-time	Maintenance worker	$5.25/hr.	1,000 hrs.	5,250

OTHER ANNUAL OPERATING EXPENSES

Acquisitions	$14,000
Supplies	2,225
Utilities	3,500
Maintenance	2,750
Other (please specify)	—

Library Budget Survey

Municipality ___Town of Lansdale___

	Job Title	Salary	Number or Hours	Cost
PROFESSIONAL STAFF				
Full-time	Head librarian	$32,500	1	$32,500
	Reference librarian	29,750	1	29,750
	Assistant librarian	28,500	1	28,500
Part-time	Reference librarian	14,500	1	14,500
	Assistant librarian	13,750	1	13,750
OTHER STAFF				
Full-time	Circulation clerk	19,500	4	78,000
	Maintenance worker	15,400	1	15,400
Part-time	Page	5.25/hr.	3,300 hrs.	17,325

OTHER ANNUAL OPERATING EXPENSES

Acquisitions	$124,000
Supplies	34,000
Utilities	6,780
Maintenance	3,600
Other (please specify)	12,500*

*Saturday children's programming and Sunday afternoon foreign film series.

Library Budget Survey

Municipality   <u>Town of New Bremen</u>

	Job Title	Salary	Number or Hours	Cost
PROFESSIONAL STAFF				
Full-time	Head librarian	$27,000	1	$27,000
	Assistant librarian	$24,500	1	$24,500
Part-time				
OTHER STAFF				
Full-time	Circulation clerk	16,500	1	16,500
	Maintenance worker	15,500	1	15,500
Part-time	Circulation clerk	$5.75/hr.	1,560 hrs.	8,970
	Page	5.25/hr.	2,300 hrs.	12,075

OTHER ANNUAL OPERATING EXPENSES

Acquisitions	$35,700
Supplies	4,300
Utilities	3,800
Maintenance	5,625
Other (please specify)	—

Budget Request Form

Administrative Unit: Adams County Library

Item	FY 1 Request

Questions

1. What was the aggregate budget for all preconsolidation Adams County libraries?

2. Did you achieve the mandated 3 percent savings? If not, why not?

3. Assume that you are a member of the board of supervisors. What questions would come to your mind as you reviewed this line-item budget? Is there any information you would like to have that this budget does not contain?

4. In general, what are the strengths and weaknesses of the line-item format?

Exercise 13

Performance Budgeting

BUDGETING FOR EFFICIENCY

Although line-item budgets are very useful, especially in maintaining control and accountability in expenditure, they do not always provide as much information about what government is actually doing with its money as some decision makers would like to have. Budgets may tell us, for instance, that the Department of Parks and Recreation is proposing to spend $1,750 on grass seed and fertilizer but offer no clue as to whether it is an efficient use of public money. What exactly are we getting for this $1,750? Have expenses for playing field maintenance been proportionate to the number of people who use the fields? Questions like these, which line-item budgets fail to address, are made to order for a *performance budget.* Because performance budgets are built around the *activities* in which a government engages rather than the commodities it buys, a person who reviews a budget in this format is able to ascertain the relative efficiency of public undertakings. Indeed, it is for this reason that a performance budget is often called an *activity budget.*

Although the groundwork for performance budgeting was laid as early as the report of President William Howard Taft's Commission on Economy and Efficiency (1912), it was not until the New Deal that performance budgeting became prominent. As the scale of government grew and its programs became more complex and far-flung, a need was felt for a budget system that offered more than control over expenditures. Budgeting processes should help *manage* as well as control, it was argued; budgets should tell us what services we are getting for our money and point out where there are inefficien-

cies. Although later budget reforms have stolen the limelight from performance budgeting, this format received widespread attention from all levels of government from the 1930s through the 1950s. Moreover, many of the concepts it introduced remain part of contemporary budget systems.

CLASSIFYING ACTIVITIES

How exactly do performance budgets work? The key is the way expenditures are classified. Instead of listing, line by line, every item that an organization buys, expenditures are grouped according to the organizational function or task they help fulfill. Thus, the first step in the preparation of a performance budget is to pose and answer the following simple question: What exactly are the activities or functions of this organization? If you ask this question of the city sanitation department, for example, you will probably get answers such as "collects trash," "cleans streets," and "removes snow." If you are dealing with a state department of agriculture, answers might include "issues crop reports," "encourages soil conservation," "promotes exports," and "preserves farmland." Note that the answers always begin with active verbs: *collects, cleans, removes, issues, encourages, promotes, preserves,* and so on. These are the activities or—to use the professional jargon—the *outputs* of government.

Having determined the activities of the unit to be budgeted, the next step in constructing a performance budget is to identify the expenditures that are necessary to produce the activities. These are the "items" in a line-item budget or the "inputs" that correspond to the "outputs." All of the commodities

Table 13.1 Program Costs: Department of Parks and Recreation

Activity	FY 1999–2000	FY 2000–2001 (Request)
01. Administration	$54,000	$62,000
02. Playground Maintenance	33,500	36,200
03. Adult Softball	11,000	11,500
04. Arts and Crafts	21,300	23,000
05. Golf Course Maintenance	37,675	38,700
06. Tennis Court Management	15,800	21,400
07. Swimming Pool Operations	66,125	69,700
TOTAL	$239,400	$262,500

that an organization buys should be allocated, in whole or in part, to one of the activities in the performance budget. Obviously, this is not done randomly. In compiling a performance budget, one seeks to assign all the costs—and only those costs—that actually go into performing an activity.

To illustrate this process, let us reexamine the budget for the Department of Parks and Recreation used in Exercise 12. Suppose that our research has found that the department engages in the following activities: It maintains playgrounds, runs an adult softball program, coordinates summer arts and crafts programs for children, manages one public golf course and four tennis courts, and operates an outdoor swimming pool; of course, it also engages in certain general housekeeping or administrative functions. Our identification of these programs or activities represents the first step in the process. For the second step, we have investigated and learned that the costs of the programs are as presented in Table 13.1.

Table 13.1 represents the bare bones of a performance budget for the Department of Parks and Recreation. Note that all of the cost data from the original line-item budget (Table 12.1) have been reassigned to the various activity classifications. How exactly was this done? Although for the purposes of this illustration the calculations are not shown here, we simply determined which expenditures were necessary to complete each of the activities. For instance, the $36,200 required by the playground maintenance category had appeared in

the line-item budget (Table 12.1) as parts of four different lines: $16,000 for maintenance, $14,300 for seasonal maintenance, $4,600 for equipment maintenance, and $1,300 for grass seed and fertilizer. This gives us a budget that tells us not just what things we plan to buy but what specific activities will be accomplished by our expenditures.

One more step is necessary to produce a true performance budget, however. The third step requires the budget maker to devise specific measures of performance for each activity in which an organization engages and to calculate the unit cost of each. In the Department of Parks and Recreation, we might want to measure the performance of the tennis program by estimating the number of hours the courts are actually used; when this number is divided into the overall cost of the program ($15,800 in FY 1999–2000), we get a unit cost for each court-hour.

This process is repeated for each activity. The idea, of course, is to identify meaningful measures that managers can use to judge the efficiency of the organization's operations. It accomplishes little to generate statistics unrelated to the central purposes of the agency's programs. Table 13.2 provides a more complete version of a performance budget for the Department of Parks and Recreation, including unit cost information.

It should be emphasized that the techniques of performance budgeting are used not simply to display data in budget requests. A good performance budget is used to control costs as well as to estimate

Table 13.2 Program and Unit Costs: Department of Parks and Recreation

	Activity	FY 1999–2000	FY 2000–2001 (Request)
01.	Administration	$54,000	$62,000
	Cost per citizen	1.08	1.23
02.	Playground Maintenance	33,500	36,200
	Cost per acre	42.66	46.12
03.	Adult Softball	11,000	11,500
	Cost per player	25.04	25.00
04.	Arts and Crafts	21,300	23,000
	Cost per child	87.22	106.18
05.	Golf Course Maintenance	37,675	38,700
	Cost per round played	7.35	7.82
06.	Tennis Court Management	15,800	21,400
	Cost per court-hour	5.67	6.73
07.	Swimming Pool Operations	66,125	69,700
	Cost per user-hour	4.21	5.09
	TOTAL	*$239,400*	*$262,500*

future expenditures. If we find, as Table 13.2 seems to indicate, that the arts and crafts program is costing markedly more over time for each child taught, we may want to reconsider funding this activity; at least we will be spurred to investigate why unit costs are rising so precipitously. Conversely, once we are able to identify a stable pattern of unit costs, we can use estimates of demand for compiling our budget requests. If we know that it costs approximately $25 for each adult who participates in the softball program and can estimate that 460 people will sign up for the leagues next year, we know our budget request must be $11,500 for the program.[1]

---

[1]These calculations have been simplified for the purpose of this illustration. Most performance budgets distinguish between fixed and variable costs. Fixed costs are those that remain constant regardless of the level of the activity performed; variable costs fluctuate as activity levels change. Certain costs are fixed in operating a public swimming pool, for example, even if very few people use it: Insurance and utilities must be paid, certain basic pool maintenance must be undertaken, basic lifeguard costs must be absorbed. Other costs vary with the number of users: Additional lifeguards must be hired or more chlorine must be purchased, and so on.

FURTHER READING

One of the classic texts in performance budgeting is Jesse Burkhead, *Government Budgeting* (New York: Wiley, 1956). Also of interest is the symposium on performance budgeting, "Performance Budgeting: Has the Theory Worked?" in *Public Administration Review* 20 (Spring 1960). The symposium material, together with other articles of interest on performance budgeting, is reprinted in Albert C. Hyde and Jay M. Shafritz, eds., *Government Budgeting: Theory, Process, Politics* (Oak Park, Ill.: Moore, 1978).

Performance budgeting has gotten something of a new lease on life in recent years in the guise of "productivity budgeting." See, for instance, Jack Rabin, ed., "Symposium: Budgeting for Improved Productivity," *Public Productivity Review* 10 (Spring 1987). This journal in general publishes many articles related to the topic of monitoring and measuring the performance of government. Also worth consulting is Michael Connelly and Gary Tompkins, "Does Performance Matter? A Study of State Budgeting," *Policy Studies Review* 8 (Winter 1988).

Overview of Exercise

The Adams County Library has now been functioning for one year. Although the Board of Supervisors is generally pleased with the results of the merger, there have been undercurrents of dissatisfaction, especially among some library-oriented citizen groups who have charged that the new system is inefficient, that money that could have bought new books has been wasted on administrative overhead. In fact, a group that calls itself the Friends of the Clear Creek Library has begun circulating a petition that asks Clear Creek's mayor either to renegotiate the merger or to explore ways to reestablish the village library unilaterally.

In an effort to head off more serious conflict and to demonstrate the advantages of the consolidated library, Budget Director Johnson has again asked you, her trouble-shooting deputy, to apply your skills as a budget analyst. Your task this time is to provide technical assistance to the library's administrative staff in developing a performance format for the library's next budget submission.

INSTRUCTIONS

Step One

Review the preliminary activity classification developed by the library administrative staff as presented on Form 60. Note any modifications you think necessary. (Hint: Is "personal services" an activity?)

Step Two

Using the data provided on Form 61, together with the budget data you compiled in Exercise 12, recast your FY 1 budget into a performance format on Form 62. This is mainly a process of deciding how to allocate line-item costs to performance categories. Be sure to include appropriate performance measures and unit costs. (Because the line-item budgets prepared in Exercise 12 can differ, each student will be working with slightly different numbers in this exercise, unless your instructor chooses to reproduce and distribute a standardized budget such as the one in the *Instructor's Manual*.)

Step Three

Complete Form 62 by preparing budget projections for FY 2. Again, use the data provided on Form 61 to make your estimates. Assume a 3 percent increase in all staff salaries and a 5 percent increase in supply, utility, and maintenance expenses. Assume no increases in average book prices.

IT Option

- Prepare your performance budget on an Excel spreadsheet.

Step Four

Answer the questions on Form 63.

Budget Request Form

Administrative Unit: Adams County Library

	Activity	FY 1	FY 2 (Request)
01.	General Administration		
02.	Acquisitions		
03.	Cataloging		
04.	Circulation		
05.	Reference		
06.	Special Programs		
07.	Personal Services		

Adams County Library Data Sheet

- At the time of the merger, the Adams County Library system had total holdings of 1,652,000 volumes. In FY 1, 18,000 additional volumes were acquired. It is anticipated that 21,500 volumes will be acquired in FY 2.
- In addition to cataloging all new volumes, the library system has met and expects to continue to meet its goal of recataloging 10 percent of its holdings each year to convert to the Library of Congress system.
- The combined circulation figures (in volumes) for all branches of the system are as follows: FY 1, 752,000; FY 2, 776,000 (anticipated).
- In FY 1, 421,000 patrons used the library system (including repeat visits). It is expected that 423,400 visits will be recorded in FY 2.
- In FY 1, the reference departments of all library branches answered 67,800 patron questions. It is expected that the reference departments will handle 71,500 questions in FY 2.
- Twenty-four special after-school programs were conducted by the system in FY 1, attended by 1,200 elementary and secondary school pupils. The same figures are expected for FY 2. In addition, 12 of the system's branches conducted Great Books discussions for adults over a ten-week period in FY 1, with a total participation of 127; this program will be discontinued for FY 2. A Sunday film series at three of the branch libraries attracted 4,500 viewers in FY 1. Approximately 6,000 are expected in FY 2.
- Total staff levels in the library system have remained constant since the merger, with no changes in the distribution of job classification (that is, you can assume that the figures from Form 58 are still accurate).
- A recent time study of library employees indicated that branch librarians spend 35 percent of their time on general administration, 25 percent on reference, 20 percent on special programs, 15 percent on acquisitions, and 5 percent on circulation. Assistant librarians devote 30 percent of their time to cataloging, 25 percent to reference, 25 percent to circulation, and 20 percent to special programs. The director of county libraries devotes all his time to general administration, as do his secretaries and administrative assistant. Pages and circulation clerks spend 100 percent of their time on circulation, reference librarians 100 percent of their time on reference.
- It may be assumed that maintenance, supply, and utility costs are borne equally by all library activities in proportion to their share of staff costs (as measured by salaries).

Budget Request Form

Administrative Unit: Adams County Library

Activity	FY 1	FY 2 (Request)

Questions

1. What, if anything, was wrong with the activity classification on Form 60? If you found something wrong, what modifications did you make?

2. Do your unit cost calculations indicate that the Adams County Library is becoming more or less efficient? Is this true of all programs? What might account for this pattern?

3. What additional measures or statistics would be useful to have to assess the performance of the Adams County Library?

4. Assume that you are a member of the board of supervisors. What questions would come to your mind as you reviewed this performance budget? Is there any information you would like to have that this budget does not contain?

5. In general, what are the strengths and weaknesses of the performance format?

Exercise 14

Program Budgeting

BUDGETING FOR PURPOSE

As we learned in Exercise 13, performance budgeting assesses the efficiency of government operations by examining the unit costs of public services. Although this information can be very useful for certain purposes, efficiency alone is seldom enough. One can walk through the woods very efficiently but get lost nonetheless. With government programs as with walking in the woods, we need to know if we are headed in the right direction, not just how fast we are getting there.

Program budgeting is designed in large part to tell us just that. A program budget forces policymakers to identify and evaluate the goals of public programs and to develop means that are optimally suited to reaching those goals. Where performance budgeting focuses on inputs and outputs, program budgeting encompasses inputs, outputs, *and impacts or results.* Thus a program budgeting system is a decision-making system. Program budgeting encourages public officials to weigh alternatives systematically and to choose policy strategies that most effectively meet public purposes.

As with line-item and performance formats, the key to program budgeting lies in the organization and presentation of budget data. Program budgets are distinguished by the fact that budget requests are arranged, as the name suggests, by programs. That is, rather than grouping together all personnel costs and all supply costs as line-item budgeting requires or classifying activities after the fashion of performance budgeting, program budgeting requires that budget managers think in terms of agency missions or goals. The broad set of goals for an organization (or, more usually, an entire govern-

mental jurisdiction) provides a set of categories for organizing and evaluating public expenditures. This arrangement is designed to serve as a reminder that day-to-day operating costs or even organizational activities are not ends in themselves. The purpose of government is to provide certain services, to accomplish things. Program budgets focus attention on what those things are and make it easier for officials to determine if government is delivering what it is supposed to deliver.

The structure and logic of program budgeting can be illustrated by reference to our hypothetical Department of Parks and Recreation. You will recall that the final performance budget for the department (Table 13.2) classified expenditures according to seven key activities, such as playground maintenance, adult softball, and arts and crafts; moreover, for each of these activities, unit costs were calculated. To create a program budget for this department, we have to refocus our thinking and ask ourselves, "What are the goals or purposes of this unit of government with respect to parks and recreation?" Subgoals might include providing organized recreational opportunities for adults and supervised recreational opportunities for children, maintaining public spaces for general recreational use, and offering various instructional sports programs. The various subgoals provide a framework for our program budget.

Each subgoal would then be further broken down into more detailed goals, for which specific programs would be planned and developed. The terms used to describe this nested hierarchy of goals and subgoals are *program, subprogram, element,* and *subelement,* with program the most general and subelement the most specific. A summary budget

PROGRAM: 5.0 Recreation

DESCRIPTION: This program provides a wide range of public recreational opportunities and services for county residents. The goal of the program is to make possible structured and unstructured leisure-time activities that promote health, physical fitness, and social interaction.

ADMINISTRATIVE UNIT(S): Department of Parks and Recreation

SUBPROGRAM: 5.1 Athletic Instruction
This subprogram provides basic and intermediate instruction for residents of the county in several different sports, including tennis, golf, and swimming. The goal of this subprogram is to encourage residents to pursue vigorous and healthful physical activity by teaching skills basic to such sports.

SUBPROGRAM: 5.2 League Sports
This subprogram provides coordination of and support for athletic leagues in the county. The goal of this subprogram is to create opportunities for residents to participate in team sports.

SUBPROGRAM: 5.3 Open Recreation
This subprogram provides for the maintenance and operation of public recreational space in the county. The goal of this subprogram is to ensure the availability of public space, including playgrounds, parks, and athletic facilities, for the pursuit of recreational activities by county residents.

Figure 14.1
Sample Program Budget Summary

for the recreation program might appear as illustrated in Figure 14.1.

Note that the various subprograms identified in Figure 14.1 may be understood as more carefully specified goals to be pursued in furtherance of the general goal of "providing a wide range of recreational opportunities and services to area residents." Note also that the overall budget is framed without regard to a specific organizational unit or department: The focus is on recreation, not on a particular agency. Although some governments may be organized in a way that permits program budgets to be constructed with a one-to-one correspondence with departments and agencies, pure program budgets often cut across organizational lines, with various units contributing to each of the program categories. This means that budget officials must create additional documentation (called *crosswalks*) that translate program data into departmental operating budgets.

To appreciate the distinctiveness of program budgeting, however, it is necessary to look beyond such a broad summary of planned expenditures. Figure 14.2 provides a sample page from the program budget of our fictional municipality that focuses on a specific subelement of the recreation program.

Figure 14.2 presents budget information of subelement 5.111, tennis instruction. If we had the full budget in front of us, we would find a separate page for subelements 5.112 (golf instruction), 5.113 (swimming instruction), and so on. Indeed, there would be detailed information provided for every subelement of every element of every subprogram of every program in the county. Note that the entry defines the subelement, specifies its objective, and

PROGRAM: 5.0   Recreation
SUBPROGRAM: 5.1   Athletic Instruction
ELEMENT: 5.11   Lifelong Sports (Adult)
SUBELEMENT: 5.111   Tennis Instruction

Description: This subelement is concerned with the provision of tennis instruction to adult residents of the county for the purpose of encouraging participation in a vigorous, lifelong activity that enhances fitness and social interaction.

Objective: To provide introductory and intermediate group tennis lessons to all interested adult residents.

Administrative Unit: Department of Parks and Recreation, Division of Recreation.

		Five-Year Plan			
	1999–2000	*2000–2001*	*2001–2002*	*2002–2003*	*2003–2004*
Residents served	700	750	790	825	850
Hours of instruction	1,400	1,500	1,580	1,650	1,700
Cost	$9,800	$11,200	$11,950	$12,560	$13,230

Summary Analysis:
To meet the anticipated increase in demand for tennis instruction over the next five years, the department initially considered four alternative strategies: (1) maintain the current level of service at no charge to students, (2) maintain the current level of service with a small user charge, (3) increase the size of the instructional groups so as to instruct more students in the same number of hours, and (4) eliminate all intermediate lessons.

The department recommends that alternative 1—maintain the current level of service at no charge to students—be fully funded as indicated in the five-year plan. This will require two additional seasonal staff positions.

Alternative 2 was rejected because the calculated costs of administering a user fee system would require that the fee be set at a level that would exclude a significant percentage of interested residents.

Alternative 3 was rejected because analysis of comparable public and private instructional programs indicates that adequate instruction cannot be provided to groups larger than five students.

Alternative 4 was rejected both because it was deemed inconsistent with subelement objectives and because a survey of area residents indicates increasing interest in instruction beyond the introductory level.

Figure 14.2
Sample Program Budget Page

identifies the administrative unit responsible for meeting the objective. Note that it also displays cost and service data for a five-year period. Such multi-year cost projections are a central part of program budgets; their purpose is to force decision makers to weight long-term costs when considering program alternatives.

Perhaps the most important part of Figure 14.2 is the section titled "Summary Analysis." It is here that we find the heart of program budgeting. Given the goal of providing introductory and intermediate group tennis lessons to all interested area residents, budget officials have systematically analyzed various alternative strategies. The first alternative, maintaining the current level of service at no charge to the student, is recommended for funding because it most effectively meets the specified objective. The other three alternatives—instituting a small user charge, increasing the size of the instructional groups, and eliminating intermediate lessons—were found wanting for the reasons specified.

Of course, what we see here is only a brief summary of the analysis that was done; depending on the relative importance of the issue and the rules of the jurisdiction, a fuller and more detailed analysis might well accompany the budget request. This summary makes our point effectively, nevertheless: Program budgets are designed to draw the attention of decision makers to the relationship between the goals or purposes of government and the means available to reach them. Public officials are thereby encouraged to evaluate goals, weigh alternative programs systematically, and choose policy strategies that best meet public purposes. It should be stressed in this context that there is no single methodology or analytical tool that can be used to sort out alternatives in a program budget. Some budget problems lend themselves readily to highly quantitative decision-making devices, such as cost-benefit or cost-effectiveness analysis (see Exercise 16). Other questions require budget officials to rely on "softer," qualitative analyses. Which tool is used will depend mainly on how easy it is to quantify the impact or benefit of a particular set of programs (*costs* can almost always be calculated or estimated in "hard," dollar terms, of course). Although some advocates of program budgeting have been criticized for their excessive attachment to quantification, program budgeting itself does not require any such excess.

As with other budget formats, variations on program budgeting are multitudinous. In general, though, governments that use program budgeting follow the basic pattern described here. That is, all budget requests must be justified in terms of their effectiveness in reaching agency goals. Although program budgeting places heavy demands on agency officials and requires them to spend considerable time and energy gathering and analyzing information, it can pay great dividends. After all, a Department of Parks and Recreation that relied only on performance or efficiency measures might never even think about the adequacy of its tennis instruction program. From an efficiency standpoint, the more people on a court, the better!

Program budgeting became popular in the public sector in the 1960s, following Robert McNamara's use of the system to aid his management of the Department of Defense in the Kennedy administration. McNamara's system, officially termed PPBS (for Planning-Programming-Budgeting System), was extended to all federal agencies by President Lyndon Johnson in 1965. Although PPBS met great resistance from many agency officials, who found it overly complex and cumbersome, and although the formal use of PPBS was suspended in 1971 by Nixon Budget Director George Shultz, the logic and techniques of program budgeting have thoroughly penetrated the routines of government budgeting systems, including those at state and local levels.

FURTHER READING

One of the best places to begin additional reading in the area of program budgeting is with V. O. Key's classic article, "The Lack of a Budgetary Theory," *American Political Science Review* 34 (December 1940); although Key does not deal with PPBS per se, his elaboration of the central problems in public budgeting provides the foundation for all later work.

Accounts of the operation of program budgeting in the Pentagon are offered in Alain C. Enthoven and K. Wayne Smith, *How Much Is Enough?* (New York: Harper & Row, 1971), and Charles J. Hitch and Roland N. McKean, *The Economics of Defense in the Nuclear Age* (Cambridge, Mass.: Harvard University Press, 1967).

Good general treatments of PPBS include Allen Schick, "A Death in the Bureaucracy: The Demise of Federal PPB," *Public Administration Review* 33 (March-April 1973), and the relevant chapters in Aaron B. Wildavsky and Naomi Caiden, *The New Politics of the Budgetary Process,* 3d ed. (New York: Longman, 1997). Also see the section in Albert C. Hyde and Jay M. Shafritz, eds., *Government Budgeting: Theory, Process, Politics* (Oak Park, Ill.:

Moore, 1978); it contains the articles by Key and Schick as well as other useful selections. Finally, the essays in Fremont J. Lyden and Ernest G. Miller, eds., *Planning, Programming, Budgeting: A Systems* *Approach to Management,* 2d ed. (Chicago: Markham, 1972), though more technical, are worth reading.

Overview of Exercise

In this exercise, you will first help design an overall program structure for the Adams County Library system. To do so, you must outline a set of program goals that the library is trying to achieve to serve as a framework for the budget. You will then review a request from a member of the library staff to buy a new bookmobile and to fund associated operating expenses. In response, you will write a memo explaining how the request should be stated in terms of a program budget.

INSTRUCTIONS

Step One

Assume that you are A. C. Andrews, deputy budget director for Adams County. Read the memo addressed to you from Budget Director Johnson (Form 64), and use Form 65 to outline a set of subprograms for the Adams County Library that could be used as a program budgeting framework. Because the purpose of this exercise is simply to get

you to think in program budgeting terms, there is no expectation that you have any detailed knowledge of library administration. Just draw on your general experience with public (or college) libraries, and ask yourself: What do libraries do? What services do they try to provide? (Note: Although this information isn't necessary to complete this exercise, to provide continuity with Exercises 12 and 13, assume that you are now in FY 3; if you like, fill in appropriate dates on memos.)

Step Two

Review Form 66 and formulate a response to Budget Officer Tome on Form 67. Remind Tome that such requests must be submitted in a program format, and make some suggestions as to how this might be done. (Hint: Are there any alternative ways to meet these service goals?)

Step Three

Answer the questions on Form 68.

25 February 20__

TO: A. C. Andrews
          Deputy Budget Director

FROM: Sarah T. Johnson
          Budget Director

RE: Revisions in Library Budget Format

Now that we finally seem to have gotten everyone to agree on program categories for the new format, we need to move ahead and devise appropriate subprograms, elements, and subelements. Although most of this work will be carried out by the staff in each operating unit, it is important that we provide some technical assistance at this stage of the process. Despite our training sessions, most of the department heads still do not understand program budgeting.

I'd like you to act as technical liaison with the library people. Your help with their performance budget gave you good insight into what's going on over there.

Here's what I would like you to do: Try to get the library staff to stop thinking in line-item and performance terms. Help them categorize library services by program, by what they are trying to accomplish. Disabuse them of the notion that "cataloging" is a public service! But don't develop the entire budget structure for them. Confine your efforts to the subprogram level. Identify a set of subprograms and provide a brief set of definitions and objectives.

As you know, the library has been designated the sole administrative unit responsible for the program category "Library and Information Services." The library's entire operating budget is to be presented in this category.

Draft Program Budget Summary

PROGRAM: Information and Library Services
ADMINISTRATIVE UNIT: Adams County Library

SUBPROGRAM:

SUBPROGRAM:

SUBPROGRAM:

SUBPROGRAM:

SUBPROGRAM:

April 23, 20__

TO: L. C. Tome, Budget Officer
        Adams County Library

FROM: J. Stacks, Head Librarian
        Main Branch

RE: Funds for a New Bookmobile

We have received increasingly insistent requests from residents of North Waynesfield to open a new branch library. They point out, quite accurately, that the closest library facilities are over 6 miles away and that the steadily growing population in North Waynesfield warrants better and more convenient library services.

I think we need to do something for these people this year. Consequently, I am submitting a supplemental budget request for a new bookmobile unit. The estimated costs are as follows:

Bookmobile truck	$31,000
Driver-librarian salary	23,000
Books and periodicals	11,000
Maintenance expenses	5,000

Although the total costs for the first year will be fairly high ($70,000), once we have the additional truck it won't be so expensive in future years. Also, I figure we'll have to use this truck in North Waynesfield only about half time; we can use it to fill service gaps in other areas of the county when it isn't in North Waynesfield.

2 May 20__

TO: L. C. Tome, Budget Officer
          Adams County Library

FROM: A. C. Andrews, Deputy Budget Director
          Adams County

RE: Bookmobile Request

Questions

1. What advantages, if any, do you see in using a program budget format? Would library services likely be improved if the Adams County Library used the subprogram structure you devised? If so, in what ways? If not, why not?

2. What was the problem with the budget request that Stacks submitted to Tome? Do you think a program format would help Tome make a more intelligent decision?

3. Given the analytical difficulties presented by program budgeting, do you think it is worthwhile to justify all budget requests every year in program terms? Would it be better to limit detailed program analyses to "big ticket" or expensive items and have other things presented in a simpler, incremental fashion?

4. Who benefits from program budgeting? Do you suppose it would tend to give more political and administrative power to some officials than others? If so, which ones?

5. Assume you are a member of the county board of supervisors. Would you rather see a budget submitted in a program format or have a line-item or performance presentation?

Zero-Base Budgeting

BUDGETING FOR PRIORITIES

Zero-base budgeting (ZBB) is the most recent innovation in the budget process. Developed in 1969 for the Texas Instrument Corporation, ZBB gained widespread attention when President Jimmy Carter mandated its use by federal agencies in the late 1970s. Although the Reagan, Bush, and Clinton administrations have not required its use, many federal agencies continue to use ZBB when preparing budget requests. ZBB is also widely used at state and local levels of government.

Although the term *zero-base budgeting* implies a very comprehensive, from-the-ground-up system, ZBB does not in fact require administrators to start from zero and justify every dollar. Indeed, some of ZBB's popularity derives from its relative simplicity, especially in contrast to the intricate calculations and projections of PPBS. As this exercise makes clear, the heart of ZBB lies in comparing and ranking alternative packages of expenditure against one another. ZBB directs the attention of managers to the relative value of different programs by forcing them to set priorities when they make their budget requests.

DECISION UNITS AND DECISION PACKAGES

As with all budget formats, there are many different ways to implement a ZBB system; the specific approach will vary with the needs of the particular jurisdiction. In essence, though, all ZBB systems involve four basic steps:

1. Identify decision units.
2. Analyze programs and alternatives.
3. Prepare decision packages.
4. Rank decision packages.

In the language of ZBB, a *decision unit* is the organizational entity that prepares a budget. An agency as a whole may be designated a decision unit for ZBB purposes, or it may be subdivided into several decision units. How does one decide what constitutes a proper decision unit? Unfortunately, there is no sure-fire method. According to the U.S. Office of Management and Budget, decision units should be designated at the lowest levels of organization where officials "make significant decisions on the amount of spending and the scope and quality of work to be performed."[1] The main idea is to involve in the budget process line officials who have major program responsibilities. In our Department of Parks and Recreation, we might decide that the Grounds and Maintenance Division constitutes one logical decision unit, the Recreation Division another, and the central administrative offices a third; alternatively, we might decide to break the divisions down into smaller decision units by designating an adult recreation decision unit and a children's recreation decision unit within the Recreation Division. What we decide will depend on the structure of the organization and on how responsibilities are arrayed. On balance, ZBB tends to decentralize budget-making power and responsibility; PPBS, by contrast, has centralizing tendencies.

The second step in ZBB, once the decision units have been designated, requires that the programs of each decision unit be identified and analyzed and that alternatives to these programs be investigated. In effect, managers ask themselves, "Why are we operating this program? What purposes does it serve? Are there better ways to accomplish our

---

[1] Fremont J. Lyden and Marc Lindenberg, *Public Budgeting in Theory and Practice* (New York: Longman, 1983), p. 99.

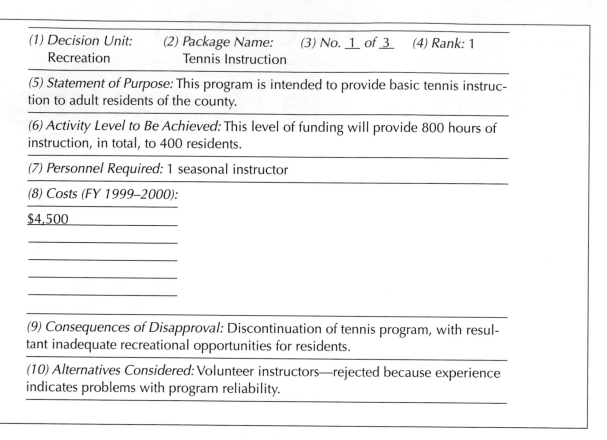

(1) Decision Unit: *(2) Package Name:*   *(3) No.* _1_ *of* _3_   *(4) Rank:* 1
    Recreation   Tennis Instruction

(5) Statement of Purpose: This program is intended to provide basic tennis instruction to adult residents of the county.

(6) Activity Level to Be Achieved: This level of funding will provide 800 hours of instruction, in total, to 400 residents.

(7) Personnel Required: 1 seasonal instructor

(8) Costs (FY 1999–2000):

$4,500

(9) Consequences of Disapproval: Discontinuation of tennis program, with resultant inadequate recreational opportunities for residents.

(10) Alternatives Considered: Volunteer instructors—rejected because experience indicates problems with program reliability.

Figure 15.1
Sample Decision Package

goals?" For those who have completed Exercise 14, these questions should be familiar, for they are very similar to those raised by PPBS. The difference in ZBB lies mainly in the amount of analysis required. Analysis of alternatives to ZBB tends in practice to be more limited; in some jurisdictions, it is only perfunctory. Where PPBS frequently insists on complex mathematical models to demonstrate cost-effectiveness, with consequently burdensome information requirements, ZBB asks only that the purposes of a program be clearly stated and that some effort be made to ascertain that current activities are justified in terms of these purposes. As with performance budgeting, ZBB formats generally request specific measures of agency activities.

Having identified the programs and purposes of their decision units, managers next prepare sets of *decision packages.* A decision package is a document that specifies a level of service to be achieved given a particular level of funding. Decision packages also summarize the objectives of a program and indicate alternative methods considered by the decision unit for reaching program goals. A sample

decision package prepared by the Recreation Division of the Department of Parks and Recreation for the tennis instruction program is provided in Figure 15.1.

This decision package states that 800 hours of basic tennis instruction can be provided to 400 area residents at a cost of $4,500. It also indicates the consequences of disapproving the funding request and displays alternatives to the tennis instruction program that were considered.

Generally, decision unit managers prepare several decision packages for each program within their unit. Although practices vary from jurisdiction to jurisdiction, three types of packages are common:

1. *Minimum- or reduced-level decision packages* prescribe the level of service below which program operations cease to be feasible.

2. *Current-level decision packages* specify the level of service to be delivered assuming no change in funding from the current fiscal year.

3. *Enhanced-level decision packages* project levels of service to be achieved given specified incremental increases in funding.

DECISION UNIT: Recreation
DECISION PACKAGE: Tennis Instruction

Package 1 of 3 $4,500 (base cost)
Provides 800 hours of basic tennis instruction to 400 area residents.

Package 2 of 3 $3,200 (incremental cost)
Provides an additional 300 hours of basic tennis instruction, accommodating an additional 150 area residents.

Package 3 of 3 $2,100 (incremental cost)
Provides an additional 300 hours of basic and intermediate tennis instruction to an additional 150 residents.

Figure 15.2
Summary of Decision Packages

In a sense, this means that managers have to prepare three spending plans for each program they supervise. Each spending plan, or decision package, says, in effect, "If you give me x number of dollars, I can provide y level of service." This is what item 3 ("No. 1 of 3") refers to in Figure 15.1: that this is the first (minimum level) of three decision packages for the program. In other words, there are two other decision packages that have been prepared for the tennis instruction program, each somewhat more costly, each providing a somewhat higher level of service. Figure 15.2 provides a summary of these three packages.

RANKING DECISION PACKAGES

To understand why budget requests are broken down into separate decision packages, we must move to the final step of the ZBB process, which is ranking. At this stage, all decision packages are ranked against one another in order of their priority. Packages considered more important by managers are ranked above those considered less important. Suppose that the recreation decision unit is responsible for four programs: tennis instruction, swimming instruction, softball, and arts and crafts; we will label these, respectively, TI, SI, SB, and AC. For each program, three decision packages have been prepared, as in Figure 15.2, for a total of 12 decision packages. The decision packages may be represented as TI-1,

TI-2, TI-3, and so on. The manager of the recreation decision unit must rank all 12 decision packages according to his or her priorities. Table 15.1 shows what such a ranked list would look like.

This ranking is, of course, only illustrative. A decision unit manager may submit any ranking that reflects his or her sense of what constitutes the most appropriate pattern of expenditure. The only rule that

Table 15.1 Sample Ranking of Decision Packages

Decision Unit(s): Recreation Division   Manager: J. T. Smith

Priority Ranking

Rank	Package	Incremental Cost	Cumulative Cost
1	TI-1	$ 4,500	$ 4,500
2	SI-1	16,000	20,500
3	TI-2	3,200	23,700
4	AC-1	7,500	31,200
5	TI-3	2,100	33,300
6	SB-1	6,000	39,300
7	SI-2	4,000	43,300
8	SI-3	3,250	46,550
9	AC-2	5,100	51,650
10	SB-2	2,800	54,450
11	SB-3	2,700	57,150
12	AC-3	1,750	58,900

must be followed in ranking decision packages is that more basic packages must be ranked above additional increments. That is, a TI-1 must always be ranked above a TI-2, which must always be ranked above a TI-3. This rule is only common sense, for one must have a minimum package (represented by the "1") before one can have increments (represented by the "2" and "3"). It is perfectly proper, though, to rank an increment of one package higher than the minimum level of another package; this is simply a way of communicating the fact that you would rather have a lot of one program than a little of two.

This process of ranking decision packages is repeated all the way up the organizational hierarchy. Upper-level managers take the ranked decision packages submitted by lower-level decision units, combine them into "consolidated decision packages," and produce another ranked list. Upper-level managers are free to change the priorities set by their subordinates, although in general the lower-level judgments are left unchanged.

It should now be apparent that the essence of ZBB lies in the process of ranking the separate decision packages. Although ZBB does not remove politics or bureaucratic game-playing from the budget process, it does tend to undercut the common budget strategy of claiming that all programs are equally crucial. Managers are forced to lay their cards on the table and set clearly stated priorities among their programs. Moreover, once managers learn how much money has been appropriated for their agency, they should be able to turn to their ranked list of packages, draw a line under the cumulative dollar figure corresponding to the appropriation, and be prepared to discontinue any programs that fall below the line. For instance, if the Recreation Division were granted $47,000, packages AC-2, SB-2, SB-3, and AC-3 (in Table 15.1) would be excised.

Although most public managers do not actually have that much discretion because legislative appropriations often require certain programs to be fully funded, the ZBB process can be a very useful way of redirecting or refocusing an agency's attention. Several years ago, for instance, the U.S. Environmental Protection Agency decided, after a thorough ZBB review, that its noise pollution program was not worth its cost; it was deemed better to have that money go to enhanced air, water, and solid waste pollution abatement projects and to run a few programs at a high level rather than a lot of programs at a low level. Similarly, our Department of Parks and Recreation might decide that a fully funded swimming program is more important than half a swimming program plus half a tennis program. Although ZBB provides no "correct" solution to such problems of resource allocation, it does encourage decision makers to think about the issues in a responsible fashion.

FURTHER READING

One of the most useful references on ZBB is a short article by Peter Pyhrr, the man largely responsible for developing the system: "The Zero-Base Approach to Government Budgeting," *Public Administration Review* 37 (January-February 1977). The collection of essays edited by Albert C. Hyde and Jay M. Shafritz, *Government Budgeting: Theory, Process, Politics* (Oak Park, Ill.: Moore, 1978), contains nine pieces on ZBB, including case studies of its implementation in New Mexico, New Jersey, and Wilmington, Delaware. A similar broad array of articles may be found in Joseph L. Hebert, ed., *Experiences in Zero Base Budgeting* (New York: PBI, 1977). For a more detailed how-to-do-it look at ZBB, see L. Allan Austin and Logan M. Cheek, *Zero-Base Budgeting: A Decision Package Manual* (New York: AMACOM, 1979).

Overview of Exercise

In this exercise, you will translate part of the performance budget you developed for the Adams County Library into a ZBB format. In doing so, you will first develop three summary decision packages for each of five specified decision units. You will then rank the 15 decision packages against one another in

any order you consider reasonable given the information provided.

It should be noted that the exercise involves two major departures from the real world of zero-base budgeting. First, it is assumed that each decision unit prepares only one set of decision packages.

Normally, of course, decision units prepare several sets of packages, as they are often responsible for more than one program. Second, because you have only limited information about each decision unit and its activities, you are not required to prepare comprehensive and detailed decision packages (as illustrated in Figure 15.1). Instead, you will generate summary decision packages, following the stated instructions, that will provide a minimum of information about service levels and costs. Were you to prepare an actual zero-base budget for this organization, you would have to undertake far more analysis and provide considerably more detail about program objectives and alternatives.

INSTRUCTIONS

Step One

Assume again that you are A. C. Andrews, deputy budget director for Adams County. Read the memo addressed to you from Budget Director Johnson (Form 69).

Step Two

Assume that your FY 2 budget request figures from Exercise 13 (Form 62) were approved. Transfer the figures to the appropriate column on Form 70. Note that to simplify the exercise, the "General Administration" category has been excluded as a decision unit; simply ignore the costs in constructing your decision packages. If for any reason you did not complete Exercise 13, your instructor will provide you with a set of figures that you may use.

Step Three

Assume a 3 percent across-the-board increase for FY 3. Do the appropriate arithmetic and complete the second column of Form 70. The figures for FY 3 thus calculated will provide the basis for constructing your ZBB decision packages in this exercise. (Note: The extrapolation is necessary because Exercise 14 did not require the generation of actual budget figures for this fiscal year.)

Step Four

Use Forms 71a–e to construct summary decision packages for each of the five decision units. All the information necessary to prepare these decision packages is contained either in Director Johnson's memo or in the data you generated for Form 70. Again, you are to use your FY 3 figures from Form 70 as the basis for your decision package cost calculations. In addition, you should use the performance and unit cost measures you calculated in Exercise 13 to figure out the level of service provided by different decision packages; assume, for the purposes of this exercise, that the basic unit cost ratios have not changed since FY 2. (Note the additional implicit assumption in Director Johnson's memo that a 90 percent level of funding will yield a 90 percent level of service, a 110 percent level of funding, a 110 percent level of service, and so on. This assumption is made for the purposes of this exercise to simplify calculations, although it is unrealistic in that it fails to differentiate between fixed and variable costs. Were you to prepare an actual zero-base budget, you would have to take the distinction between these costs into account in order to calculate projected service levels. See footnote 1 in Exercise 13 for a more detailed explanation of fixed and variable costs.)

Step Five

Use Form 72 to rank your decision packages. Provide the incremental and cumulative cost data as required. Although there is no one "correct" order of priority, try to rank the packages in a way that reflects your sense of their importance.

Step Six

Assume that the library winds up receiving only 95 percent of its total FY 4 requests, as represented in Form 72, for the activities encompassed by these five decision units (exclude monies for "General Administration" when you make your calculations). Draw a line on Form 72 below the last decision package that would be funded under these circumstances.

Step Seven

Answer the questions on Form 73.

23 March 20__

TO: A. C. Andrews
         Deputy Budget Director

FROM: Sarah T. Johnson
         Budget Director

RE: ZBB Format for Library

As you know, the board of supervisors voted last week to discontinue our program budget format. Although I remain convinced that the benefits of this approach outweigh its costs, the supervisors were sensitive to complaints that filtered back to them from department heads about the alleged administrative difficulties of program budgeting. Fortunately, I have been able to convince them that we should not return to a routine, line-item budget system. They are willing to allow us to use a zero-base budget format this fiscal year, at least on a trial basis.

Because you are more familiar with this approach than virtually anyone else in County government and because you have worked closely with the library staff on budget questions in the past, I'd like you to supervise a ZBB trial run for the library budget for the coming fiscal year (FY 4). Use the Acquisitions, Cataloging, Circulation, Reference, and Special Programs budget categories (the principal ones we used to use in the days of performance budgeting) as the bases for your decision units; ignore the General Administration category, though—this is a special case that we'll deal with later. Prepare one set of three decision packages for each of these decision units (for a total of 15 decision packages): a minimum-level package, a current-level package, and an enhanced package. For ease of implementation, I suggest you use a fixed 90 percent of current (FY 3) expenditures to calculate the minimum-level packages and a fixed 110 percent of current expenditures to calculate the enhanced-level packages—in other words, the "base" decision package in each case should be 90 percent of current expenditures, the first incremental package (the one labeled "2 of 3") should represent the difference in dollars between the base and current expenditures, and the final incremental package ("3 of 3") should represent the difference in dollars between current expenditures and 110 percent of current expenditures. You should be able to derive the level of service figures from previous library budget submissions. I will, of course, want to see your final ranking of these 15 decision packages.

Budget Worksheet

	FY 2 (from Form 62)	FY 3
Budget Categories		
Acquisitions		
Cataloging		
Circulation		
Reference		
Special Programs		

DECISION UNIT: Acquisitions Department
DECISION PACKAGE: Book Acquisitions (BA)

Package 1 of 3   (Base Cost)

Package 2 of 3   (Incremental Cost)

Package 3 of 3   (Incremental Cost)

DECISION UNIT: Cataloging Department
DECISION PACKAGE: Book Cataloging (CA)

Package 1 of 3   (Base Cost)

Package 2 of 3   (Incremental Cost)

Package 3 of 3   (Incremental Cost)

DECISION UNIT: Circulation Department
DECISION PACKAGE: Book Circulation (CR)

<u>Package 1 of 3</u>   <u>(Base Cost)</u>

<u>Package 2 of 3</u>   <u>(Incremental Cost)</u>

<u>Package 3 of 3</u>   <u>(Incremental Cost)</u>

FORM 71d

DECISION UNIT: Reference Department
DECISION PACKAGE: General Reference (RE)

Package 1 of 3   (Base Cost)

Package 2 of 3   (Incremental Cost)

Package 3 of 3   (Incremental Cost)

DECISION UNIT: Office of Special Programs
DECISION PACKAGE: Special Programs (SP)

Package 1 of 3   (Base Cost)

Package 2 of 3   (Incremental Cost)

Package 3 of 3   (Incremental Cost)

Adams County Library
Decision Package Ranking Sheet

	PRIORITY RANKING		
Rank	Package	Incremental Cost	Cumulative Cost
1			
2			
3			
4			
5			
6			
7			
8			
9			
10			
11			
12			
13			
14			
15			

Questions

1. Which programs would likely be eliminated if your budget recommendations were adopted?

2. What are the advantages and disadvantages of ZBB for line managers vis-à-vis central budget officials?

3. What are the relative advantages of ZBB versus PPBS?

4. Assume that you are a member of the board of supervisors. Which budget format—line-item, performance, program, or ZBB—would you prefer that the county's administrative agencies use?

PART FOUR

Decision Making and Policy Analysis

ADMINISTRATORS AND THE POLICY PROCESS

The classical view of American constitutional democracy that is presented in high school civics textbooks does not have much to say about bureaucracy and public administration. Congress, we are told, follows the wishes of the citizenry and makes the law, while the president, under the watchful eye of the Supreme Court, implements it. To the extent they are recognized at all, public administrators are understood to be somewhere in the background, working under the direct control of the executive to carry out the technical details of legislation. Elected officials make policy; administrators simply administer it.

Unfortunately, this is not a very accurate description of the actual relationship between politics and administration in the United States–or anywhere, for that matter. It seriously understates the role of public administrators in the governmental process. Administrators do not just carry out policy; they make policy. Indeed, few areas of American life and few Americans are untouched by administrative decisions. From highway safety and the regulation of prescription drugs to the processing of social security checks and student loans, public administrators make choices that have significant effects on all of us.

The term that we use to describe the latitude or freedom that administrators have to act on their own is *administrative discretion,* a concept we explored in some detail in Exercise 5. How is it that administrators have come to exercise such discretion? The Constitution, after all, creates no such role for them. The main reason is the complexity of modern government. It is no longer possible (and perhaps no longer desirable) for legislators and other elected officials to issue precise and detailed instructions to administrators about many questions of public policy. Even if they were so inclined, they have neither the time nor the expertise to do so. Consequently, they delegate their authority to administrators. Although Congress and the president still try to set the broad goals of public policy (for instance, "air transportation should be as safe as possible"), they often leave it to professional administrators to make the rules that give the policy meaning ("airlines must install seats and carpeting made only of noncombustible materials").

Administrators play a role in the policy process even in the absence of such formal delegations of authority, however. Bureaucracies are the eyes and ears of government. It is often the bureaucracy that first becomes aware of problems in need of governmental attention. And it is the bureaucracy that is asked to investigate and report on the nature of the problems. The administrator who defines a problem and structures the information on which a decision is made has a subtle, though powerful, impact on the decision itself. Although politicians in an open society have multiple sources of information—the press, interest groups, and individual citizens—public administrators occupy a strategic position. At least part of America's misadventure in Vietnam may be explained by misleading and inaccurate reports from the field (encouraged, to be sure, by politicians) that contributed to a belief that the United States was "winning" the war.

Bureaucracy also constitutes the arms and legs of government, to pursue the metaphor. Policy decisions are seldom self-implementing. Administrators are the ones that actually have to get their hands dirty and put decisions into effect. They have to identify and clean up toxic waste dumps, plan soil conservation projects, manage job training schemes, and fly reconnaissance aircraft. Even given clear goals and even absent formal delegations of authority, administrators cannot do these jobs without exercising considerable discretion. No statute no matter how detailed, no rule book no matter how thick can anticipate all contingencies and program all administrative actions.

The point of this analysis is very simple: Administrators are key actors in American government. Directly and indirectly, formally and informally, they make decisions and take actions that fundamentally shape the character and direction of public policy. This implies that we, as students of public administration, need to pay close attention to the processes of administrative policy formulation and implementation. It further implies that we have a special obligation to see that administrative discretion is applied as competently and responsibly as possible. The three exercises in Part Four introduce techniques that, when used properly, help harness administrative discretion for public purposes.

FURTHER READING

Two useful overviews of the role of public administrators in the political process are Kenneth J. Meier, Politics and the Bureaucracy: Policymaking in the Fourth Branch of Government, 4th ed. (Fort Worth: Harcourt Brace, 1999); and James W. Fesler and Donald F. Kettl, The Politics of the Administrative Process, 2d ed. (Chatham, N.J.: Chatham, 1996). For a classic analysis of the roots and implications of administrative power, see Norton E. Long, "Power and Administration," Public Administration Review 9 (Autumn 1949). A critical view of the dispersion of power in American government (from Congress and into the hands of bureaucrats and interest groups) is offered in Theodore J. Lowi, The End of Liberalism, 2d ed. (New York: Norton, 1979). Michael J. Hill offers a broadly theoretical overview of policy making in The Policy Process in the Modern State, 3d ed. (London: Prentice Hall, 1997).

Exercise 16

Rational Decision Making

WHAT IS RATIONALITY?

Rationality is a commodity highly prized in Western culture. We all like to believe that we think and act rationally and resent it if someone suggests we are doing otherwise. But what exactly does *rational* mean? In everyday discourse, we use the term fairly loosely and say that someone is rational if he or she acts reasonably, logically, and normally. We label as irrational or nonrational any behavior that we find strange or abnormal, which, depending on one's perspective, may encompass everything from paying $50 for a rock concert ticket to exhibiting active fantasies about being chased by creatures from Venus.

For the student of public administration, rationality has a more precise meaning. We say that a decision is rational if there is a systematic relationship between an end being pursued and the means used to get there. More specifically, a rational decision is one that entails selecting the best alternative to reach a particular goal.

Most discussions of this subject treat rational decision making in administration as a four-step process:

1. Goals are clarified and ranked.
2. All alternatives are surveyed.
3. The consequences of each alternative are weighed.
4. The alternative that best meets the goal is chosen.

You may object that this definition of administrative rationality isn't really much more precise or objective than the definition of rationality in general. After all, who is to say what alternative is best in any particular circumstances? Doesn't it depend a lot on the values we hold?

This objection has some merit. It is certainly true that estimates of the worth of an alternative will vary from person to person or from agency to agency. It is even true that we often don't know what our goals are, much less which alternative might best get us there. Moreover, any effort to apply this definition in an administrative context has to come to grips with the fact that decisions are often made collectively, with many different people applying many different values to many different goals. It is for these reasons, in fact, that some scholars have argued that it is not worthwhile even to talk about rationality in administrative decision making. Even if we could agree on what it looks like, they say, we wouldn't find it.

These arguments cannot and should not be dismissed lightly. They should caution us against uncritical acceptance of any technique that promises to deliver a "rational" decision. At the same time, we should not assume that because values are often diverse and goals unclear that all decisions are equally wise. While it may be impossible to make (or even identify) purely rational decisions, it is possible and necessary to try to make relatively or intendedly rational decisions. In fact, it may be useful to talk not about rational *decisions* but about rational *decision making*. This underscores the fact that the best we can do is to try, in the face of heavy odds, to act rationally. It draws our attention to the fact that rationality inheres in the process, not the outcome. If we make an effort to clarify and rank our goals and then search for and evaluate alternatives, we may not always be pleased with the outcome. But chances are that we will be better off than we would have been had we proceeded blindly, with no attention to goals, alternative strategies, or consequences.

No decision-making technique, no matter how carefully drawn, can guarantee success, however. A belief that it can is a form of hubris that leads quickly to disaster. David Halberstam's description in *The Best and the Brightest* of the "rational decision making" that surrounded American prosecution of the war in Vietnam is a compelling case in point.[1] The trick is to balance systematic analysis with humility and open-mindedness. The most rational decision makers are those who recognize that their systems are subject to failure.

The list of various techniques of rational decision making is virtually endless. It includes, among other things, simulations and game theory, operations research, systems analysis, linear programming, and decision trees, as well as a myriad of techniques bequeathed by microeconomists. Although each item has a distinctive flavor and is suited for only certain limited applications, all have in common the purpose of expanding the decision maker's awareness of choices and their consequences.

COST-BENEFIT AND COST-EFFECTIVENESS ANALYSIS

Cost-benefit analysis is one of the most common techniques of rational decision making. It is aimed at determining whether a particular investment of public funds is worthwhile. As its name suggests, cost-benefit analysis requires the decision maker to compare the total costs and benefits of a proposed program. Wherever possible, hard, quantifiable measures of both benefits and costs are to be used. If the ratio of benefits to costs is favorable—that is, if the investment has a net positive return—the program is justified.

Cost-benefit analysis first came into widespread use by the federal government in water resource management programs in the 1930s. The U.S. Army Corps of Engineers and Bureau of Reclamation used variations of this technique when deciding where and how to construct municipal water, irrigation, and flood control projects. Cities often use cost-benefit analysis today when considering major cap-

ital investments, such as constructing a new municipal parking garage or a convention center.

Cost-effectiveness analysis is an outgrowth of systems analysis. Although related to cost-benefit analysis, cost-effectiveness analysis is more concerned with the systematic comparison and evaluation of alternatives. The question for the cost-effectiveness analyst is, given the goal of reaching *x*, which of alternatives *a*, *b*, and *c* (or which combination thereof) will accomplish the job at the least cost? Note that the benefits of *x* are assumed. Cost-effectiveness analysis is often used in policy areas, such as social welfare or defense, where benefits are taken for granted but are not subject to hard measurement. This shifts attention to the relatively solvable problem of achieving these benefits at the lowest possible cost.

The relative benefits conferred by each alternative, even if not precisely quantifiable, cannot be totally ignored, however. For instance, a state agriculture department may set for itself the goal of eliminating avian influenza within certain affected counties. It "costs out" three main alternatives (see Figure 16.1), each of which is probably capable of accomplishing the goal (nothing is certain, of

1.	QUARANTINE	
	Income loss	$2,300,000
	Tax loss	460,000
	Administration	500,000
	Total	$3,260,000
2.	LIMITED INSPECTION	
	Income loss	$ 600,000
	Tax loss	90,000
	Administration	1,500,000
	Total	$2,190,000
3.	FLOCK DESTRUCTION	
	Income loss	$2,300,000
	Tax loss	460,000
	Administration	3,000,000
	Total	$5,760,000

Figure 16.1
Cost-Effectiveness of Avian Influenza Remedies:
Three Alternatives

[1]David Halberstam, *The Best and the Brightest* (New York: Random House, 1972).

course): (1) a total import-export quarantine on the affected areas, (2) a limited inspection and flock destruction program, and (3) destruction of all poultry within the target areas.

Should they now just pick the cheapest alternative (apparently alternative 2, all things considered)? Not necessarily. Alternative 3, though more expensive, confers additional benefits to the extent that it offers a greater probability of success. Alternative 1 is cheaper than 3 but may be slightly less beneficial. But who knows? One of the reasons the state agriculture department is using cost-effectiveness analysis is that it cannot quantify benefits precisely. The point of the example is that ends and means or objectives and program strategies can never be wholly separated, even in the most careful analyses. Because we can never be sure of consequences and because we find it difficult to calculate benefits, we almost always find ourselves trading off a little of our objective here for a little of an alternative there. This is the essence of systems analysis. Ends and means are in a constant and constructive state of flux as one searches for an optimal balance. Where does this leave the state agriculture department? Not with any easy answers, to be sure, at least not if it has approached the analysis with the proper humility. But the act of undertaking the cost-effectiveness analysis will have helped officials think through their objectives and clarify their alternatives. And at least they'll have something to point to when the governor calls and asks why irate farmers are picketing the executive mansion.

FURTHER READING

Classical theoretical discussions of administrative decision making may be found in David Braybrooke and Charles E. Lindblom, *A Strategy of Decision* (London: Collier-Macmillan, 1963); Charles E. Lindblom, "The Science of 'Muddling Through,'" *Public Administration Review* 19 (Spring 1959); and Herbert A. Simon, *Administrative Behavior,* 3d ed. (New York: Free Press, 1976).

A good introduction to and survey of techniques of decision making is Richard D. Bingham and Marcus E. Ethridge, eds., *Reaching Decisions in Public Policy and Administration: Methods and Applications* (New York: Longman, 1982). Warren Walker, *The Policy Analysis Approach to Public Decision-Making* (Santa Monica, Calif.: Rand, 1994), also provides a useful introduction to much of this material. Peter House and Roger Shull, *Rush to Policy: Using Analytic Techniques in Public Sector Decision Making* (New Brunswick, N.J.: Transaction Books, 1988), provides some cautionary notes.

Many technical treatises on cost-benefit analysis are available. Two of the most accessible are Richard Lyard and Stephen Glaister, *Cost-Benefit Analysis,* 2d ed. (New York: Cambridge University Press, 1994), and Alan Abouchar, *Project Decision-Making in the Public Sector* (Lexington, Mass.: Heath, 1985). Also interesting is R. Shep Melnick, *The Politics of Benefit-Cost Analysis* (Washington, D.C.: Brookings Institution, 1991).

Overview of Exercise

You are J. La Rue, senior policy analyst in the Community Transportation Planning Division of the State Department of Transportation (SDOT). One of your major responsibilities is to work with local communities in the state to help them assess their transportation needs and to make appropriate recommendations for state action. At the top of your agenda is a request for assistance from the city manager of East Wallingford, a rapidly growing community of 45,000 people that has been plagued by chronic traffic congestion. As an ace cost-effectiveness analyst, your task in this exercise is to analyze

East Wallingford's transportation situation and decide which of four main alternatives—a northern bypass, a southern bypass, street widening, or a bus-plus-perimeter-parking system—should be supported.

INSTRUCTIONS

Step One
Study the map of greater East Wallingford provided on Form 74 and familiarize yourself with the physical structure of the community.

Step Two

Read the "Preliminary Problem Analysis" memo (Form 75) prepared for you by your assistant, M. Ubahn. It provides important information about the dimensions of East Wallingford's traffic problem, including a discussion of certain political constraints. You may, if you wish, fill in the date of the memo with the current year.

Step Three

Complete Form 76, "Construction and Maintenance Cost Worksheet," by calculating the basic construction/acquisition and maintenance/operating costs of each alternative. Use the information provided on Form 77, "Cost Specifications," as a basis for your computations. Note that these costs represent costs to the state; for the purposes of this analysis, additional costs to be borne by other levels of government are ignored.

Step Four

Complete Form 78, "Environmental and Social Cost Worksheet." Note that you are to assign a cost figure, from zero to 100, for each alternative. The figures represent your estimates of the relative costs of each of these strategies. Although there are no right or wrong answers here, try to arrive at reasonable estimates based on your reading of the situation in East Wallingford. As the instructions on Form 78 indicate, take into consideration the likely environmental damage (air and water pollution, noise pollution, etc.) and social dislocation that will follow from each alternative.

Step Five

Complete Form 79, "Analytical Worksheet I." This form allows you to combine your cost calculations from Forms 76 and 78. Note that it is necessary to translate your costs from the "Construction and Maintenance Cost Worksheet" (Form 76) into terms compatible with a 100-point scale. You can do this easily by dividing your total for each alternative from Form 76 by 10,000. Note that you also have to decide on weights for each of the costs on Form 79. See the instructions on Form 79 for details.

Step Six

Complete Form 80, "Analytical Worksheet II." Refer again to Ubahn's memorandum and calculate the cost per minute of reducing average trip times by following each of the outlined alternatives; for instance, Ubahn estimates that the Northway will reduce travel time from 30 minutes to 10 minutes; as you have already calculated the cost of constructing this highway, simply divide the cost by the minutes saved (20). These calculations provide you with a set of *cost-benefit ratios,* which you should use as a basis for deciding which alternative to recommend.

Step Seven

Based on the cost-benefit ratios you calculated on Form 80 and any other information you consider pertinent, choose an alternative. Use Form 81 to outline and justify your choice by composing a brief memorandum to your supervisor, the director of the Division of Community Transportation Planning of the State Department of Transportation (SDOT).

Step Eight

Answer the questions on Form 82.

Map of East Wallingford

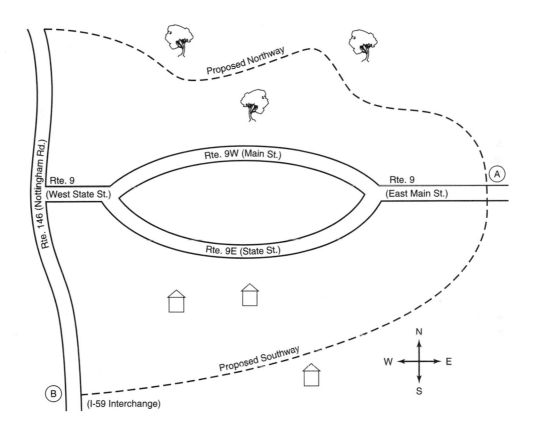

Rte. 146 (Nottingham Rd.)

Rte. 9W (Main St.)

Rte. 9
(West State St.)

Rte. 9
(East Main St.)

A

Rte. 9E (State St.)

Proposed Northway

Proposed Southway

B

(I-59 Interchange)

N
W — E
S

FORM 75

17 June 20__

TO: J. La Rue
        Senior Policy Analyst
        Community Transportation Planning

FROM: M. Ubahn
        Junior Policy Analyst
        Community Transportation Planning

RE: Preliminary Problem Analysis, East Wallingford

In response to your request for a preliminary analysis of East Wallingford's traffic problems, I spent three days in East Wallingford last week, at which time I interviewed city officials and initiated a traffic flow study. My findings can be summarized as follows:

1. East Wallingford is served by two state highways. Route 146 (Nottingham Road), a north-south arterial, passes through the western side of the city. Route 9, an east-west arterial, passes through the center of East Wallingford and connects to Route 146, which is its western terminus. In the central business district, Route 9 is actually divided for 1.5 miles to allow for one-way traffic flows. Route 9E is known as State Street; Route 9W is known as Main Street.

2. Three miles south of the central business district on Route 146 is an interchange for Interstate 59.

3. Traffic flows are unacceptably heavy on Route 146 and on Main (Route 9W) and State (Route 9E) Streets. During peak travel hours (7:30 AM to 9:30 AM and 4:00 PM to 6:00 PM), average trip times are far below State standards for a community of this size. Trips between Point A and Point B in either direction (see map), a distance of 4.5 miles, require 30 minutes on average.

4. City officials want average trip time in this corridor to be reduced to 15 minutes. While this seems to be a reasonable goal, application of SDOT standards in this case suggest it should be seen as a target rather than as an absolute cutoff.

5. Federal highway money is available on a matching basis for highway construction, of course, but people in the major residential districts south of the city have opposed building a "Southway," a 4-mile-long link from East Main Street to lower Nottingham Road near the Interstate interchange (projected trip time: 6 minutes).

6. On the other hand, local environmental groups interested in preserving the undeveloped streams and woodlands above East Wallingford have argued vociferously against a "Northway," a 5-mile-long stretch from East Main Street to upper Nottingham Road that would cut through the forest (projected trip time: 10 minutes).

7. Widening Main Street and State Street has received some support as an alternative, but local business people have objected that this project (3 miles of street widening in total) would be disruptive for their trade in the short term (estimated two years of construction) and would probably cause them to lose valuable parking spaces in front of their stores in the long term (projected trip time: 16 minutes).

8. Perimeter parking, in conjunction with increased bus service, has been discussed as a fourth possibility, although it is not clear that this would alleviate the problem entirely. I estimate that the city (with state aid) would have to purchase five new buses and construct two 1-acre parking lots to relieve congestion to near-tolerable levels (projected trip time: 20 minutes).

Construction and Maintenance Cost Worksheet

Alternatives	Costs		
	Construction/ Acquisition	Maintenance/ Operating	Total
Southway			
Northway			
Street widening			
Perimeter parking			

Cost Specifications

Annualized Construction/Acquisition Costs*
Highways constructed mainly in residential areas. $200,000/mile
Highways constructed mainly in undeveloped areas. $100,000/mile
Street widening. $100,000/mile
Parking lot construction $10,000/acre
Bus acquisition $30,000/bus

Maintenance/Operating Costs
Highway maintenance $10,000/mile/year
Additional maintenance for widened streets $10,000/mile/year
Parking lot maintenance $1,000/acre/year
Bus maintenance $1,000/bus/year
Bus operation $30,000/bus/year

*Although construction/acquisition expenditures are, in a sense, "onetime" costs, these figures represent annual costs to the state given the manner in which the investments would be financed. This allows you to sum construction/acquisition and maintenance/operating costs and to compare expenditures on an annual basis. Moreover, to simplify the analysis, these costs have already been standardized to account for the differential depreciation of these investments; thus the fact that buses need to be replaced more often than highways is already reflected in this cost structure. Finally, these figures represent costs to the state; additional costs borne by other levels of government are ignored in this exercise.

Environmental and Social Cost Worksheet

Alternatives	Costs	
	Environmental	Social
Southway		
Northway		
Street widening		
Perimeter parking		

Instructions: Review the map of East Wallingford, reread Ubahn's memorandum, and use any other resources you like to estimate the relative environmental and social costs of these four alternatives. Assign a number, from 0 to 100, to each alternative for each type of cost (0 = low cost; 100 = high cost). There is no one "correct" set of answers to these cost calculations. You should, however, try to assign costs that reflect the situation in East Wallingford as accurately as possible. The easiest way to do this (although not necessarily the most precise way) is to rank the alternatives against one another (1 through 4) on each dimension; then assign cost figures that reflect the ranking.

Analytical Worksheet I

Alternatives	Weighted Costs			
	Economic (Construction/ Acquisition & Maintenance) (EC) Weight =	Environmental (EN) Weight =	Social (S) Weight =	Total (TC)
Southway				
Northway				
Street widening				
Perimeter parking				

Instructions: This form allows you to combine your cost calculations from Forms 76 and 78. To complete this form, you must (1) translate your construction and maintenance costs into numbers compatible with a 100-point scale and (2) assign weights to each of the three costs (EC, EN, and S) in this table.

To translate your construction and maintenance costs, simply divide each of the totals from Form 76 by 10,000. Do this now and make a note of your answers on a separate sheet of paper.

Now you must assign weights to each of the three costs in this table. To do this, first think about the relative importance of economic factors, environmental factors, and social factors in a decision of this kind. Are they equally important? Is one slightly more important than the other two? Is one far more important than the other two? Your answer will depend on your own (or your organization's) values. After you have thought about this, choose numbers that reflect your evaluation. For instance, if you think that economic factors are twice as important as environmental and social factors, assign a weight of 2 to EC and weights of 1 each to EN and S. If you think they are all equally important, assign weights of 1 to each. Feel free to use fractions: for example, you might weight EC at 1.5, EN at 1, and S at 1.25.

Note the weights you have decided on in the appropriate spaces in the table. Then multiply the weight times the cost (from Forms 76 and 78) and enter the product in the table. Finally, add across the rows to determine the total costs (TC) of each alternative.

Analytical Worksheet II

Alternatives	Costs	
	Reduction in Trip Time (RTT)	Effectiveness (TC/RTT)
Southway		
Northway		
Street widening		
Perimeter parking		

Instructions: Calculate the effectiveness of each alternative by dividing the total cost (TC) (from Form 79) by the reduction in trip time (RTT) (from Ubahn's memo, Form 75). This cost-benefit ratio (TC/RTT) should then be used to guide your selection of the appropriate alternative. The lower the cost per mile, the more attractive the alternative—other things being equal.

Date:

TO: City Manager
East Wallingford

CC: Director, Division of Community Transportation Planning,
State Department of Transportation

FROM: J. La Rue
State Department of Transportation

RE: Proposed Resolution of Traffic Congestion

Questions

1. Do you think that your decision about East Wallingford's transportation problem was rational or at least was made rationally? Why or why not?

2. Does this imply that the rejected alternatives should be considered irrational or nonrational? Elaborate.

3. What is the relationship between the values of the analyst and "objective" data in rational decision making? Is it possible to exclude your own biases entirely when making choices of this sort?

4. Although it would seem from the facts presented in this case that none of the alternatives would satisfy all groups in East Wallingford, do you think that this is just an artifact of the exercise? That is, if you had more time and access to more information, do you believe an "optimal" solution to this problem could be found? In general, do most conflicts over public policy arise simply from misunderstanding and a lack of information such that good rational analysis will provide acceptable solutions?

Policy Implementation

WHAT IS IMPLEMENTATION?

Sometimes the decisions we make are self-executing. That is, once we make a choice, everything falls into place automatically. If you are standing in a cafeteria line, for instance, and decide you want some yogurt and a fruit cup, you just reach up and put them on your tray. Or, after you've thumbed through the registration guide and selected a set of courses for the upcoming semester, you simply complete the appropriate form and drop it off (and keep your fingers crossed that you're not closed out of that one course you need to graduate!).

Unfortunately, most decision-making situations are not that simple, especially for public administrators. The act of making a decision is only the first step on a very long road that leads—it is to be hoped—to the realization of public policy. *Implementation* is the translation of policy choices into action. As one pair of scholars has put it, implementation refers to "those activities that occur after the issuing of authoritative public policy directives."[1]

In some respects, "implementation" is simply another term for "public administration." After all, the ultimate ends of budgeting, personnel administration, organization theory, and all the other subfields of public administration are the achievement of agency goals, which are in turn the institutionalization of policy choices. It is worth focusing on implementation apart from these day-to-day activities of public administration, however, to remind ourselves that what we want to do, as embodied in the choices we make, is not always easy to accomplish. It takes more than a well-designed and well-oiled administrative machine to make a program work.

Indeed, the main reason that processes of implementation have received increased attention from students of public policy in recent years is the recognition that many well-intentioned (and seemingly well thought out) government programs have gone awry. From antipoverty and environmental protection programs to initiatives in housing, health care, and defense, lofty ambitions have too frequently met with frustration and failure. Although some observers have taken this as evidence that government has overreached its grasp and tried to do too much, others would argue that the real problem has been inattention to processes of implementation. We've made the right choices, but we've not followed through on them.

Implementation is about follow-through. It involves recognizing that programs unfold in complex and uncertain environments. The success or failure of a venture depends not only on the initial program decisions of administrators (and legislators and political executives) but also on the subsequent decisions and actions of myriad others: clients, interest groups, officials in other agencies or other levels of government. Similarly, unanticipated political, economic, or demographic changes can wreak havoc with a perfectly well intentioned program.

Think for a minute about the problem of foreign policy. We all recognize that it is seldom a simple matter for the United States (or any other country) to achieve its objectives in the world. In trying to encourage peace and stability in the former

---

[1] Daniel A. Mazmanian and Paul A. Sabatier, *Implementation and Public Policy* (Glenview, Ill.: Scott, Foresman, 1983), p. 4.

Yugoslavia, for instance, American foreign policy-makers must try to deal with a multitude of warring Serb, Croat, Bosnian, and Kosovar factions, not to mention other interested parties (the United Nations; the British, French, and other EU governments; the Russians; etc.). As much as we might like American policy to succeed, our expectations are never very high because we know so many variables are beyond our control. The same could be said of American policy in Central America, Southeast Asia, the Middle East, and so forth. Making foreign policy is like playing darts in the dark: Even if you have a rough idea of where the board is, the best you can do is throw and hope.

Domestic policy, we are learning, is not much different. Decision makers in the large domestic agencies of Washington (or Harrisburg, Sacramento, or St. Paul) frequently discover that they have no more control over the situations they are trying to manage than their colleagues in the State Department. Although lawsuits, bureaucratic inertia, and out-and-out noncooperation substitute for bombs and bullets, the sense of facing an uninterested or even hostile world remains the same.

Why is this so? The main reason is that power in America is fragmented. It is a very rare occasion, indeed, when any one agency has the political and administrative resources to impose its will without reference to other actors in the policy system. Even when there are no serious jurisdictional disputes between agencies at the same level of government, the nature of American federalism requires coordination and a sharing of power among levels of government. Interagency and intergovernmental bargaining, negotiation, and compromise are integral parts of the policy process.

Moreover, even in the unlikely event that governmental actors up and down the federal structure are in agreement on a policy initiative, the independent power of target populations and interest groups must be reckoned with. Because some people benefit and others lose, most governmental programs generate opposition as well as support. The fact that Congress has approved and the Department of Health and Human Services is prepared to administer a new health services program for migrant workers, for instance, does not mean that private physicians, hospitals, and agricultural interests are going to roll over and do their best to see that it

works. Nor does a decision to reduce sulfur emissions from coal-fired generating plants mean that industry will jump to purchase the necessary scrubbers. It more likely means that opposition to these decisions will continue in new arenas with new tactics. While it may be that a "decision" has been made, it would be a mistake to assume that the battle is over.

More than almost any other administrative problem for which (partial) technical solutions have been developed, the dilemmas of policy implementation are intractable or very nearly so. Failing a wholesale change in the nature of our political system, in directions that few of us would countenance, the best that administrators can hope for is to anticipate and plan for problems of implementation from the earliest stages of the decision process. "Assume the worst and then do your best to avoid it" is probably the soundest administrative advice in the circumstances.

IMPLEMENTATION AND THE CRITICAL PATH METHOD

Having provided adequate warning about the dangers of unguarded optimism in policymaking, it must be said that all is not lost. Some policies do get implemented; some programs do achieve their goals. Open-eyed planning seems to make a difference. Administrators who have a clear grasp of the goals of their policies and who have tried conscientiously to anticipate and avoid bottlenecks stand at least a fighting chance of seeing their programs work as intended.

Although sound implementation planning can take many forms, one technique that has become increasingly popular in recent years is known as the *Critical Path Method* (CPM). Sometimes called *network analysis* or *PERT charting*,[2] CPM provides a way of representing graphically, in an easy-to-grasp form, the steps required to implement a policy decision. As two exponents of CPM have put it, this method "facilitates logical thought by permitting the

---

[2]PERT, an acronym for Performance Evaluation Review Technique, was a management system developed in the 1950s for the U.S. Navy as part of the Polaris submarine program.

Figure 17.1
Basic Critical Path Model

administrator . . . to recognize more fully the relationships of the parts to the whole." Through a simple system of circles and arrows, a policy planner can depict the flow of policy and predict likely impediments to smooth implementation "before they actually occur."[3]

Part of the appeal of CPM is its simplicity. CPM networks are composed of just two elements: *events* (represented by circles) and *activities* (represented by arrows). An event is defined as the start or completion of a task; events consume no resources and simply mark time in a CPM network. Activities represent the flow of tasks themselves; activities, by definition, consume resources. To create a CPM network, the analyst merely identifies the set of events that must occur to implement a policy and links them together in the proper sequence with activity arrows. Each activity arrow represents the amount of time (or other resources) that must be consumed to produce an event.

Figure 17.1 represents a simple three-event, two-activity CPM network. This network indicates that beginning with event A, activity 1 must be completed to reach event B; activity 2 must be completed to reach event C. Moreover, because event B intervenes between A and C, you can infer that it is a necessary part of the sequence; that is, you cannot get to C without finishing B.

To use a less abstract illustration, let's assume that you and your roommates have decided to throw an end-of-the-semester party for your friends in the dormitory. As a first step in the party planning process, you decide, very sensibly, to make a list of the things that need to be done:

1. Order beer keg, tap, ice, and bucket
2. Purchase potato chips and pretzels

3. Compose guest list
4. Buy invitations
5. Mail invitations
6. Pick up beer, tap, ice, and bucket
7. Reserve room

You next ask yourself, in what order do we need to do these things? You could just run around and try to accomplish them randomly, but it seems that a certain order would be appropriate. After all, you don't want to send out invitations before you know whether you can reserve a room for the party. And you can't send out invitations before you buy them and make up a guest list, nor can you pick up the beer and related supplies before you order them. So you need to work out a sequence of activities that makes sense. Figure 17.2 provides a CPM network that does exactly that. Each of the activities is represented by one of the arrows. The events (circles) designate the beginning or end of an activity. Note that "reserve room" and "compose guest list" have been combined into a single activity sequence because we decided that both could be undertaken prior to any other events (other than the decision to hold the party).

There are alternative ways to schedule these activities, of course. If you were really conservative, for instance, you might not want to commit yourself

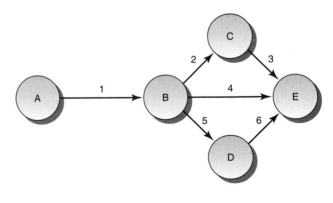

Event	Activity
A – Decision to hold party	1 – Reserve room and compose guest list
B – Room reserved and guest list composed	2 – Buy invitations
C – Invitations purchased	3 – Send invitations
D – Beer supplies reserved	4 – Buy potato chips and pretzels
E – Party	5 – Reserve beer supplies
	6 – Pick up beer supplies

Figure 17.2
Critical Path Network for Party Planning

[3]Anthony J. Catanese and Alan W. Steiss, "Programming for Governmental Operations: The Critical Path Approach," in Richard D. Bingham and Marcus E. Ethridge, eds., *Reaching Decisions in Public Policy and Administration: Methods and Applications* (New York: Longman, 1982), p. 388. Originally published in *Public Administration Review* 28 (March–April 1968).

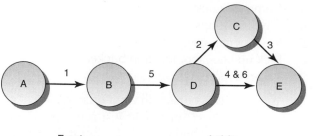

Figure 17.3
"Conservative" Critical Path Network for Party Planning

Event	Activity
A – Decision to hold party	1 – Reserve room and compose
B – Room reserved and	guest list
guest list composed	2 – Buy invitations
C – Invitations purchased	3 – Send invitations
D – Beer supplies reserved	4 – Buy potato chips and pretzels
E – Party	5 – Reserve beer supplies
	6 – Pick up beer supplies

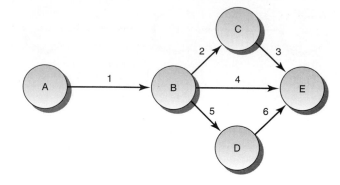

Activity	Time Estimate (days)
1	2
2	2
3	3
4	1
5	2
6	1

Figure 17.4
CPM Network with Time Estimates

to buying potato chips and pretzels (Activity 4) or buying and sending invitations (Activities 2 and 3) until you found out whether or not you could reserve the beer supplies (Activity 5). In that case, your CPM would look like Figure 17.3.

But let's assume that you're willing to live dangerously, and you adopt the schedule of Figure 17.2. What exactly does the CPM network of Figure 17.2 tell you? Frankly, not much at this point. All it really does is represent schematically what you already plan to do. The real utility of CPM lies in taking the additional step of estimating the amount of time it will take to complete each activity and produce the next event. This allows the analyst to anticipate the flow of action and manage resources as efficiently as possible.[4] The time estimates are obtained simply by making reasonable judgments about each activity. The analyst figures out (or asks a knowledgeable observer) how long an activity is likely to take. Figure 17.4 reproduces Figure 17.2 with a set of time estimates attached to each activity.

Before we can put the information about time estimates to good use, however, it is important to note one additional point. If you examine Figure 17.4 carefully, you will see that there are three pos-

sible routes, or paths, that you can trace between event A and event E: A-B-E, A-B-C-E, and A-B-D-E. You can think of them as paths through a forest, marked by arrows, that lead you from your starting point to your destination.

The idea of multiple paths to a destination is central to CPM. Unlike finding the way in a real forest, however, the main purpose of CPM is to identify the *longest* path that connects your starting point with your destination. Because you will walk all these paths simultaneously (a difficult feat in a real forest), the time required to complete the longest path is equal to the time required to complete the total project. The longest path in a CPM network is called the *critical path*. This is because timely completion of the entire project hinges on the successful execution of this sequence of activities as scheduled; any delays along the path will necessarily delay the project. Thus it is critical that these activities proceed expeditiously. Because the other paths are, by definition, shorter than the critical path, delays in the execution of their scheduled activities will not necessarily impede the project (unless, of course, the delays become so serious that the total time consumed by the path exceeds the original critical path).

The term used to describe the excess time available on the noncritical paths is *slack*. The amount of

[4]Normally, three separate time estimates are made for each sequence of activities: (1) the most *optimistic* time (t_o), (2) the most *pessimistic* time (t_p), and (3) the *most likely* time (t_m). The mean of these three times then is used as the *average expected time* (t_e) for the activity.

slack on any path is equal to the amount of time consumed by the critical path minus the amount of time consumed by the path in question. Although a little slack in planning may be desirable (it allows you to handle unanticipated contingencies without throwing the whole project off schedule), too much is inefficient. In the most carefully planned projects, administrators arrange activities to obtain the maximum use of resources, allowing as little "down" or idle time as possible.

Armed with this information, let us turn again to Figure 17.4. We now know that the critical path in this network is A-B-C-E. Again, this is because it is the longest path in the network. The expected time of completion for this project is seven days, the length of the critical path. Paths A-B-E and A-B-D-E are three days and five days long, respectively, which means that A-B-E has four days of slack and A-B-D-E two days. Thus, if we want to keep the party on schedule, we've got to make sure that there are no delays in reserving the room, making up the guest list, and buying and mailing the invitations. As far as arranging for the food and beer is concerned, we have a little room to maneuver. In fact, it might be wise to put those activities off for a day or two until we're sure that the room reservation and invitations are under control.

Although you may decide that it is not worth the trouble to construct a critical path chart to plan a party, this methodology can prove very useful when attempting to manage the implementation of a complex administrative decision. Consider, for instance, the avian influenza problem outlined in Exercise 16. No matter which alternative state agriculture department officials choose to pursue (quarantine, limited inspection, flock destruction), implementation will be far smoother and the success of the policy far more assured if the multitude of discrete activities necessary to bring it to completion is carefully planned and coordinated. If a quarantine is chosen, for example, it will be necessary to write and publicize regulations; identify and monitor target areas; hire and train new enforcement staff; procure additional field equipment, including vehicles; contract or otherwise arrange for fowl testing with state or private laboratories; coordinate activities with adjacent states and with other agencies within the state; and perhaps establish a compensation program for farmers. The other two

alternatives would entail equally complex planning. Because many of the steps are interdependent, such that a failure to complete one will cause delays all down the line, use of the critical path technique (or similar methodology) could save valuable time and resources. Indeed, it would be hard to imagine a program this complex achieving its objectives without such systematic implementation planning.

Programs of this complexity are not atypical in the public sector. If anything, this brief discussion of the steps involved in a hypothetical avian influenza program considerably understates the uncertainty and complexity most public administrators face. Although no technique, including the critical path method, can guarantee that policy decisions will actually be implemented, not to undertake some sort of systematic planning in these circumstances is to court disaster.

FURTHER READING

Among the classic works in the field of policy implementation are Jeffrey Pressman and Aaron Wildavsky, *Implementation: How Great Expectations in Washington Are Dashed in Oakland* (Berkeley, Calif.: University of California Press, 1984); Erwin Hargrove, *The Missing Link* (Washington, D.C.: Urban Institute, 1975); Carl Van Horn, *Policy Implementation in the Federal System* (Lexington, Mass.: Heath, 1979); Eugene Bardach, *The Implementation Game* (Cambridge, Mass.: MIT Press, 1977); and Daniel A. Mazmanian and Paul A. Sabatier, *Implementation and Public Policy* (Glenview, Ill.: Scott, Foresman, 1983). A more recent compilation that is also excellent is Malcolm Goggin et al., *Implementation Theory and Practice: Toward a Third Generation* (Glenview, Ill.: Scott, Foresman, 1990).

One of the technical articles on the critical path method most useful for students of public administration is Anthony J. Catanese and Alan W. Steiss, "Programming for Governmental Operations: The Critical Path Approach," *Public Administration Review* 28 (March-April 1968); it has been reprinted in Richard D. Bingham and Marcus E. Ethridge, eds., *Reaching Decisions in Public Policy and Administration: Methods and Applications* (New York: Longman, 1982).

Overview of Exercise

In this exercise, you reassume your role as J. La Rue, senior policy analyst in the State Department of Transportation. After considering your recommendations (from Exercise 16), the city of East Wallingford has decided to construct the Northway. Although preliminary approval has been granted by the state, final authorization to proceed with construction will not be given until a series of hurdles has been cleared.

Your job is to coordinate the initial implementation of the Northway decision. In particular, you are to undertake a critical path analysis of the steps leading up to the start of Northway construction. In so doing, you will design a critical path network, calculate the time of completion of various sequences of activities, identify the critical path, and estimate the amount of slack in noncritical paths.

INSTRUCTIONS

Step One

Study the memorandum (Form 83) prepared by M. Ubahn, your assistant. It contains all the information you need to design a CPM network for the Northway project. Use Form 84 to draw your network. Remember that the first event (circle) in your network should be the Northway decision; the last should be the beginning of construction.

Step Two

Complete Form 85 by calculating the estimated time of completion of each event, identifying the critical path, and computing the amount of slack in the noncritical path(s).

Step Three

Answer the questions on Form 86.

15 September 20__

TO: J. La Rue
Senior Policy Analyst
Community Transportation Planning

FROM: M. Ubahn
Junior Policy Analyst
Community Transportation Planning

RE: Northway Preconstruction Planning

Per your instructions, I have assembled the data necessary to produce a CPM implementation analysis of the Northway project. Herewith is a summary:

1. Preliminary highway design, required for all subsequent action, should require 45 days.

2. Preparation of a draft Environmental Impact Statement (EIS) will require 60 days.

3. Following release of the EIS, two days of public hearings must be scheduled prior to submission of documentation to the Environmental Protection Agency (EPA). An additional three days will be necessary to pull together all paperwork after the hearings.

4. EPA approval will require approximately 60 days.

5. Formal approval of the preliminary design by our highway counterparts in SDOT [State Department of Transportation] should require only five days from submission. They don't need to wait for the EPA results, of course.

6. Because of the new state Agricultural Lands Preservation statute, we'll need to clear the preliminary design with DOA [State Department of Agriculture]. It will take approximately 30 days to prepare the paperwork after the preliminary design is completed for the DOA submission. An additional 30 days will be required for DOA consideration, interagency coordination, and approval.

7. Following EPA, DOA, and SDOT responses to the preliminary design, 60 days will be necessary to make modifications and prepare the final highway design. This includes the time necessary to clear any changes with the interested agencies.

8. Once the final highway design has been prepared and approved, two further activities can commence: land acquisition and contract preparation and bidding. These activities can proceed independent of one another. It will require 90 days to acquire the necessary land and 65 days to prepare and award construction contracts.

9. Once all necessary land has been acquired, SDOT surveyors will require 14 days to complete their work.

10. After all contracts have been prepared and bid, 21 days will be required to certify and award contracts.

11. Construction can begin once contracts have been certified and awarded and once the survey work is completed.

CPM Network For Northway Planning

CPM Calculations

1. Identify below the amount of time it will take to complete each event in your CPM network. You can determine this by summing the time consumed by all the necessary activities preceding the event.

Event   Expected Time of Completion

2. Identify the *critical path* in your CPM network. How long will it take to begin construction?

3. Identify the *noncritical paths* in your CPM network and calculate the amount of *slack* in each.

Questions

1. What are the advantages of creating CPM networks? What limitations, if any, do you see in this technique?

2. Is CPM better suited to some policy implementation situations than others? If so, in what ways?

3. What resources, other than time, might usefully be represented by activity arrows in CPM networks for the purposes of planning policy implementation?

Exercise 18

Policy Evaluation

THE IMPORTANCE OF POLICY EVALUATION

As far as most casual observers of American politics and public affairs are concerned, the policy process ends once a decision has been made—when a bill has been approved, a regulation promulgated, an executive order signed, and so forth. Those more familiar with the intricacies of policy implementation, as we learned in Exercise 17, tend to be more skeptical and to wait until various administrative problems have been ironed out before they feel satisfied that the policy process has run its course.

Although a concern for implementation is laudable, we should not assume that an implemented policy—even a perfectly implemented policy—signals a fitting end to the policy cycle. Public policy is not an end in itself; it is a *means* to an end. Policies are designed, at least in theory, to accomplish goals or solve problems. Once a policy is in place, public administrators must always ask themselves, What has the policy accomplished? Did we reach the goal we set forth? Has the problem the policy was designed to solve been ameliorated?

Questions such as these are central to *policy evaluation,* which may be formally defined as "the objective, systematic, empirical examination of the effects ongoing policies have on their targets in terms of the goals they are meant to achieve."[1] Policy evaluation is important for the very simple reason that it helps us know whether our policies have worked. Absent some effort to gauge the effects of public policy, we are not only throwing darts in the dark, to pursue the metaphor used earlier; we never even find out if we hit the board.[2]

[1]David Nachmias, *Public Policy Evaluation: Approaches and Methods* (New York: St. Martin's, 1979), p. 4.

POLICY AS THEORY

A useful way to understand the problems (and importance) of policy evaluation is to think of a policy as a theory, or better, as a hypothesis or set of hypotheses derived from the theory. When we formulate a public policy, we are in a sense formulating a hypothesis. We are assuming that an action we take will have a specific and measurable effect: "If we do *x,* then *y* will happen" or "If we raise the drinking age to 21, then highway fatalities will decline." This is exactly the logic that applies in a laboratory: "If we heat this metal to a temperature of 550 degrees Fahrenheit, then hydrogen gas will be emitted."

Although this analogy is sound logically, it is troublesome empirically. Working in a laboratory, we can control conditions quite precisely. We can make sure that the gas we are looking for (and no other gas) has in fact been emitted; we can also take measures to ensure that other factors are not responsible for the presence of the gas (e.g., our lab assistant did not accidentally open a canister of hydrogen).

This is not easy to do with public policy. Even when our policy (the *if* part of the hypothesis) is clear and unambiguous, it is often hard to know what sort of changes are going on (the *then* part of

[2]A persuasive case can be made that many participants in the policy process, as well as most citizens, don't really care about the effects of public policy, at least not in the sense implied here. It can be argued that policy is to be understood mainly as a set of symbols, disseminated to engender popular acquiescence in the status quo; nothing fundamentally changes or is meant to change. For an elaboration of this argument, see Murray Edelman, *The Symbolic Uses of Politics* (Urbana: University of Illinois Press, 1964). For the purposes of this chapter, it will be assumed that policymakers do intend to achieve the effects stated in the policy.

319

the hypothesis) out there in the real world. Not only do we often have difficulty measuring social effects in general, but also we can seldom be sure what is producing them.

To illustrate this point, suppose that your state has decided to try to stimulate urban redevelopment by designating a series of "enterprise zones" in the state's largest cities. The legislature has passed and the governor has signed a bill exempting businesses that locate within the zones from all state and local property taxes for a period of three years. The theory, of course, is that this sort of tax break will encourage investment in otherwise undesirable areas: "*If* we give businesses tax incentives, *then* they will invest in areas that need redevelopment."

A year or so passes, and the governor asks you to assess the effectiveness of this policy. How should you proceed? The laboratory model is not much help. You lack the rigorous controls and precise instruments available to experimental scientists. You can of course try to do before-and-after comparisons of income, employment, vacancy rates, gross sales, and so forth in the zones. But will such data be available? How reliable will they be? Anyway, what should you try to measure? The legislature spoke of "redevelopment." This seemed clear enough at the time, but what exactly does it mean? Does any kind of economic activity qualify as redevelopment? Is it important to look at income distribution as well as income in the aggregate? The odds are that if you go back and try to reconstruct the intent of the legislature by reading debates and committee reports, you will find more than one definition of redevelopment. That is, you will discover that there was something less than complete agreement on what the policy was and what it was intended to accomplish.

Moreover, even if you solve these preliminary problems and decide that redevelopment, by whatever definition, has indeed taken place within the enterprise zones, what inferences will you draw? It would be premature to conclude that the policy has worked. After all, is it not possible that other factors (general economic conditions, bank lending policies, interest rates, energy cost and availability, social attitudes, spillovers from business activity outside the zones), alone or in combination, have produced the effect? Maybe the law had nothing to do with it. Indeed, maybe the redevelopment

occurred *despite* the law and even more redevelopment would have taken place without it. That is not likely, perhaps, but it is possible. And it is important to know. If we just assume that the law was responsible, supporters of enterprise zones will undoubtedly use this evidence of "success" to justify similar actions in the future. If their theory is wrong, unnecessary social costs will have been incurred for no tangible benefits. But how can you make such causal inferences? The social world is not like a laboratory; everything else does not come to a dead stop while a policy is being implemented. Variables are many; constants are few.

None of this is to suggest that policy evaluation is impossible. Policy can and should be evaluated. The point is that evaluation is complicated. Social science research (and this is exactly what policy evaluation involves) is far more difficult, owing to the uncertainties involved, than research in a laboratory. Good evaluation research requires a special sensitivity on the part of the evaluator. Great care must be taken in identifying and clarifying policy goals, adducing appropriate measures of success, collecting valid and reliable data, and drawing correct (and appropriately qualified) inferences.

EVALUATION PROCEDURES

For better or worse, though, there is no one policy evaluation technique that may be learned and applied in all circumstances. Because a policy is like a theory, all the multitudinous methodologies and techniques available to test theoretical hypotheses may be brought to bear in policy evaluations. Controlled social experiments can be run; statistical analyses using historical or comparative data can be undertaken; mathematical models can be built; citizens and policymakers can be interviewed; qualitative assessments can be made. Which methodology or set of methodologies should be used will vary with the situation.

In the end, learning to do sound policy evaluations is the same as learning to do sound research. The trick lies in putting together a sensible research design, in asking the right questions in the right way. This is far more important than learning a particular methodology or technique.

But what does it mean to put together a sensible research design? From the foregoing discussion we can distill several steps:

1. *Identify clearly the policy to be evaluated.* This means understanding both the goal, or intent of the policy, and the instruments of policy. What was the policy supposed to accomplish? Precisely how was it to be done? Treat the policy as a theory and derive from it testable hypotheses. Use the "if, then" form to remind yourself of the hypothesized relationship between action and outcomes.

2. *Devise valid measures.* Restate policy goals and instruments in ways that can be measured. Remember that most policies—to attract support and minimize opposition—state goals only in very general terms that cannot be measured directly. You must translate broad aims like "urban redevelopment" into measurable variables, such as occupancy rates, employment, and income. In doing so, make sure that your measures are valid—that they measure what you think they measure (see Exercise 9).

3. *Collect empirical data.* For each of the measures of each of the variables in your policy hypothesis, collect the most reliable information you can find. This may mean sifting through government statistics or conducting interviews or other field research.

4. *Analyze your data.* Does there appear to be a causal relationship between the independent variable (the policy) and the dependent variable(s) (the outcome)? That is, is a change in the former variable associated with a change in the latter?

5. *Consider competing theories.* This is actually part of step 4, but it is so important that it deserves special emphasis. In analyzing your data, consider whether the changes you observe could be attributed to other causes. Is the redevelopment we have seen a function of tax incentives or of something else? To answer this question, it will be necessary conceptually to start over at step 1 and follow all the procedures outlined. Before you can say that a policy has worked, you must be prepared to reject all plausible alternative explanations. This is not always easy to do. It requires controlling for (or holding constant) some variables while you look at others. Absent experimental conditions, you will probably have to undertake some comparative research (e.g., look at similar neighborhoods *not*

designated urban enterprise zones and see how they have fared) or otherwise try to isolate the policy from other effects.

6. *Look for unintended consequences.* Even though a policy may be aimed at one target, it may hit another accidentally. Urban enterprise zones may (or may not) stimulate economic activity, but they may (or may not) also displace poor people and contribute to the problem of homelessness, create new pockets of poverty as businesses shift areas of operation, reduce state and local revenues beyond levels anticipated, and so on. Our knowledge of the complexities of the social world is so limited that we should expect the unexpected in public policy. Sound policy evaluations look for unintended as well as intended consequences.

By following these general rules, a fair start can be made at evaluating public policy. It will be necessary, of course, to choose specific analytical techniques appropriate to the problem at hand. And it will also be necessary to remember that no evaluation study, no matter how carefully executed, can ever be considered definitive; too much uncertainty is involved all along the line. But these techniques do provide a basis for a reasonably systematic evaluation, which is better than an unsystematic evaluation or no evaluation at all.

One final (and frustrating) question must be posed, however: What do we do with policy evaluations once we get them? If the "we" refers to American policymakers and various attentive publics in general, the answer is, unfortunately, "Not much." If they are executed well, policy evaluations can and should serve as valuable feedback to the policy system. We can learn what we are doing right and what we are doing wrong. But the feedback is often ignored. Many people stop paying attention to a policy once the initial decision is made; some new issue or problem grabs the headlines and relegates the policy to the quiet recesses of the bureaucracy. Others ignore the fruits of evaluation research because they are less interested in policy outcomes than they are in the policy itself. Businesses that lobby for tax credits may bolster their arguments with rosy pictures of social benefits, for example. But it is the credits that count, not the benefits; once the tax concessions are obtained, systematic evaluation is likely to loom only as a threat.

This should remind us that policy and politics are inseparable. Policy evaluation is no more a neutral, value-free activity than any other administrative process. While public policies can, for analytical purposes, be treated like scientific hypotheses, they ultimately represent the codification of certain social values, which more often than not are in conflict with other social values. As long as people disagree about what government should do (and good democrats hope that that will be a very long time indeed), people will disagree about what government has done. The questions that frame a policy evaluation will unavoidably reflect some values and ignore others, if only to the extent that some questions are never asked.

Consequently, it is not surprising that policy evaluators do not always find an eager and credulous audience. Those interested in policy evaluation may take some solace, though, from the fact that settled social consensuses do occasionally develop in particular policy areas. As that happens, as values converge, policy evaluations become more widely accepted. Moreover, as one well-regarded scholar of policy evaluation has put it:

> *Decision makers are not monoliths. . . . As time goes on, if confirming evidence piles up year after year on the failures of old approaches, if mounting data suggest new modes of intervention, this will percolate through the concerned publics. When the political climate veers toward the search for new initiatives, or if sudden crises arise and there is a scramble for effective policy mechanisms, some empirically grounded guidelines will be available.*[3]

FURTHER READING

Although somewhat dated, one of the best introductions to policy evaluation for students of public administration is still David Nachmias, *Public Policy Evaluation* (New York: St. Martin's Press, 1979). A more advanced treatment of policy evaluation by one of the leading figures in the field is Peter Rossi, *Evaluation: A Systematic Approach* (Newbury Park, Calif.: Sage, 1993). *The Handbook of Practical Program Evaluation* (San Francisco: Jossey-Bass, 1994), edited by Joseph Wholey, Harry Hatry, and Kathryn Newcomer, contains 25 essays on designing, conducting, and using evaluation studies—all from a very practical perspective, as the title suggests. Several other edited volumes that contain more theoretically inclined articles are Stuart Nagel, ed., *Policy Theory and Policy Evaluation* (New York: Greenwood Press, 1990); Leonard Rutman, ed., *Evaluation Research Methods: A Basic Guide* (Newbury Park, Calif.: Sage, 1984); and William Shadish Jr. et al., eds., *Foundations of Program Evaluation* (Newbury Park, Calif.: Sage, 1991). For a nice collection of articles that consider the political dimension of program evaluation, see Dennis J. Palumbo, ed., *The Politics of Program Evaluation* (Newbury Park, Calif.: Sage, 1987). Finally, two interesting sets of articles on comparative (i.e., non-American) experiences with policy evaluation may be found in J. Mayne et al., eds., *Advancing Public Policy Evaluation* (Amsterdam: North-Holland, 1992) and Ray C. Rist, ed., *Policy Evaluation: Linking Theory to Practice* (London: Edward Elgar Publishing, 1995).

Overview of Exercise

In this exercise, you will design a strategy to evaluate the transportation policy chosen in Exercise 16 and implemented in Exercise 17. It will require you to think about the intent of the policy, devise appropriate measures of policy success or failure, and suggest ways that data might be gathered and analyzed.

INSTRUCTIONS

Step One
Review the material presented in Exercises 16 and 17, especially Forms 74 and 75, and generally refamiliarize yourself with the situation in East Wallingford.

Step Two
Identify the policy goal(s) articulated by East Wallingford and state officials. Working on the

[3]Carol H. Weiss, "Evaluation Research in the Political Context," in Elmer L. Struening and Marcia Guttentag, eds., *Handbook of Evaluation Research I* (Newbury Parks Calif.: Sage, 1975), p. 24.

assumption that the alternative you recommended in Exercise 16 was in fact adopted (i.e., disregard the premise of Exercise 17 that the Northway was chosen), briefly describe the policy itself. Record the information in the appropriate spaces on Form 87, "Design for Policy Evaluation."

Step Three

Describe how you might go about measuring the extent to which these policy goals have been met. What indicators of success would you use? Use Form 87 to record your comments.

Step Four

Given the indicators you described in Step Three, discuss how you would collect the necessary data.

Feel free to use your imagination—but be sure to factor feasibility into your recommendations. Use Form 87 to record your comments.

Step Five

Assume that you find some evidence that your policy goals have been met, in whole or in part. Outline some plausible competing explanations (reasons other than the policy you recommended) for the outcome, and describe how you might go about deciding which explanation ultimately to accept. Use Form 87 to record your comments.

Step Six

Answer the questions on Form 88.

Design for Policy Evaluation

Policy Goal(s):

Policy Adopted:

Measure(s) of Policy Success/Failure:

Data to Be Used in Evaluation:

Alternative Hypotheses:

Questions

1. Assume that you actually had to undertake the evaluation you designed for this exercise. How difficult do you think it would be to carry out? What would be the major difficulties?

2. What unintended consequences of this policy do you think it would be important to look for in your study? How would you go about it?

3. How much confidence would you have in the results of your study? How much confidence do you think others in East Wallingford or in the State Department of Transportation would have? Why?